LUXURY
WORLD

LUXURY WORLD

The past, present and
future of luxury brands

MARK TUNGATE

KOGAN PAGE

London and Philadelphia

Publisher's note

Every possible effort has been made to ensure that the information contained in this book is accurate at the time of going to press, and the publishers and authors cannot accept responsibility for any errors or omissions, however caused. No responsibility for loss or damage occasioned to any person acting, or refraining from action, as a result of the material in this publication can be accepted by the editor, the publisher or any of the authors.

First published in Great Britain and the United States in 2009 by Kogan Page Limited

120 Pentonville Road	525 South 4th Street, #241
London N1 9JN	Philadelphia PA 19147
United Kingdom	USA
www.koganpage.com	

© Mark Tungate, 2009

The right of Mark Tungate to be identified as the author of this work has been asserted by him in accordance with the Copyright, Designs and Patents Act 1988.

ISBN	978 0 7494 5263 6
E-ISBN	978 0 7494 5856 0

British Library Cataloguing-in-Publication Data

A CIP record for this book is available from the British Library.

Library of Congress Cataloging-in-Publication Data

Tungate, Mark, 1967–
    Luxury world : the past, present and future of luxury brands / Mark Tungate.
        p. cm.
    Includes bibliographical references and index.
    ISBN 978-0-7494-5263-6
    1. Luxury goods industry. 2. Brand name products. 3. Luxuries–History. I. Title.
    HD9999.L852T86 2009
    338.4'7–dc22
                                        2009027020

Typeset by JS Typesetting Ltd, Porthcawl, Mid Glamorgan
Printed and bound in Great Britain by MPG Books Ltd, Bodmin, Cornwall

For Géraldine.
Or perhaps I should say, for
Madame Géraldine Dormoy-Tungate.
It was a very good year.

Contents

Acknowledgements

The great luxury of working on a project like this is that you aren't on your own – in fact, you are obliged to get in touch with a wide variety of advisors and facilitators. On that score, I'd particularly like to thank Francesca Barba, who not only looked after me in Monaco, but also introduced me to several people who specialize in serving the very wealthy. A warm word of thanks, too, to Paul Coleman, whose excellent contacts led to two valuable interviews. Similarly, the persistence of Alexandre Wehrlin at Piaget made my visit to that company possible. Evelyne Resnick uncorked her extensive knowledge of wine. Genevieve Flaven of S-Vision was on hand, as ever, to provide advice and inspiration. I also owe a debt of gratitude to Jon Finch at Kogan Page, who remained patient in the face of missed deadlines. And of course none of it would be worth doing without Géraldine, whose love and support have a value beyond measure.

Finally, thanks to all my interviewees. They will find their names in the pages that follow. Here are those who worked behind the scenes: Anais Caietta, Joanna Derain, Iris le Floc'h, Piyatchat Jiemvitayanukul, Alix Leonard-Morgan, Julia Marozzi, Karin de Mulder, Monica Paolazzi, Waike Papke, Emanuelle Perrier, Jimmy Pihet, Carole de Poix, Laetizia Saubesty, Alexia Uri. I wish you all the best of *luxe*.

Introduction:
The evolution of luxury

'I can't afford to buy cheap things.'

It's 10 am on a sunny Sunday morning and for once the Avenue des Champs Elysées is quiet. Normally the distant Arc de Triomphe is obscured by a haze of exhaust fumes rising from two crawling lines of traffic, but today the view up the avenue from the Place de la Concorde is diamond clear. One can almost imagine tumbleweed blowing across the attractively cobbled thoroughfare.

The avenue is not entirely deserted, however. A motorcade of three large black automobiles makes its stately way to the Louis Vuitton flagship store at the corner of Avenue George V. The cars sigh to a halt outside the emporium, which has been specially opened for the occasion. A uniformed chauffeur emerges and opens the rear door of the middle car. From its cool dark interior emerges a vision in a cerise velour tracksuit. The tiny figure's neck and wrists are weighed down with gold jewellery. In her arms, she cradles a chihuahua. The girl is barely 17 years old, and she is a princess from one of the Gulf States.

The princess is escorted into the store, where a personal shopper is on hand to help her. Although he speaks a handful of languages, his linguistic skills are not required. When the princess sees something she likes, she simply points. By the time she has left the store, she has spent tens of thousands of euros.

This incident – sketched from life, with only minor embellishments – captures the essence of the luxury industry: an elite brand doing its utmost to provide a personalized service to a high-spending client. For most of us, the world inhabited by the princess is impossibly distant from our daily lives. And yet every year luxury brands spend millions trying to convince us otherwise.

They've been at it for a long time. Certainly since the turn of the last century, when couturiers who made wildly expensive dresses for a narrow market of wealthy women began to diversify in order to boost their incomes. The fashion designer Poiret launched a perfume called Rosine – named after his eldest daughter – in 1911. Chanel No 5 was created in 1921. The house of Worth launched another famous fragrance, Je Reviens, in 1932. These pretty glass bottles were prisms through which everyday consumers could glimpse a life of luxury. Other accessories followed. In the 1970s, Cartier launched a range of affordable trinkets called 'Les Must': lighters, pens, watches and key rings, all trafficking the jeweller's premium values.

At the beginning of the 21st century, when established luxury brands fell into the hands of giant corporations with profit-hungry shareholders, this courtship of the mass market accelerated and intensified. Sunglasses, sneakers, scarves, belts and billfolds: lower-priced items put luxury tantalizingly within our reach. We found that we could enter the Louis Vuitton store on the Champs Elysées, purchase a relatively affordable gift (say, a US $260 monogrammed passport cover) and be treated with only slightly less deference than the teenage princess. The crystal-encrusted tentacles of luxury descended to caress our souls, and we grasped them.

This development changed the luxury game. As Michel Chevalier and Gérald Mazzalovo observed in their 2008 book *Luxury Brand Management*, the traditional definition of a luxury brand was one that was 'selective and exclusive... almost the only brand in its category, giving it the desirable attributes of being scarce, sophisticated and in good taste'. The scarcity and 'aristocratic dimension' of these brands went hand in hand with a lofty price tag, making them inaccessible to most people. But with the democratization of luxury, that definition had evolved. The sophistication remained, but the selectivity was less apparent. Now there were two sorts of luxury: the inaccessible and the mass. The factors that bound them were 'an additional creative and emotional value for the consumer' and the promise of quality – which was occasionally fulfilled.

The rise of accessible luxury stoked a fascination with the sector that generated books, documentaries, magazines and even celebrities. For what was Paris Hilton if not a goddess of accessible luxury, sent down from the paradise of the rich to entertain the masses? The trend also provoked suspicion that the word 'luxury' had become devalued. The journalist Dana Thomas argued as much forcefully, in her 2007 book *Deluxe: How luxury lost its lustre*. 'The luxury industry... has sacrificed its integrity, undermined its products, tarnished its history and hoodwinked its consumers,' she wrote. 'In order to make luxury "accessible", tycoons have stripped away all that has made it special.'

'Luxury' had become a synonym for 'overpriced' – so-so products sold at huge margins in order to pay for the glitzy marketing that surrounded them. Those who worked in the trade began casting around for alternative terms. Tyler Brûlé, founder of the upmarket magazines *Wallpaper* and *Monocle*, offered 'über-premium', which he described as 'a blueprint for the new luxury'. The idea was to take luxury back to its original form, 'sourcing the rarest raw materials, reducing the number of items made, and [returning to] single-door availability'. Brûlé suggested shutting down chain stores in favour of 'one amazing space on Madison Avenue'. It didn't matter if the product was available only in, say, Tokyo: 'You're going to have to buy that Japan Airlines flight if you want to purchase' ('Über-premium separates the Have Lots from the Have Nots', *The Age*, 10 December 2006).

London department store Selfridges also rejected the L-word when it launched a space devoted to premium products in September 2007, instead christening it The Wonder Room. 'We wanted a word that conveyed something special, accessible and exciting,' the store's creative director, Alannah Weston, told the *Financial Times*. 'Luxury seemed dated to me' ('What luxury means now', 7 September 2007).

The credit crunch and ensuing global financial crisis heralded a new phase. As the economy spiralled into recession, most consumers were forced to cut back on luxuries – accessible or otherwise. But the concept of luxury was too alluring to be banished altogether.

BEYOND BLING

While ordinary people curbed their dreams in order to get a handle on reality, luxury brand consultants – a breed that had proliferated with the democratization of the sector – advised their clients to concentrate on the super rich: in other words, the über-premium market. The number of billionaires had risen dramatically in the preceding years, and their individual wealth continued to grow relative to that of the rest of society.

The media's fascination with the sector remained undimmed. Indeed, they had an interest in promoting luxury goods. Many newspapers had launched 'luxury lifestyle' supplements to mine advertising income from premium brands. The trend arguably began with the *Financial Times' How To Spend It* magazine, launched in 1994. More recent additions to the genre include *Time Style & Design* (2003) the *New York Times' T* magazine (2004) and *The Wall Street Journal*'s *WSJ*, launched on the very cusp of recession in September 2008. The latter seemed a risky proposition, but luxury advertisers are attractive to publishers precisely because their most expensive products are held to be recession-proof.

It's worth noting that, even in their darkest hour, the luxury brands spoke of a 'slowdown' rather than a collapse. After all, they had a long way to fall. In 2007, Verdict Research estimated that the global market for luxury goods was worth US $263 billion. Two years later, in the depths of economic gloom, Hermès announced a modest rise in profits. Louis Vuitton parent LVMH said the brand had posted 'double digit gains' in Asia – home to almost 40 per cent of the world's luxury consumers. While the global luxury market slumped, sales in the Middle East and China grew by 2 per cent and 7 per cent respectively. The recession shook the luxury giants, but they comforted themselves with the thought that they were somewhat sheltered from the storm.

An article in the *International Herald Tribune* captured the mood of brittle confidence. The fashion designer Karl Lagerfeld said recession was merely a time for 'moral and physical' spring cleaning. 'There is no creative evolution if you don't have dramatic moments like this,' he pronounced, adding: 'Bling is over.' In the same piece, Frédéric Verbrugghe, director of the food hall at upmarket department store Le Bon Marché, offered a more measured interpretation. He said customers would now look for luxury products that had *savoir faire* rather than flash ('In the lap of luxury, Paris squirms', 15 January 2009).

This parallels the 'flight to quality' theory: given the choice of buying an expensive hand-crafted product that will last or a cheap off-the-rack one that will fall to bits a few months later, the discerning customer takes the former option. As an elegantly dressed man once said to me in a Paris department store, when we had agreed on the doubtful quality of a selection of ties, 'I can't afford to buy cheap things.'

Lack of affordability does not seem to limit our appreciation of luxury. We are tempted to despise those who enjoy sybaritic lifestyles, but somehow it feels like cheap jealousy. In a separate interview – this time with BBC Radio 4's *Today* programme – Lagerfeld observed: 'If you have no dreams... people would ask why they get up in the morning... If you want only things you can afford, it's boring... It is very ugly to think [things] shouldn't exist because you cannot buy them' (2 February 2009).

Finally, there remains the argument that true luxury is beyond price. 'Definitions of luxury change according to era, location and who you ask,' observes Lorenz Bäumer, who designs jewellery for Louis Vuitton. He mentions the Vélib rental bike scheme in Paris, which allows users to borrow a bicycle free of charge, provided they pay a refundable deposit with their credit card. 'Today, it's possible to pick up a bicycle anywhere in Paris and cycle through the city, for nothing. That, to me, is a great luxury.'

The aim of this book is to consider different interpretations of luxury by taking a closer look at a variety of goods and services. What is the history of these brands? How do they communicate with their customers? What, if anything, do they have in common? And how are they weathering these turbulent times?

THE NECESSITY OF LUXURY

It may well be that luxury is a basic human need – a way of winning something back against the cruelty of life. The urge appears to have been there from the beginning. In his 1992 book *Histoire du Luxe en France*, Jean Castarède mentions a 30,000-year-old ivory figurine known as the 'Venus of Brassenpouy'. He notes that she has braided hair. 'As bizarre as it might seem, one of the first concerns of man (or woman) was not clothing or protection, but seduction.' Ornamentation predates clothes and weaponry, he argues.

Castarède also points out that early man shared another of our basic urges, which is to dream. Dreams and longings provoke not only self-expression through art, but also the impulse 'to single oneself out through ornamentation, make a mark through monuments, seduce others by acquiring or giving rare objects, and finally to better enjoy life by improving one's food and surroundings. *Voilà le luxe.*'

In other words, man has aspired to better things since he first glimpsed the stars.

The primitive impulses behind our desire for luxury also nudge us towards a clearer definition of this slippery word. As Castarède suggests, luxury is often associated with the realm of the senses: voluptuous images, tastes, odours and sensations. Indeed, sensuality is a key component of many luxury brands.

Christopher J Berry offers further clues in his book *The Idea of Luxury* (1994). He writes that luxury is often, erroneously, perceived as all that is superfluous. But 'if it takes six screws to secure a shelf then more than that number are redundant... [and] a seventh screw is not a "refined" luxury good.' Instead, Berry submits the idea that a luxury is a refinement on something that already exists. It is not superfluous, but it *is* substitutable. In other words, any second-hand jalopy will get you from A to B, but driving a Bentley provides an additional sensual pleasure.

Berry remarks that luxuries generally have a wide appeal, even though they remain out of reach of the majority. Antiquarian books and rare stamps may be extremely precious to niche groups of collectors, but despite their value they are not considered luxuries. All of us, however, can imagine enjoying a weekend at a five-star hotel. For Berry, luxury falls into distinct categories: food and drink, clothing and accessories, shelter and leisure. I would add transport to the list. These are areas where the basics are available to most of us, but where luxurious substitutes are available to a few.

I used the categories above as a guide when structuring this book. But I also wanted to consider less tangible ideas of luxury. For many of us in the developed world, 'luxury' is not just about expensive goods. It's also about time. Perhaps it makes more sense to save the money we would have spent on a frippery from Dior and lavish it on getting our shirts laundered, so we have time to talk to our kids or read a book instead of doing the ironing. There's also the luxury of experience. I'm all for breakfast on the balcony and cocktails by the pool, but an eco-voyage up the Amazon or a tour of Florence with an expert in Renaissance art are also luxury vacations. And thanks to our hectic working lives, the acquisition of knowledge has itself become a luxury.

One thing that all successful brands share is a great story. The luxury sector, particularly, is full of rags-to-riches (and often finery-to-riches) sagas. Stuart McCullough, head of sales and marketing at Bentley, pointed this out after relating the history of the automotive brand. 'The same narrative lies behind almost any luxury brand you care to examine. There's always a hero. That hero needs to have struggled against great adversity. They rise nobly to the challenge. And today's success is the ultimate realization of their dream.'

Relating some of these stories became one of my goals. It also enabled me to meet a few of the people behind luxury brands.

SAVOIR FAIRE

The real inspiration for this book was Paris, which has been my home for the best part of a decade. There are many sides to the city, but its facade, at least, is opulent. From the shop windows of Avenue Montaigne to the chic students who combine H&M with Dior, from the jewellery boutiques of Place Vendôme to the jewel-like macaroons in the window of Ladurée, I see flashes of luxury almost every day. This constant exposure to a world that lay – most of the time – just beyond my reach prodded me to investigate further. I barged through the gilded doors using the only means at my disposal: a press card and a list of questions.

And while I'll admit to a certain bias, it seems fair that any inquiry into the world of luxury should devote a large percentage of space to the French capital. In fact, there is a strong case to be made for Paris as the birthplace of modern luxury.

In his 2001 love letter to the city, *Le Flâneur*, the writer Edmund White notes: 'The French invented the idea of *luxe* and have always been willing to pay for it... A ritual of Parisian life is trading *les bonnes addresses* – the names and locations of some talented upholsterer or hat-maker or re-caner of straw bottomed chairs or of a lovely little neighbourhood seamstress.'

Although the city had long been associated with pleasure (even the Romans praised its temperate climate), the systematization of luxury began with Louis XIV. As the historian Jean Castarède puts it, under the Sun King 'French luxury became a profession'. In the mirrored fastness of Versailles, Louis set the bar of opulence so high that even the wealthiest nobleman was unable to compete with him. He devoted hours to his toilet and literally dictated the fashions of the day. 'One word from him was enough to ensure that a doublet with too many slashes was revised, or that a fashion that was not to his taste vanished,' writes Castarède.

Louis' vanity sprung from a familiar psychological driver: insecurity. As a boy, his life had been threatened by the Fronde (named after a type of slingshot), a political insurrection that had brought the mob to the very gates of the Palais Royal. One of the rebels made it as far as the king's bedchamber – but was disconcerted by the sight of the sleeping 12-year-old boy. The precocious Louis later quelled the uprising by taking control of parliament (*'L'état, c'est moi'*) and paying off the rebel leaders. But the king never forgot that the people could turn against him. He abandoned Paris for a former hunting lodge in the suburbs, turning it into a glittering carapace. The court of Versailles effectively became a theatre in which Louis played the leading role – and always wore the most exquisite costumes.

But the king's tastes spread beyond fashion to influence architecture, gardening, furniture and the decorative arts. His passion for luxury ensured that an entire industry grew up to serve him.

Henceforth, Paris was eternally linked with *le luxe*, even after the revolution. But before we reach that point we should mention another personality who used Versailles as a private playground: Marie Antoinette. 'This child of 15,' as Castarède describes her, 'thrown into the intoxicating environment of the loftiest and most stunning court in the world… from her arrival in France mistakenly saw life as a costume ball and royalty as a succession of fashion shows.'

At first, the queen and the city seemed made for one another. In her 2001 biography of Marie Antoinette, Antonia Fraser observes 'Paris was a city dependent on the financial support of the noble and rich to maintain its industries, which were in the main to do with luxury and semi-luxury goods… In a country where details of appearance, costume and presentation were "vital matters"… Marie Antoinette was an appropriate consort.'

We know where the queen's extravagant lifestyle led her – but post-revolutionary France did not entirely lose its taste for luxury. And Napoleon was in no position to offer a remedy, judging by the loot he brought back from his European victories and the opulent balls he threw to celebrate them. As for his personal tastes, the emperor was a client of the watchmaker Breguet and a fastidious wearer of cologne. In this respect he was almost as fragrant as his empress, Josephine, who launched the French perfume industry practically single-handed.

It was during the Second Empire – under Napoleon III – that French luxury began to take the shape that is familiar to us today. Many brands that remain the essence of French chic were founded in the 19th century. Louis-François Cartier established his jewellery business in 1847, later handing it over to his son Alfred. The firm moved to a prestigious address in Rue de la Paix – not far from the Ritz hotel and its stream of wealthy clients – in 1899, where it remains. Only six years earlier, Boucheron had moved to the nearby Place Vendôme, where visitors can still gaze into its sparkling windows. Thierry Hermès had founded his celebrated saddlery and equestrian supplies business in 1837. In 1880 it transferred to its current address at 24 Rue du Faubourg Saint-Honoré – close, at the time, to the homes and stables of the aristocracy.

In 1854 a trunk-maker called Louis Vuitton opened his atelier a stone's throw away from Cartier and Boucheron. Vuitton's designs were a reflection of his times. Traditionally, travellers' trunks had curved tops, designed to sluice off the rain when they were strapped to the roofs of stagecoaches. But Vuitton's trunks were flat – the better for stacking in the baggage cars of trains or the holds of steamships. They were made of durable poplar and sheathed in grey waterproofed canvas. The design became so commonplace that Vuitton began printing his own name on the canvas in a symmetrical pattern, transforming his trunks into branded accessories.

Today, of course, Louis Vuitton is part of the massive LVMH (Moët Hennessy, Louis Vuitton) conglomerate. A former real-estate entrepreneur named Bernard Arnault took control of the group in 1989. A couple of years earlier he had acquired Boussac, the textile firm that owned the Christian Dior fashion house, laying the foundations for what was to become a luxury empire.

The presence of LVMH is another reason for the pre-eminence of France in the world of luxury. There are actually three such conglomerates, which together have transformed luxury from the domain of discreet craftspeople into a multi-billion dollar industry. They are, in size order, LVMH, Richemont and PPR (owner of the Gucci Group, which alongside Gucci itself embraces a slew of premium brands, including Boucheron, Yves Saint Laurent, Bottega Veneta, Balenciaga, Stella McCartney and Alexander McQueen). These are unquestionably the most powerful players in luxury – and all three of them are based in Paris.

Italy can make a very serious claim to the luxury throne – with its potent ready-to-wear and leather goods brands – but France is far stronger in the areas of wines and spirits, fragrances and cosmetics, watches, jewellery and tableware.

In short, Paris lies at the heart of the luxury world. And that is where our journey begins.

1

The dream weavers

'As long as there is a society, there will always be fashion.'

It was not surprising that the funeral of Yves Saint Laurent resembled a fashion show. In front of the Eglise Saint Roch – a break in the narrow boutique-lined canyon of Rue Saint Honoré – the tiered bank of photographers was an irresistible reminder of the battery of lenses that bristles at the end of every catwalk. And, of course, nobody was getting into the church if they weren't on the list.

But Yves Saint Laurent was also a French national treasure, so efforts had been made to include the public. Although the street was closed to traffic, we could watch the fashion firmament arriving from behind the steel barriers that kept us at a safe distance. A giant screen outside the church projected images of the funeral procession, and later of the service itself.

The 5th of June 2008 was overcast, the grey sky seeming to press down on the onlookers cramming the little street. Opposite the church, wizened black-clad ladies ventured onto the balconies of their apartments, like figures auguring rain on a weather clock. More ladies of a certain age lurked in the crowd, the mothballs shaken out of their Saint Laurent dresses. The atmosphere was solemn, with an odd undercurrent of pride. It would be difficult to imagine another country's citizens responding so emotionally to the passing of a fashion designer. 'Thank goodness it started at 3.30,' said a man standing next to me. 'I had time to finish lunch.'

Leading designers came to pay their respects: John Galliano, Jean-Paul Gaultier, Hubert de Givenchy, Christian Lacroix, Kenzo Takada, Valentino... soon the church held more brand names than a department store. The actress Catherine Deneuve, whose screen appearances in Saint Laurent helped to define the label's coolly sophisticated image, climbed the steps clutching a sheaf of green wheat. Embracing Pierre Bergé, she wiped away a tear. Bergé was the business mastermind behind the Yves Saint Laurent brand, and for many years the designer's partner in life as well as work. President Nicolas Sarkozy appeared with Carla – first lady and former Yves Saint Laurent model.

Finally, the gleaming oak coffin arrived. As it was carried into the church, the crowd broke into applause. The great designer had made his last journey down the catwalk. There wouldn't be another like him, everyone said. It was the end of an era.

THE ROAD TO READY-TO-WEAR

'In fashion, it's always the end of an era,' points out Didier Grumbach, president of the Fédération Française de la Couture, which organizes the Paris collections, educates the next generation of designers and is generally the keeper of the flame of French fashion. 'It was the end of an era, too, when [Cristóbal] Balenciaga closed his fashion house in 1968. And yet today the Balenciaga brand is back and thriving. Fashion is merely a reflection of society. As long as there is a society, there will always be fashion.'

What Grumbach does acknowledge, however, is Saint Laurent's huge influence on the fashion of the late 20th and early 21st centuries. 'Modern women's clothing owes a great debt to Saint Laurent. The descendents of his designs are the foundation of the wardrobes of many millions of women.'

For this and other reasons, Yves Saint Laurent is an ideal figure to study when looking at the long journey of luxury fashion from haute couture to high street. But in order to appreciate the pivotal role he played, we first need to take a look at some of his precursors. The archetype of the fashion designer owes a lot to the example of an Englishman named Charles Frederick Worth, who left London in 1847 with five pounds to his name and rose to become an outfitter of empresses.

Traditionally, French couturiers had been humble suppliers whose creations depended more on the caprices of their clients than on their own imaginations. A possible exception was Rose Bertin, a haberdasher and couturière who had become personal stylist to Marie Antoinette. Bertin had entered court circles thanks to her numerous aristocratic clients. The patronage of a megastar like Marie Antoinette lifted her reputation to stratospheric heights, allowing her to play the diva in her shop on the Rue Saint Honoré. When a snobbish customer came calling, Bertin sniffed 'Show madame my latest work for her majesty.' She may have been nicknamed 'the minister of fashion', but it is not clear how much Bertin called the shots when faced with a queen of style. They occasionally have the air of mischievous confidantes daring one another to go a step further.

Worth, on the other hand, was a fashion tyrant. He cajoled his clients into following his tastes and was determined that his designs should resemble those of no other dressmaker. 'My mission is to invent: creativity is the secret of my success,' he boasted. This single-mindedness was apparent from the start, when he was working as an assistant at the Paris drapery house of Gagelin and Opigez. Visitors admired the fit of the dresses Worth had made for his wife, who also worked at the store. Soon he had his own fashion house and was promising to liberate women from their crinolines, warning them that he alone possessed the skill to refine their silhouettes. This was made-to-measure with an extra touch of self-aggrandizement. At the turn of the century, mere couture made way for haute couture.[1]

Worth and his successors – Poiret and Vionnet among them – founded the first fashion brands. But although the designs of these Paris fashion houses were adapted and interpreted by provincial dressmakers, the couturiers were still effectively tailors, making individual items to fit specific clients. Haute couture was strictly by appointment only. The concept of mass-produced clothing hanging in stores did not exist. However, the mechanization of the textile industry and the emergence of department stores had combined to make the next step inevitable: ready-to-wear was just around the corner.

Yves Saint Laurent was by no means the originator of ready-to-wear (or prêt-à-porter, to use the French term), but he was probably its most creative exponent. As Didier Grumbach's own 1993 book on the subject, *Histoires de Mode*, reveals, couturiers had been experimenting with branded series of garments since at least the 1920s. During that decade, Madeleine Vionnet signed an agreement with an independent Paris atelier to make labelled reproductions of her designs – with the proviso that no more than three of each were ever sold. And just after the Second World War, under the Marshall Plan devised by the Americans to speed Europe's economic recovery, there was briefly a project to establish a factory that would produce labelled versions of French couturiers' designs for export. At the time, the Paris fashion houses baulked at the idea.

A few years later, in 1950, a group of fashion insiders (among them Jean Gaumont-Lanvin, nephew of the designer Jeanne Lanvin) formed a company called Couturiers Associés. This would produce high-quality ready-to-wear lines based on patterns provided by designers. The label would bear the designer's name as well as the name of the company. This time, five designers signed up: Jacques Fath, Robert Piguet, Paquin, Carven and Jean Dessès. Each designer would deliver seven patterns per season. The clothes were run-up in dressmaking ateliers. To promote the collections, fashion shows were held in selected department stores, casinos and hotels across France.

The company was the precursor of today's luxury fashion empires – but it only existed for three years. The market for expensive mass-produced fashion was still small, and it was impossible to predict which garments would sell. This was an age before concerted marketing efforts and media coverage dovetailed to create the concept of 'trends'. Market research was undertaken, but it came too late. Lack of capital, internal squabbling and failure to seduce an adequate target market combined to put an end to the experiment.

A far more successful approach to prêt-à-porter was devised by a designer forever linked with the Swinging Sixties as one of the popularizers of the mini skirt: André Courrèges. In a decade when technology was fashionable and fashion was being inspired by the street, Courrèges saw no reason why industrially produced garments should not coexist alongside hand-finished haute couture creations. Indeed, he showed both collections on the catwalk as a way of demonstrating that a less wealthy public could also get a taste of Courrèges style.

'Courrèges was the first to understand that haute couture drove the dream,' says Didier Grumbach today. 'The haute couture collection established the necessary premium image of the brand, which then rubbed off on the prêt-à-porter line.'

The strategy worked. In 1967, Courrèges opened his first prêt-à-porter boutique in Paris. Over the next decade he expanded globally, opening 28 stores in the United States, 20 in Germany, 17 in Japan and three in Hong Kong. Sales rocketed from 17 million francs in 1970 to 68 million by 1973. Clearly, this level of output could not be entrusted to the Paris dressmaking ateliers. In 1972, Courrèges built his own factory in Pau, the town in the southwest of France where he was born. During the fuel crisis of the mid-1970s, the company was forced to retrench, but by then Courrèges had become one of the first global ready-to-wear brands.

It's no coincidence that Courrèges is associated with 'futuristic' outfits like trapezoid dresses and shiny moon boots. Ahead of his time, he understood the importance of quality control when it came to brand image.

Even today, few ready-to-wear labels make their own clothing. A designer label is just that: the name of a designer sewn in to a garment made in a factory. Naturally, the manufacturers keep a low profile. Take Staff International, for example. The company was founded in 1985 in Noventa Vicentina, in Italy. Owned since 2000 by the Diesel group, it makes clothing for designers such as Martin Margiela, Marc Jacobs, Vivienne Westwood and Sophia Kokosalaki. Other names woven into its history include Karl Lagerfeld, Valentino, Costume National and Missoni. Through services like its 'knitwear atelier', the company ensures that the clothes we end up wearing match the designers' original vision. But it helps them with other matters too: every brand has a dedicated team working on products and styling, research and development, sales and production. Staff International also has a press and communications division that advises on PR, brand strategy and advertising. And its distribution arm ensures that the clothes find their way into the right stores.

The production (or 'confection' as it's known in France) of prêt-à-porter clothing has a long history. Didier Grumbach himself has been involved in the manufacturing of garments for designers. In 1954, as he recounts in his book, the young Grumbach joined C Mendès, a business started by his grandfather Cerf Mendès-France 80 years earlier. Over the years the company made clothing for the likes of Jeanne Lanvin, Jean Patou, Emanuel Ungaro, Guy Laroche, Givenchy, Balenciaga – and Yves Saint Laurent.

THE YSL LEGACY

Saint Laurent was the first designer to make ready-to-wear seem as desirable and – crucially – as prestigious as haute couture. Perhaps that's because, despite his otherworldly demeanour, he was at heart a populist. Late in his career, he half-joked that he wished he'd invented the denim jean. He was born into a well-off family in Algeria, then a French colony, in 1936. In 1953 he arrived in Paris – a skinny 17-year-old kid with a bunch of sketches under his arm, demanding and getting an appointment with Michael de Brunhoff, the editor of *Vogue*. After taking one look at the sketches, or so the legend goes, de Brunhoff dispatched Saint Laurent to Christian Dior.

And there the precocious designer stayed, taking over at the helm of the house when Dior died prematurely in 1957. After creating six collections, some of which divided critics, he was called up to fight for France in the Algerian war of independence. Anybody could tell that Saint Laurent was constitutionally unsuited to military service. He was hospitalized after just 20 days with severe depression. By the time he emerged, at the end of 1960, he had lost his job at Dior. But now he was ready – or at least as ready as this timorous figure could ever be – to establish his own fashion house. And his partner Pierre Bergé was at his side, taking care of business while the designer wove his dreams.

The pair soon realized that Paris fashion could not afford to maintain its courtly posture – not in the fast and loose atmosphere of the 1960s. They created a separate brand called Yves Saint Laurent Rive Gauche and in 1966 opened a small boutique in Saint Germain. The name and the location were carefully chosen. At the time, the Left Bank of Paris was considered bohemian, literary and faintly unruly: two years later, its students would be at the centre of the May riots that almost toppled the government. It was certainly a world away from the glittering haute couture *maisons* and their haughty clientele. As such, it was an ideal rallying point for a fashion revolution that would put women in safari jackets, tuxedos and trouser suits.

In her 2002 biography of Yves Saint Laurent, the journalist Laurence Benaïm evokes the boutique's uncluttered red and black lacquer interior and its angular Mies Van der Rohe Barcelona chairs. The long, narrow, former bakery was reconfigured by Isabelle Hebey, a designer who considered steel and laminate the contemporary version of wood panelling. 'It quickly became a Paris nightclub for the daytime,' writes

Benaïm. As for the clothes, they were 'not the luxury of wealth, but of attitude'. Pierre Bergé observed that while Chanel liberated women, Saint Laurent gave them power. Long before the statement shoulder pads of the 1980s, he created a palette of styles for the independent woman.

Yves Saint Laurent Rive Gauche was far more than a spin-off line, as Didier Grumbach recounts: '[Saint Laurent] brought a new significance to prêt-à-porter. He discovered that the work of couture – solitary, constantly demanding perfection, immediately consumable – is, all things considered, less creative than that of prêt-à-porter... which anticipates the desires of women by proposing, in advance, new styles... From the very first season, he outpaced couture with his brilliance, mastery and invention, imposing with prêt-à-porter his [vision of] fashion on the entire world.'

Through a franchise system, Yves Saint Laurent Rive Gauche grew into a global network of stores. YSL also adopted the licensing strategy that later tarnished the images of some designers. Its most enthusiastic exponent was Pierre Cardin, another Parisian prêt-à-porter pioneer. Cardin licensed his name to the manufacturers of all manner of objects, from pens to cooking pots. Designers had realized that, with haute couture creating an ethereal dream at the top end of the market, they could make a fortune by chopping the dream into little pieces and selling it in the form of – often quite shoddy – branded goods at the bottom. Finally realizing the damage this was doing, most fashion brands reined in their licences in the 1990s. Today, while the majority of their profits still come from the sales of fragrances, sunglasses and other accessories, they keep strict control over the design and production of items that bear their names.

Although Yves Saint Laurent was happy to feed this hunger for licences, he fared better than most, launching highly successful perfumes like Rive Gauche (1971) and Opium (1978). In fact, according to Laurence Benaïm, by the time the Paris fashion house celebrated its 30th anniversary in 1992, no less 82 per cent of its income derived from fragrances and cosmetics. Of the 2,993 people who worked there, only 533 were concerned with couture. This reflects, in microcosm, the structure of the entire fashion industry. It was a clear confirmation that YSL had transcended the material: to millions of people around the world, the three letters evoked an enviable Parisian lifestyle that could be bottled and packaged. Inevitably, the house became embroiled in the brand-acquisition fever that gripped the fashion industry throughout the 1990s – and which is still having an impact on the sector today.

Elf-Sanofi acquired the fragrances and beauty arm of Yves Saint Laurent in January 1993, with Saint Laurent and Pierre Bergé retaining control of the fashion house. Six years later, however, both the beauty business and the fashion house were acquired by François Pinault and his retail group PPR. The same group soon beat LVMH in a tussle to take control of Gucci. The fashion world had changed – firms that had begun as small, almost familial, concerns were now part of well-oiled business machines – and Saint Laurent found that it no longer suited him. By the time he died, he'd effectively been retired from fashion for six years.

Towards the end of his life, however, he had a chance to see how other designers might interpret his legacy. First, PPR brought in the American designer Tom Ford to oversee the YSL brand. Ford had become a star by transforming Gucci from a faded purveyor of upmarket bags to a sexpot fashion brand, complete with stores clad in black marble and sweaty 'porno chic' advertising. But Ford's risky balancing act between sophistication and vulgarity did not sit well with the Yves Saint Laurent brand, which had a cooler, more ambiguous image. Saint Laurent and Pierre Bergé signalled their disapproval by pointedly staying away from Ford's YSL shows. Although the charismatic American had done a great job with Gucci, his magic was not having the desired effect at YSL. Eventually, Ford left PPR for new projects – including the creation of his eponymous fashion brand – and Yves Saint Laurent was ripe for another overhaul.

This time, the chemistry worked. Ford's second-in-command at YSL was a tall, elegant Milanese named Stefano Pilati, who'd joined the brand from Prada in 2000. Rising to the top slot in 2004, Pilati, after a hesitant start, made the brand his own. Yet his sharp, urbane designs deliberately channelled the Saint Laurent spirit. The founder himself was said to approve.

A whole raft of historic French fashion brands have had to deal with this transition from creator to successor: Chanel, Dior, Givenchy, Balenciaga, Lanvin – the list goes on. Indeed, most of them have churned through several designers by now, with varying degrees of success. The challenge for the newcomers is to remain true to the essence of the brand while updating it and expressing their own creativity.

Pilati puts his wobbly beginning down to the fact that his initial designs were somewhat ahead of the curve. His tulip-shaped skirts were derided when he showed them in 2004, only to be appropriated by other designers later on. He admits 'When I was 17, the design director at Nino Cerrutti, who was my first mentor, taught me that to be too much ahead is to be behind. The most important thing is to be right on time' ('At Yves Saint Laurent, a chic for tough times', *International Herald Tribune*, 30–31 August 2008).

For a brand, the most important thing is to be profitable – a box that YSL had failed to tick at the time of writing. It lost €60 million in 2004 and managed to break even four years later. The dramatically improved picture may have something to do with Pilati's creativity – but the strategy put in place by the brand's new chief executive Valerie Hermann when she arrived in 2005 should not be discounted. Hermann felt that, in contrast to the licence-mania of the Saint Laurent era, the brand was not producing enough accessories. She encouraged Pilati to design a bag. The resulting creation, called Muse, was a bestseller. Pilati has since followed up with more accessories and footwear. He is dynamically creative, but not divorced from reality. In the *IHT* article quoted above, he first states 'I am not a businessman', before changing his mind: 'I have become a businessman. The times require that.'

THE FUTURE OF COUTURE

Yves Saint Laurent took luxury fashion out of stuffy salons cluttered with gilt chairs and put it onto the streets. Ironically, the vitality and creativity of prêt-à-porter eclipsed haute couture, which began to look like an overblown anachronism. Now fashion had democratized, who wanted to spend a hundred thousand dollars on a dress? By the end of the 1990s it was suggested that there were fewer than 500 haute couture customers worldwide. A number of designers had packed away their sketchpads, unable to make a profit. Some commentators thought haute couture would disappear altogether. Others felt it was worth saving. After all, haute couture was the wellspring. It was the fairytale, the glittering spectacle whose pixie dust rubbed off on the rest of the fashion industry. Could anybody breathe life back into haute couture?

In his position at the helm of the Fédération Française de la Couture, Didier Grumbach was in an ideal position to see what should be done. Haute couture is an official appellation, rather like Bordeaux or champagne. In order to enter this exclusive club (it's called the Chambre Syndicale de la Haute Couture) a designer had to have 'made-to-measure dressmaking activity in the Paris area'. But in 1997 membership was broadened to include 'guest designers', who would be voted in by existing members. They would show made-to-measure clothes alongside experimental ready-to-wear pieces.

Grumbach notes that the first guest designers to send collections down the runway during the haute couture shows – which are held at the end of January and the beginning of July – were Thierry Mugler and Jean-Paul Gaultier. Many others have followed. A recent selection included Cathy Pill, Felipe Oliviera Batista, Josep Font and Alexis Mabille (of whom we'll hear more later). All these guests have added dynamism to a calendar that would otherwise have thinned out to only a handful of designers. There are also 'correspondent members' whose clothes are hand-made, but not in Paris: they include Valentino and Giorgio Armani.

Some designers who started out making ready-to-wear have since entered the world of haute couture. Jean-Paul Gaultier has progressed from 'guest designer' to full membership of the Chambre Syndicale, showing an haute couture collection every season. Giorgio Armani made his debut in 2005, showing 35 pieces in a collection that he called Giorgio Armani Privé. According to UK newspaper the *Daily Telegraph*, Armani had invested in an entire dressmaking atelier. Customers seduced by the pieces on the catwalk could expect to undergo three fittings before walking away with their own bespoke version, which would cost them anywhere between £12,800 and £46,500 ('Armani plots a new French revolution', 25 January 2005).

For haute couture these prices were considered accessible. The vertiginous cost of an haute couture dress is also the price of an entire system: the designer's salary, those of the women who hand sew and embroider the pieces, the cost of the runway show, the boutique and the personal shoppers who greet VIP customers in private salons... the haute couture client is paying for individuality and creativity, certainly – but for many other things besides. This inaccessibility drives the brand dream, which explains its appeal to designers. 'Once upon a time, designers created haute couture and diversified into prêt-à-porter,' points out Grumbach. 'Now it's the other way around.'

A number of contemporary fashion brands have adopted the strategy pioneered by the original couturiers: a pyramidal structure with haute couture as a shining lure at the apex and bags and perfume being hawked at the base. But designers also use haute couture as a field of experimentation – the ultimate expression of their art. The shows put on by John Galliano at Dior and Karl Lagerfeld at Chanel often feature creations that have little to do with what the average person thinks of as 'clothing'. This artistic element allows couture to escape the accusations of excess, irrelevance and frivolity that are often directed at other sectors of the luxury business.

I asked rising designer Alexis Mabille for his take on the future of couture. Now in his early 30s, Mabille knows the Chambre Syndicale de la Haute Couture intimately, as he studied fashion design at its school. With his long dark hair and impeccable dress sense – which often features long coats and a bow tie – Mabille could easily be a couturier from another age. Which is perhaps not a coincidence, as in the mid-1990s the school still had a somewhat 19th century feel about it.

'Most of the teachers had worked at the traditional couture houses like Givenchy and Balenciaga, so they were very skilled and extremely strict,' he recalls. 'We learned how to do everything by hand. In fact, there were only about three sewing machines in the entire place. Your seams, hand sewn, had to be perfectly straight. And if the garment was not perfect, you were obliged to take it apart and start again.'

This is the sort of *savoir faire* that will be lost if haute couture dies, he argues. The school is more modern now, but Mabille admits that he's glad he learned the old-fashioned way. 'As a result I'm very demanding when it comes to my prêt-à-porter collections. In fact there are certain problems that can only be resolved by hand.'

He got bitten by the couture bug early, making outfits for theatre productions and friends while growing up in his native Lyon. When he came to Paris he made ends meet by designing wedding dresses. After leaving fashion school, he did short apprenticeships with Ungaro and Nina Ricci before joining the design team at Christian Dior, where he stayed for nine years. Originally he worked in the licensing department – and this was before the brand had become more exigent about the quality of the products that bore its name. 'It was pretty depressing,' he says. 'I won't even describe some of the horrors they came up with.'

Under Mabille's influence the range of licensed goods improved, edging closer to the vision of Dior's new designer, John Galliano.

When Galliano asked who was behind the change, he was introduced to Alexis Mabille. The young apprentice soon found himself working directly with the boss, notably designing a line of jewellery. This, eventually, gave him the confidence to launch his own fashion house. 'It's very familial,' he says. 'I founded the business with my mother and my brother. The press seemed to find that quite intriguing, along with the fact that my collections are fairly accessible.'

He dismisses any suggestion that he has a flair for marketing – though he's clearly a favourite of the French media – but he has a talent for devising simple yet amusing concepts. One of his collections featured variations on the bow tie in unusual fabrics, at a time when it was possibly the most outmoded accessory imaginable. Mabille commissioned a series of photographs and sent them off to 40 or so fashion journalists. The images were subsequently reproduced everywhere, to the extent that the bow tie sneaked back into some masculine wardrobes. Mabille has since adopted it as a motif. He also likes to blur the boundary between masculine and feminine dress, although he flinches at the word 'androgynous'. 'I simply believe that both sexes should have access to the same variety of colours, materials and forms. Men should be able to wear a grey suit one minute and a sequinned pink tank top the next – and women too.'

Here we get to the nub of Mabille's prescription for haute couture. 'It's all about erasing the silos,' he says. 'It's ridiculous to assume today that a woman who can afford a €30,000 haute couture dress from Dior is not also going to buy a simple pair of jeans from time to time. So when I was invited to show haute couture as a guest, I happily mixed it with prêt-à-porter. I even went a step further and mixed spring–summer with autumn–winter. I called the collection "No season, no reason". The press loved it.'

But to his dismay, Mabille has watched the silos multiply. 'As well as seasonal collections for men and women, there are pre-collections and cruise collections. The workload for designers is crushing.'

This trend is driven by the battle for profits. The fashion journalist Suzy Menkes has suggested that the industry is constantly on the verge of a nervous breakdown. 'These companies are so huge that they can't ever say that they've lost it, that they've lost the plot, that they don't know what they're doing. So they just cast around desperately, they pay all these zillions to stylists or pop stars, for people to come and sit in the front row. Anything, really, to try and keep in the swim' ('Suzy Menkes & Stefano Tonchi', *Self Service* magazine, fall–winter 2008).

With so much at stake, the prêt-à-porter shows have become blatantly commercial. So Paris haute couture season is evolving into the last pole of experimentation: for the big fashion brands, certainly, but also for younger designers with fresh ideas. Their clothes are not necessarily hand-sewn in traditional ateliers, but they are unique in a different way. They have an artisanal, spontaneous feel about them. Their collections combine imagination, innovation and pure craft. Mixing and matching has breathed life back into haute couture.

NOTE

1. For more on Charles Frederick Worth, see *Fashion Brands: Branding style from Armani to Zara* (2nd edition, Kogan Page, 2008).

2

The last artisans

'If I wanted to get rich, I would do something else.'

Any sentence containing the word 'luxury' often features the word 'authenticity' not far behind. There's a strong chance that the word 'craftsmanship' will crop up as well. In today's wired world, when the human hand is more likely to be poised over a computer keyboard than grasping a tool, the ancient figure of the artisan has taken on a nostalgic glow. The luxury goods business, like almost every other, has become commoditized. So it's only natural that an object created in a cramped atelier by the sure and nimble fingers of a skilled craftsman should be prized for its purity.

Marketers, of course, are aware of the enhanced importance of authenticity. At the end of 2007, Harvard Business School Press published a book called *Authenticity: What consumers really want*, by James H Gilmore and B Joseph Pine II. Summarizing their work for the magazine *Advertising Age*, the pair started out on the right foot. 'Amid all the other issues advertising faces,' they wrote, 'there's a fundamental problem that has received too little attention: marketers' phoniness. Marketers and their complicit agencies can't help but exaggerate the fineness of every commodity, the greatness of every good, the superiority of every service and the memorability of every experience. Such phoniness has to stop.'

The authors went on to point out that 'in today's experience economy – where people increasingly bypass commoditized goods and services to spend time with companies that stage engaging experiences – authenticity is becoming the new consumer sensibility… People want real offerings from genuinely transparent sources.'

Suddenly, though, the article seemed to change tack, as the authors offered what appeared to be a series of tips that would enable brand owners to create an *impression* of authenticity.

> Many meaningful names readily connote authenticity. Top on the list are companies named after their founders, such as… Harley-Davidson and Levi Strauss & Co… Names also help render authenticity when they refer back to times when life was simpler, slower-paced and seemingly more authentic. Many firms, for example, have 'Main Street' in their names for this reason. Others employ words that evoke previous economic eras, including 'craft' (suggesting agrarian hands) or 'works' (suggesting industrial labour), as if every offering were handmade by a skilled craftsman in a workshop or small factory. ('Stop dishing out the phoniness, marketers', *Advertising Age*, 10 December 2007.)

For me, the implications of the article were depressingly clear: just like 'luxury' itself, the notion of authenticity was being hijacked by brands that were anything but.

THE OTHER SIDE OF FLORENCE

I'm not entirely sure why, but for me the word 'handmade' always conjures up an image of leather goods. Perhaps it's a masculine yearning for a pair of bespoke brogues or the perfectly proportioned piece of luggage. Resilient yet pliant, the latter item would slide effortlessly into an overhead locker while containing at least a week's worth of clothing. It would improve with age and attract envious glances from fellow passengers. I've been searching for that bag for so long now that I am almost certain it does not exist.

Florence seemed an ideal place to continue the quest. Everyone knows that the beautiful Italian city is the capital of fine leather goods. 'One of the world's foremost handcraft centres,' wrote Paul Hofmann, a former *New York Times* correspondent living in Italy, back in 1981.

Hofmann's article evoked a half-vanished world of skill, pride and, naturally, authenticity.

> Long before the celebrated art treasures of the Renaissance were created, the Florentine craftsmen of the late Middle Ages were famed for their skills and their products were in demand all over Europe. The wool and silk guilds, the goldsmiths and, yes, the tanners and leather cutters amassed the wealth that led to the emergence of a well-to-do craftsmen's class in Florence and, in turn, awakened interest for learning and art... The rich and powerful guilds belong to distant history, but the Florentine handcraft tradition lives on. ('The fine Italian hands of Florence', *The New York Times*, 8 November 1981.)

I read, too, of the existence of the Scuola de Cuoio, a Florentine school for artisanal leather workers. To me, the notion sounded almost as thrillingly medieval as that of the guilds. But the elegant streets of Florence also glint with the names of modern Italian luxury brands: Prada, Fendi, Gucci... These luxury titans benefit from their association with the artisanal heritage of the Italian leather goods industry. And the idea is so attractive that many of us are willing to be seduced.

'Diane Becker will never forget her visit to the Gucci prototype laboratory in Florence. Nearly all the pattern makers, marketing directors and research heads were elegant, stylishly coiffed men in their thirties, wearing charcoal suits. The one exception was a simply dressed man of around 70, a master craftsman who had learned artisanal leatherworking as a boy' ('Why it's worth spending US$2,000 on a bag', *Bene* magazine, summer 2006 issue). However, even the most romantically inclined writers are forced to admit that things are changing. From the same article: 'Most producers use synthetic thread today because it's stronger than traditional cotton... Although machines do most of the work these days, some luxury bags are still stitched entirely by hand.' A little further down the column, Patrizia Gatti, an editor at *Vogue Italia*, offered a few words of reassurance. 'The most notable names have the longest experience and use the best materials... You see it in the details, in the precision – they stay true to their traditions.'

One yearns to believe this. And yet, inevitably, there is another side to Florence. Dana Thomas revealed it in her 2007 book *Deluxe*, when she explained that most Italian luxury companies had swapped artisanal methods for factory production lines, which had dramatically improved productivity and thus boosted profits. 'Since 1995, all Gucci leather goods have been designed on computers,' she added, as if to banish from our minds the image of the old-fashioned atelier, with dust-motes suspended in shafts of light slanting from high windows.

Even consumers who missed Thomas's exposé must by now be aware that all is not what it seems in Italy. Down-to-earth British tabloid the *Sunday Mirror* got in on the act. 'Designer labels' sweatshop scandal!' a headline blared (on 2 December 2007). 'For generations,' read the accompanying article, 'Made in Italy meant just that – the chicest handbags from Milan, heels from Rome and gowns from Florence, handcrafted by Italian craftsmen. Not any more… Italy's finest fashion houses are leaning increasingly on an army of cheap Chinese immigrants who have turned Tuscany's textile powerhouse into Little China.'

The article took us to the Tuscan city of Prato, 'Italy's luxury goods capital'. The picture it painted did not resemble the Tuscany I knew. 'The air here is thick with the reek of dim sum and Chinese tobacco. Workers stand in the street to smoke, hawk and spit amid the bustle of what feels like downtown Beijing.'

The report claimed that Italian shoes selling for £900 in the United Kingdom were 'probably made by Chinese immigrants working 12 hours days for just three euros an hour'. It added that the city of 4,000 textile factories was home to 'an army of 25,000 low-wage workers', many of whom did not officially exist.

Readers of British tabloids have learned to take the articles in them with a pinch of salt, but this stark portrait sounded worryingly realistic. A few weeks later, back in Paris, I had coffee with a friend who works for an Italian fashion brand. 'Have you heard about the documentary they showed on RAI?' she asked me. 'Most embarrassing!'

The programme aired by Italy's state TV channel had shown Chinese workers stitching together handbags for leading Italian fashion brands in 'clandestine workshops' in Prato and Naples. It claimed bags that cost only about 20 euros to produce would be sold for more than 400 euros in stores. Gucci immediately refuted the report, saying in a statement: 'Whenever Gucci finds a situation that is not consistent with the internal policy and [independent watchdog] Bureau Veritas's standards, the non-compliant suppliers are immediately suspended.' But Luca Marco Rinfreschi, a member of the Prato chamber of commerce, said: 'You can't deny that this kind of situation exists… Globalization has affected

Italy like the rest of the world' ('Made in Italy... by undocumented workers', AFP, 24 December 2007).

There is a hint of prejudice about these stories. Beyond the issue of whether the Chinese workers are officially documented and properly paid lies a more shadowy insinuation, concerning their skill. There is no reason why a Chinese immigrant shouldn't learn how to make Italian leather goods. For that matter, even goods that are 'Made in China' need not be of low quality. What has irked the media is the realization that they, along with consumers, have been duped. They bought into an image of skilled craftsmen in dusty Florentine workshops, only to be confronted by the 21st-century reality of computer-aided design, factory production lines and crews of Asian workers. Where was the 'authenticity'?

Where indeed? While I was forced to accept that most luxury companies had bowed to pressure from shareholders and stepped up the production of their goods – with the subsequent loss of time and care lavished on each item – I refused to believe that artisans had vanished from the face of the earth. Somewhere, I thought, there must be a dedicated group of people making genuine luxury goods with their dextrous hands. The answer came along by accident, when I asked a friend where he had bought his splendid pair of shoes. He told me they had been hand made by Pierre Corthay, in a tiny workshop not far from the Opéra Garnier in Paris.

THE SHOEMAKER'S APPRENTICE

It was from Pierre Corthay that I learned that guilds still exist. Corthay himself apprenticed with one: the Compagnons du Devoir. This 900-year-old organization is committed to ensuring that artisans from a wide range of traditional métiers – including carpenters, bakers, stonemasons, metal workers, saddlers and shoemakers – pass on their skills to the next generation. Young people who join the guild are taught different facets of their chosen craft during a series of work placements around France. It's a win–win situation for everyone involved: established craftspeople get motivated, enthusiastic assistants, while the youngsters, many of whom have few qualifications, learn a trade.

Corthay, whose parents were actors, showed early evidence of a creative streak, nimble fingers and a sense of style. As a boy, he would make himself bracelets out of twists of leather discarded by an aunt, who used the material for sculptures. Soon he moved on to wallets. 'At first it was just a game, in the same way you might play with building blocks or modelling clay. But as the objects got more complicated it became a real passion and I realized that I wanted to make it my job.'

His apprenticeship began in 1979, when he was just 16 years old. He moved to a new town roughly once a year for six years. 'It's enormously enriching, because you learn a different technical vocabulary from each teacher. And the approach to the work is not the same in Paris, Toulouse, Lyon or Strasbourg.'

In 1984 he entered the luxury footwear sector, with a post at the atelier of John Lobb in Paris. Two years later, he was asked to run the atelier of another prestigious name, Berluti. The first year was a handover period during which the departing *chef d'atelier*, Monsieur Jean, passed on his knowledge. And the subsequent four years were spent getting to grips with the demands and eccentricities of customers who were, quite simply, passionate about shoes.

One day Corthay got a call from the owner of a small workshop in central Paris. The man was considering retirement – would Pierre be interested in taking over the business? And so, in 1990, Corthay founded his own highly niche brand. His younger brother Christophe, who had also done an apprenticeship with the Compagnons, joined him five years later. The business now employs 15 people, divided between the tiny bespoke operation in Paris and a larger atelier in the suburb of Neuilly Plaisance. The latter produces 2,500 pairs of ready-to-wear shoes each year. The scale is almost industrial compared to the 130 bespoke pairs created at the Paris workshop.

Corthay takes me on a brief tour of the Paris operation. There's a small boutique with a window facing the street, where customers can buy ready-to-wear models or come for the latest fitting of their bespoke works-in-progress. Behind the shop is just the kind of atelier I've been fantasizing about, with workbenches in a narrow leather-scented space. The workshops continue in the cellar. The smooth wooden forms of clients' feet, lined up on shelves, look faintly macabre in the jaundiced light. Corthay shows me a three-dimensional cardboard pattern that will eventually be transformed into a leather prototype. There will be at least one fitting before work on the actual shoes begins. Pierre tells me that it takes five months or between 50 and 60 working hours to complete a pair of bespoke shoes, depending on the model and the client.

'Clients tell me that the anticipation is part of the pleasure. The internet is a wonderful tool, but some things in life shouldn't be bought with two clicks of a mouse. Planning, discussion, coming back and forth for fittings – these are all elements of the experience that, in the end, magnify its pleasure.'

Once they're on your feet, however, a pair of Corthay shoes should last you 20 years. Prices range from €3,000 to as much as €7,000 for bespoke, compared to €900 for ready-to-wear.

The different aspects of Corthay's craft fascinate him, he says. 'There's the sculptural and design element, the fact that you're working with soft and hard substances, and of course the connection with others. There's something intimate about footwear that you just don't have with a bag. Designing a pair of shoes for a customer is a dialogue.'

Customization has always been an important element of luxury, from haute couture robes to monogrammed luggage. The personal touch confers status and implies respect. From the tailors of Savile Row to the customized denim jeans of Earnest Sewn in New York, consumers are willing to pay a premium to take part in the creative process.

Corthay observes that some clients have a talent for design. 'They wouldn't be able to transform the image in their heads into an object, but they have a feeling, an instinct for design. Sometimes, we're just here to translate their ideas into reality. It would be arrogant to assume that we have a monopoly on good taste.'

Like most niche luxury brands, Corthay gets a lot of his custom via word of mouth. But he doesn't sniff at more sophisticated marketing approaches either. He welcomes the media with open arms and is a charming and attentive raconteur. The brand's website is elegant, sophisticated and bilingual (www.corthay.fr). 'For us it's a window to the world. Thanks to the site, we've been contacted by clients from Japan, from the United States – all over.' He recounts an amusing tale about the site's conception. 'I'm a vehicle nut. I'm crazy about cars, trains and planes. And for me, the shoe is another vehicle. So when I had to have the shoes photographed for the website, I worked with a photographer who specialized in taking pictures of cars. The play of light on the surface of the objects is very similar.'

Partly due to the exposure afforded by the website, Corthay shoes are now stocked by a number of luxury outlets around the world: from Yohji Yamamoto in France to Bergdorf Goodman in the United States, as well as a handful of boutiques in Germany, Switzerland, Belgium, the Netherlands and – of course – Japan. The United Kingdom, which has its own strong tradition of bespoke footwear, has for the moment remained immune to the charm of French handmade shoes.

When I embarked on the research for this book, I was granted a short and sharp interview with Tina Gaudoin, editor of the *Wall Street Journal*'s luxury magazine, *WSJ*. I mentioned my conviction that craftspeople were the real purveyors of luxury, while companies that churned out production line handbags were simply mass retailers with sophisticated advertising. Gaudoin replied 'I think that's a rather easy accusation to make. If you look at groups like the Gucci Group, for instance, within that group you have Bottega Veneta, which has always been an artisanal brand and has maintained that approach. Hermès in France has done the same thing. An interest in small, artisanal brands may be a trend, but unless they have some kind of financial backing, quite frankly, they're screwed.'

I repeated this to Pierre Corthay, who shrugged. 'It depends if you want to do a job you love, or if you want to make money. If I wanted to get rich, I would do something else. Obviously the business has to turn over, to put food on the table and roofs over our heads, but our main goal is to take pleasure and pride in what we do. The notion of pleasure is, for me, fundamental. When I get up in the morning, I don't have the impression that I'm going to work. I had a similar conversation with a client of mine recently. He said "Pierre, making a lot of money is not difficult, but there is one condition: you must think only of that." Personally, I am driven by other things.'

As consumers become increasingly demanding, they are likely to look more deeply into the provenance of expensive items. And they will find that the patient skills of men like Pierre Corthay offer a reassuring alternative to all that is flashy, insubstantial and evanescent.

3

Romancing the stones

*'Jewellery has an emotional and sentimental resonance
that few other products possess.'*

There is little glamour about the Antwerp World Diamond Centre. It lies in a narrow street behind the grandiose railway station that is a monument to former wealth, but now seems out of scale with this cosy Belgian city. Along the way, you pass a cluster of diamond dealers, most of which have faded frontages that make them look as banal as tobacconists. They have names like Antwerp Or, Design Jewellery and Golden I.

The Antwerp World Diamond Centre is the heart of a square mile grid entirely devoted to the trade in precious stones. Overhead, security cameras track your progress along with that of the smart-suited dealers, who carry fortunes with them in blocky black briefcases – often handcuffed to their wrists as a movie screenplay might demand.

The tiled lobby of the Diamond Centre looks like an efficient blend of hospital waiting room and metro terminus. People come and go through metal turnstiles. Piped pop music fills the air. On the wall is a jagged fresco of interlocking polished steel plates, presumably meant to evoke the sparkle of a diamond.

For the moment, I am lost. I know that I want to find out how the diamond industry works, and where Antwerp fits into the scheme of things, but apart from that I am a rough hunk of mineral waiting to be hewn. I barely know how diamonds are formed, mined, cut or traded. I've never even bought one.

The man who can help me with all but the last matter is Philip Claes, the centre's chief corporate affairs officer, who welcomes me warmly in his office on the seventh floor. It is Philip's job to protect Antwerp from encroaching foreign competition and maintain its position as a leading brand within the diamond industry.

BRANDING ANTWERP

In the streets below us, Claes tells me, approximately 1,500 companies and four exchanges – or bourses – take care of 80 per cent of the world's trade in rough diamonds and half of all polished stones. Alongside the diamond banks there are grading labs, insurance, security and transport companies, brokers, consultants, travel agents – and the hotels and restaurants that have flourished alongside them. All in all, the Belgian diamond trade employs 34,000 people and has a turnover of almost US $40 billion a year. The obvious question, then, is why Antwerp?

'Diamonds were first traded here as early as the 15th century,' Claes says. 'But we were the second choice.'

There ensues a brief history lesson. From the very beginning, humans instinctively felt that diamonds were special. And yet these transparent gems are made of carbon, one the most common elements on earth. Perhaps their immense age gives them power. The formation of diamonds began with that of the planet itself, as it was moulded and compressed by unimaginable forces. Deep at the centre of the earth, deposits of carbon crystallized. Later, as the surface cooled, streams of liquid rock – magma – bore the diamond crystals upwards. These streams hardened into vertical pipes. Erosion later washed some of the diamonds into rivers, which was probably where they were first discovered.

The first recorded mention of diamonds dates back 3,000 years, to India, where they were prized for their ability to refract light. The ancient Greeks were the first Westerners to come into contact with them. Indeed, the very word 'diamond' comes from the Greek *adamas*, or 'unconquerable'. Meanwhile, the Romans believed that diamonds warded off evil spirits and bestowed health on the wearer. This belief lingered into the Middle Ages, when diamonds were thought to cure sickness and afford the wearer protection against the plague. In this context, the tradition of giving a diamond to a lover takes on a new significance.

The 13th century trader Marco Polo brought diamonds back to Venice from India. Dishevelled and sun-baked, the bearded vagabond conjured a rain of gemstones from the folds of his ragged cloak, confirming at least one of his tall tales. From Venice, diamonds found their way to Bruges – the Venice of the north.

'And here's where we got lucky,' smiles Claes, 'because the harbour at Bruges silted up, so trade shifted to Antwerp. In fact there is a document from 1447 regulating the diamond trade here, ensuring that the gems were only handled by certain recognized traders.'

The Antwerp trade enjoyed a second boom in the early 20th century, largely due to the Jewish community, which arrived en masse to escape the pogroms of Eastern Europe. Many hoped to travel to New York on the Red Star Line, the transatlantic steamship service that ran from Antwerp from 1873 to 1935. 'Diamonds are small, valuable and easy to carry,' points out Claes, 'so they were an obvious way of transporting wealth abroad.' However, not everyone could find a berth on the expensive and overcrowded Red Star Line vessels, while others simply decided to settle in amenable Antwerp. And so the trade in diamonds began in earnest.

A second wave of Jewish settlers arrived during the Second World War. Once again, fate was on Antwerp's side. 'Although we'd traditionally been a diamond trading centre, we'd always been in competition with Amsterdam. But the Netherlands were occupied a year longer than Belgium, so when the Belgian authorities returned from London soon after D-Day, they restarted the diamond trade in Antwerp, which gave us an edge. That was really the secret of the success that we continue to enjoy today.'

Many of the Belgian descendents of those original Jewish families are still in the trade, alongside the Indian dealers who arrived in the 1970s. Until that time, India had been better known as a source of diamonds than of dealers and cutters; now it is estimated that some 300 Indian families are active in the trade in Antwerp, providing as much as 70 per cent of the sector's total turnover. But Jewish traditions remain strong. For instance, there are no formal contracts in the Antwerp diamond district: a deal is sealed with a simple handshake known as the *mazel*, from the Jewish phrase *mazal u'bracha*, or 'good luck'.

The Antwerp World Diamond Centre also dates back to the 1970s. It was set up in 1973 to act as the official spokesman and coordinator for all the Antwerp diamond sector's activities. It runs the Belgian customs office for the import and export of diamonds. It's the industry's official liaison with international governments. And it is responsible for promoting Antwerp as the world's leading diamond centre. This presents considerable challenges, however, because the diamond sector – like many segments of the luxury industry – is feeling the pressures of globalization.

Africa is the world's top producer of diamonds, but stones also arrive in Antwerp from Canada, Australia and Russia. The best-known mining company in the business – at least to the general public – is undoubtedly De Beers, the 120-year-old concern that has joint ventures with the governments of Namibia and Botswana. Until recently, De Beers dominated the market, with a share of between 60 and 70 per cent. Now it retains about 40 per cent and competes with Russia's Alrosa, which has a slice of roughly the same size. The remainder is mostly divided between Canada's BHP Billiton, Australia's Rio Tinto and the Harry Winston Diamond Corporation.

De Beers' grip on the market loosened at the start of this decade, when its policies came under the scrutiny of regulators in the United States and Europe. After 1929, when Ernest Oppenheimer took over as chairman, the company transformed itself into a monopoly by buying up rough diamonds from its competitors. These were added to a vast stockpile worth US$5 billion by the end of the 1990s. In addition, De Beers sold only to an exclusive group of preferred clients – known as 'sightholders' – at sales called 'sights'. In 2005, the Belgian Polished Diamond Association claimed De Beers was breaking EU competition rules by artificially restricting the supply of diamonds to the market. De Beers conceded, agreeing to phase out purchases from Alrosa – its main competitor – and stop selling its rivals' gems by the end of 2009. It has also, it says, reduced its stockpile ('De Beers loosens grip on diamond market', *International Herald Tribune*, 22 February 2006).

This move ought to have brought more rough diamonds onto the open market, allowing Antwerp to consolidate its position as the industry's global hub. But things didn't quite work out that way. Keen to appear transparent in its dealings, De Beers became fussier about its 'sightholders'. It pledged to sell the bulk of its rough diamonds only to established jewellery brands, which as well as purchasing the raw stones could also undertake to cut them, polish them, mount them and finally sell them. In addition, De Beers launched its own retail network – De Beers Diamond Jewellers Ltd – in a joint venture with Louis Vuitton Moet Hennessy (LVMH). They now have stores around the world.

The move made sense because De Beers had always been far more than a trade brand. In fact, it had carefully positioned itself in the minds of consumers as the supplier of the world's finest stones. It owed this status largely to a campaign created by the New York advertising agency NW Ayer after the Second World War. In 1947, a young copywriter called Frances Gerety was asked to come up with a line for a series of De Beers visuals. After racking her brains all day, she jotted down one final line and pledged to take a fresh look at it the next morning. The note read: 'A diamond is forever.' In 2000, the magazine *Advertising Age* voted it the best advertising slogan of all time. When it finally became a retail brand, De Beers already had the perfect sales pitch.

The other big mining companies have also shifted towards this vertically integrated model, creating a closed circuit that – some smaller dealers complain – trickles the bulk of rough diamonds into the palms of a shrinking number of powerful brands.

In the face of these changes, Antwerp has been able to retain its prestige – at least in certain areas. 'Eighty per cent of rough diamonds that are sold worldwide are still traded in Antwerp,' Claes says. 'Occasionally, they are also manufactured – that's to say, cut and polished – here. But Antwerp is no longer a major manufacturing centre. In the 1960s and 70s, some 30,000 people were cutting and polishing in and around the city. Today that business has moved away to countries with lower labour costs: India, Vietnam, Thailand, Sri Lanka and so on. There are between 800,000 and one million cutters and polishers in India. There's no way we can compete with that. It's a problem familiar to almost every industry.'

However, Antwerp still has the most renowned diamond polishers in the world: around a thousand highly skilled artisans. As a result, Claes says, the 'Cut in Antwerp' label is highly prestigious. 'The very big, important, difficult rough diamonds are brought to Antwerp. In 2006, for example, the Lesotho Promise was sold and cut here. At 603 carats, it was the 15th largest diamond ever discovered.'

The diamond was sold to Graff for US$12.3 million. It was later cut into 26 stones of various sizes, which were said to command a total price tag of US $50 million. The following year, a 493-carat rough diamond from the same mine – the Letseng in Lesotho – was sold in Antwerp for US $10.4 million. (It was still a mere bauble compared to the monstrous Cullinan diamond, found in South Africa in 1905 and weighing more than 3,100 carats.)

Wherever they have been cut, at least half of the world's polished stones make it back to Antwerp, where they are graded and sold to diamond merchants and jewellers – from small local entrepreneurs to representatives of giant brands based in Paris and Milan. Ironically, many of the gemstones follow the old Red Star Line route to the United States, where 50 per cent of the world's diamonds finally arrive in – or on – the hands of consumers.

CLARITY AND CONFLICT

Far below the office where I'm sitting with Philip Claes is a laboratory where the polished diamonds that flow into Antwerp are graded according to the four Cs – carats, clarity, colour and cut – before being awarded a certificate of authenticity. (A carat, by the way, is 0.2 grams. The word has roots in Arabic and Greek and refers to the carob seed. The seeds were used to balance the scales when jewels were weighed in ancient times.) The lab operates under the traditional name of the Hoge Raad voor Diamant, or Diamond High Council. A certificate from HRD Antwerp is regarded as an incontestable assurance of quality, further enhancing the city's status.

When I tour the lab later on, I'm disappointed to find that one enters through a fairly standard set of double doors – albeit under the gaze of a security camera – rather than having to run a gauntlet of armed guards and retinal scans. The laboratory itself is a wide, open-plan space with windows along one side. 'Natural daylight' lamps on the benches are regulated to augment the subdued light of Antwerp, ensuring the perfect conditions for studying diamonds. As soon as it enters the lab, a diamond is given both an identification number and a bar code. Each time a lab worker comes into contact with the stone, they scan it in and out. That way, a diamond's exact location in the lab can easily be determined. Nobody leaves at the end of the day unless every diamond can be accounted for.

Graders have no knowledge of the owners of the diamonds they are handling, so they can't be influenced to 'upgrade' a flawed gem. At each of the four stages of its journey through the lab, a diamond is checked by three different graders of increasing seniority, using a combination of modern technology – for instance the D-Screen diamond tester, which was developed by the lab – and the traditional loupe method. (A loupe is a hand-held magnifying glass: those typically used by jewellers provide a magnification of ×10.) If there's any discrepancy between the results, the gem is passed on to two or more graders.

So what exactly are they looking for? After size comes clarity. All diamonds reveal traces of their growth history, visible as minute internal and external flaws. These 'inclusions' can occasionally be seen with the naked eye, but more often with a loupe. The best – and the most rare – quality is 'loupe clean'.

When the standard of clarity has been established, the diamond's colour comes under scrutiny. Although diamonds can occur in a variety of colours – including pink, purple, red and blue – most of them are colourless to slightly yellow. The best grade is entirely colourless, known as 'exceptionally white'. Technology can tell the graders whether a diamond's colour has been artificially enhanced – by exposing it to extremes of pressure and temperature – and of course whether the gem itself is a fake, having been synthetically created in a laboratory.

Finally come cut and finish, which are largely responsible for the fire, brilliancy and scintillation of a diamond. Here the graders are mainly checking for symmetry.

Training to become a grader takes approximately six months, including theory, hands-on experience and examinations. Looking around the lab, I'm surprised to see that the 160 or so graders are not only young, but also predominantly female.

This is by no means the case at the diamond bourse, or exchange, which I visit the same morning. It's located a little way down the street from the AWDC. Antwerp is by no means insulated from the vagaries of the global economy, and at the time of my visit delocalization and the downturn had combined to rob the city of its glitter. The level of demand for diamonds had taken an abrupt dip. On this weekday morning, the exchange had a Sunday afternoon calm.

A wide, high-ceilinged room with bench-like tables and massive north-facing windows that let in plenty of Flemish light, the bourse resembles an old-fashioned coffee house in a Central European city.

But instead of sipping espressos and tucking into pastries, the sombre black-clad figures hunched around the tables are poking with their index fingers at scatters of gemstones. Diamond trading is a profession handed down from father to son; some of these men may be the descendants of the original Jewish settlers who arrived in the early 1900s. Others may be representatives of the influential Mehta family, which has diamond businesses all over the world. Occasionally one of them holds a diamond up to the light and squints at it through a loupe. I can now see that those block-like black briefcases are stuffed with folds of paper, each of which contains a spill of diamonds.

It occurs to me that one of these little stones might easily roll off the table and onto the floor. What happens if you lose a diamond? A notice board on the wall of the bourse answers my question: several dealers are advertising lost and found diamonds. Indeed, it would be hard to steal a diamond from here. Each gem has a certificate and a unique identity. Even if you got one out of the building, you'd have to sell it. But as every dealer in Antwerp is a member of what amounts to an exclusive cabal, outsiders bearing stones are treated with suspicion. And anybody found engaging in underhand deals is immediately blackballed from every bourse on the planet. Photos of blacklisted dealers are also displayed prominently on the notice board.

Antwerp, then, considers itself a watchword for honesty as well as quality. But a few years ago, its name was tainted by two words that threatened to undermine the reputation of the entire industry: conflict diamonds.

My own scant knowledge of conflict diamonds comes from the odd newspaper article and the 2006 movie *Blood Diamond*, starring Leonardo DiCaprio. No doubt, I remark to Philip Claes, the controversy was highly exaggerated.

'Actually, no,' he says. 'The film is reasonably accurate. The issue first surfaced in around 1997, when we became aware through the NGOs that there was a problem in a number of African countries, notably Angola and the Democratic Republic of Congo, where rebel fighters were trading diamonds for weapons.'

Antwerp was heavily criticized by the United Nations for its role in the conflict diamond trade. The Fowler Report – named after Robert Fowler, Canada's ambassador to the United Nations – suggested in March 2000 that diamonds acquired from UNITA (the Angolan independence movement) in exchange for arms had ended up in the city.

'We were shocked,' says Claes, 'because we had – and we still have – the best-regulated system in the world. We in Antwerp took the first step in what later became an industry-wide process, by developing a certification process that required the monitoring of diamonds to ensure they were not used to fuel conflicts. Diamonds from Africa could not be traded in Antwerp unless they were certified conflict-free.'

As the controversy grew, the diamond industry realized it needed to act in order to reassure consumers and save its reputation. 'We did not want to find ourselves in the same position as the fur trade', Claes admits. 'A diamond is supposed to be something pure: a symbol of love. We did not want it to come to stand for corruption and bloodshed.'

In May 2000, encouraged by the United Nations, the representatives of the leading diamond producing states met in Kimberley, South Africa, to discuss ways of stopping the trade in conflict diamonds. This led to the adoption in 2002 of the Kimberley Process Certification Scheme, based on the system pioneered in Antwerp. Known as The Kimberley Process, the system is open to any country willing to implement its requirements. As of September 2007, this covered 74 countries responsible for 99.8 per cent of global diamond production (www.kimberleyprocess.com). Among the requirements, diamonds from legitimate mines must be monitored at every stage along the pipeline and transported in tamper-proof containers, along with a Kimberley Process certificate. Today, only Kimberley Process members are allowed to trade rough diamonds, thus locking out non-compliant countries. Certificates are closely studied in Antwerp to ensure that they are genuine, that the relevant authority has signed them and that the diamond in the accompanying package matches the description. In this way it is estimated that the number of conflict diamonds on the open market has been reduced to 0.2 per cent.

'The system is effective,' says Claes. 'Does that mean it's no longer possible to smuggle conflict diamonds? No, of course not: no system can be 100 per cent watertight. And by the way, other commodities have been abused in Africa: especially an ore known as coltan [columbite-tantalite], which is one of the elements used in cell phones. Nobody ever mentioned "blood mobiles". Such is the glamour of diamonds.'

Polishing the Antwerp brand is not just about battling controversy and market fluctuations. The AWDC also gets involved in more traditional marketing techniques. For instance, it runs conferences at which industry leaders gather to discuss the issues of the day. It also organizes a biennial diamond jewellery design competition that attracts hundreds of entries from across the globe. It has stands called 'diamond pavilions' at trade shows. It prints a quarterly trade magazine called *Antwerp Facets*. And it organizes backstage tours and lectures, while regular exhibitions of exotic jewellery keep it in the mainstream media. In short, over more than 35 years the Antwerp World Diamond Centre has painstakingly positioned itself as Europe's leading diamond authority – and the city as the focal point of the industry.

So what happens to the diamonds when they leave Antwerp?

DIAMONDS BY DESIGN

Place Vendôme is a distillation of the notions that bring thousands of tourists a year to Paris: architectural beauty, history, elegance and sophistication. Dominated by the Ritz hotel, the extravagantly vast square is lined with jewellery boutiques. It owes its symmetry to the architect Jules Hardouin-Mansart, who designed its grand facades at the beginning of the 18th century to mask the homes of powerful banking families. At its centre is the Vendôme Column: erected in 1810 by Napoleon, torn down by the Communards – inspired by a later regretful Gustave Courbet – during the insurrection of 1871, and replaced again three years later at the artist's expense. Today the bronze column's greenish reflection wavers in the tinted windows of passing black limousines; middle-aged women in Hermès scarves traverse its shadow while walking their tiny dogs.

The jewellers arrived in the 19th century, led by Frédéric Boucheron in 1893. Formerly based near the Palais Royal, Boucheron had noted the construction of Garnier's new opera house near the Place Vendôme and shrewdly surmised that the quarter was about to become deeply fashionable. He opened his boutique in 1893. Cartier and Chaumet followed. Place Vendôme has been a magnet for luxury brands ever since: its octagonal shape inspired the design of Chanel's first wristwatch.

The jewellery designer Lorenz Bäumer's salons offer a stunning view of the square. Bäumer himself finds the place constantly inspiring: he collects photographs from different points in its history. 'It is a theatre where Parisian life is played out,' he says. 'It has become the showcase for Parisian luxury.'

Bäumer is an ideal subject for this book because his approach represents many of the facets of genuine luxury. Still in his early 40s, he has built up a respected if somewhat insider brand. In addition, he was for some time Chanel's unofficial jewellery designer. At the time of our meeting, he has just been commissioned to design a line of jewellery for Louis Vuitton. But in a sector that has become dominated by a handful of global brands, Bäumer is still something of a rough diamond: an independent free spirit. Although he is based on Place Vendôme, he does not have a shop window. His salons – three comfortable meeting rooms, in which only a few items of jewellery are displayed – are accessible via elevator, by appointment only. He does not advertise. His clients find him by word of mouth, and he keeps them by offering a discreet personal service. They occasionally stop by to sip tea and nibble macaroons while he offers them a glimpse of his latest creations. He is a combination of haute couturier, engineer, artisan and entrepreneur.

The son of a German diplomat and a French beauty who worked in 'many different creative fields, from couture to interiors', Bäumer was born in Washington, DC. In fact he could have been born almost anywhere, as his father's career took the family meandering around the globe. Having attended a series of French schools, he arrived in Paris to take his baccalaureate exam. After that, he studied engineering at the École des Arts et Manufactures. This was by no means out of synch with his vocation. 'I specialized in innovation, design and production,' he explains. 'It's based on the life cycle of a product, from the seed of the idea to the sale. So in fact I'm doing exactly what I was trained to do.'

Bäumer has always loved making things. As a child, the young Lorenz would conjure his own toys out of odds and ends. He was forever painting and doodling. He had a knack for creating sparkly trinkets. 'I made jewellery with champagne corks and pieces of aluminium foil scavenged from the kitchen. I could feel a magic force in these pieces.'

Later, after graduating, he began creating costume jewellery under the brand name LORENZ. 'It was a great way of starting because I could express myself creatively without spending a fortune on materials. I always say that a jewellery designer needs three things: talent, time and capital. But even without the latter, costume jewellery enabled me to indulge in what was for me the ultimate in creativity. It was fairly easy to get hold of cut crystal, gilded metal and coloured stones.'

He taught himself, sculpting delicate wax models and liaising with casters and gilders to transform them into exotic pieces; he still recalls with affection the large animal brooches studded with multicoloured stones. In 1992 – four years after starting his business – Bäumer stepped onto the higher plane of fine jewellery at the request of a client. The piece was a deceptively simple swirl of gold around a diamond. Once he had entered this new world, he was determined to stay. 'Fine jewellery is unique. There's an emotional and sentimental resonance that few other products possess. A potential client might come here having bought a few items of clothing from the latest collection at Chanel. But they might hesitate before spending exactly the same amount on a piece of jewellery, because they want to think about it, ask their husband and so forth. It should be an easy decision, because an item of jewellery will last much longer than a dress. Yet there's such an emotional investment in jewellery that purchasing it feels important and significant. And here, in my view, you're touching on one of the real components of luxury – which is the experience.'

That's also why Bäumer sets such store by personal service. 'When you come to my salon, you are talking to the person who designed your jewellery, one to one. Not only that, but you can commission him to make something exclusively for you. And the end result will be with you for the rest of your life. That is something truly valuable. It's what distinguishes jewellery from other sectors of the luxury industry. For me, fine jewellery combines creativity, value and attention to detail in a way that eclipses even the most complex piece of haute couture.'

It also explains why fashion brands such as Chanel, Dior and Vuitton have entered the jewellery business over the last couple of decades. 'When fake branded T-shirts from Asia threaten to undermine their image, having a jewellery collection is an ideal way of reinforcing their premium positioning.'

Ironically, Bäumer's clients expect his designs to be both fashionable and timeless. 'They will wear the pieces now, with the fashions of today. Yet at the same time, a piece of jewellery is something passed on from generation to generation, so it can't follow current trends too closely. It's a problem unique to the sector and a balancing act that every jewellery designer must perform.'

Bäumer often thinks of himself as a performer. For instance, he says that he plays the role of 'the conductor of an orchestra' with the eight people in his atelier and various external workers. He invites me on a little tour of the 'backstage' behind his salons. And here are the young employees in their open plan office, studying beautifully detailed jewellery designs – as neat and precise as architectural plans – or revolving 3D models of them on computer screens. Bäumer designs his jewellery on paper, by hand – but it is adjusted and perfected on screen.

'Everything begins with the drawing,' says Bäumer. 'I work spontaneously. I find that if I analyse an idea too much I lose the thread. I use a small pad of paper, a pencil, and 15 or so felt-tipped pens in various colours. I draw the piece from several angles, because I need to explain the design to the team and to the client.'

Next the sketches arrive in the atelier, where technically precise images are created. 'We're in the 21st century and, in my profession as in others, information technology has revolutionized the way of working. The computer is a phenomenal tool. I can design a virtual piece of jewellery, turn it in space, instantly change the stones, the colour of the gold and so on.'

Once a virtual piece of jewellery has been created, a model-maker must transform it into a physical prototype. The models are usually sculpted in wax. After that, a caster transforms the wax into metal, using the traditional 'lost wax' method, which is said to date back as far as the ancient Egyptians. The wax model is encased in liquid rubber, which sets and is then carefully removed from the original model. Molten wax is injected into the cavity. After it has hardened, the new wax model is removed from the rubber mould. This wax form is covered in plaster of Paris and fired. The heat melts the wax, which trickles away through a tiny hole – hence the word 'lost'. Inside the hollow plaster mould, every detail of the design is perfectly replicated in negative. Molten silver (or gold) is poured in and allowed to cool. Finally, the plaster cocoon is broken open to reveal the newborn casting.

After that, the jeweller refines the piece: filing and polishing, even cutting with a laser. The stones are sourced from a handful of *diamantaires* dotted around Paris: many of them are located in the 9th arrondissement, a swift motorcycle courier's ride away from Place Vendôme. Diamonds that may have been bought in Antwerp will be cut and polished to order by these artisans, who work in unglamorous ateliers with barred windows, diamond dust settling imperceptibly on benches and shelves. 'A mere stone becomes a jewel in the hands of an expert cutter,' stresses Bäumer. In his studio, I'm shown the silver casting of a ring and the tiny diamonds that will be set into it. Setting is another skill, performed by yet another artisan. The tiny strands of metal that will hold the stones in place must be invisible to the naked eye.

Once the stones are set, the piece is polished once again. Then, finally, an engraver adds Bäumer's signature. 'Just as I explained,' he concludes, 'it's like an orchestra. If all the sections perform well, the final result makes everyone proud.'

Bäumer is deeply proud of his métier, which he clearly considers nobler than others within the luxury industry. 'You don't keep an item of clothing for years because it reminds you of your 20th wedding anniversary. And while some people might consider a car a romantic gift, I'm not sure it has the same impact as a piece of jewellery.'

He certainly agrees with one of the basic tenets of luxury marketing, which is that the products must not be easily available. 'Partly by necessity and partly by choice, I don't have and will never have a chain of boutiques. When I want to sell my products in New York or Los Angeles, I discreetly let my regular clients know that I will be in town for two or three days, so they can make an appointment with me. "Pop-up stores" are quite popular in the retail industry – the idea of opening a store for a limited time period in order to create demand – but my approach is even more ephemeral.'

As we've seen, the high cost of entry makes creating a jewellery brand a long and delicate business, especially for independent designers. But some have an almost unconscious grasp of the insubstantial elements that will make potential clients hunger for their creations. Who could resist, for instance, the story of a Frenchwoman who fell in love with the precious stones of Jaipur?

A TALE OF TWO CITIES

There is no doubt that Marie Hélène de Taillac makes gorgeous jewellery. It's there for everyone to see, in her wholly contemporary Saint Germain boutique. Although she occasionally uses diamonds, Taillac (the 'de' is dropped in correct French usage) has a predilection for coloured gemstones. But these supremely delicate drops of light become even more alluring when she tells the tale behind them. Which is, of course, why she tells it so well.

First, though, it's necessary to underline Taillac's importance to the jewellery sector. In 1996, when she launched her first collection, the world of high-end jewellery was distinctly stodgy. 'First there were the staid, overly decorated and uncomfortable stores you needed to navigate to buy jewellery. Then, there was always the feeling that the jewellery itself made you look like an ancestral portrait and somehow, never seemed to work either with jeans or with contemporary designer clothes.'

Her ambition was to create a collection that brought real, precious jewellery into the everyday lives of women. And she found the key in the capital of Rajasthan.

It was not entirely unexpected that Taillac should have been drawn to Jaipur. The glamorous Frenchwoman has had one of those restless, peripatetic lives that are the envy of the armchair traveller. Born in Libya, she was raised in Lebanon before arriving in Paris, which she still regards as somewhat haughty and inhospitable. When her parents returned from a trip to Iran with pictures of the Iranian crown jewels, she was captivated. At the age of 18, she intended to study at the Gemological Institute of America (GIA), in New York. 'I realized that my English wasn't good enough, so after my baccalaureate I decided to spend a year in London taking lessons. The school was near Victoria – I went there only once. I was used to going to London for the shopping, so I had a glamorous image of the city. When I arrived at the language school near Victoria Station, it all seemed much too grim.'

The solution, obviously, was to get a job in a shop. A chance encounter with jewellery designer Nicky Butler provided the perfect post, at the hip Fulham Road boutique Butler & Wilson. Nicky Butler and Simon Wilson had originally traded in art nouveau and art deco costume jewellery before creating their own pieces. It transpired that their big, bold, sparkly creations worked perfectly with the confrontational, shoulder-padded fashions of the 1980s. The pair soon had a cult brand on their hands.

Taillac fitted right in to this hip, bohemian environment. She eventually became the brand's press attaché and befriended influential journalists like Hamish Bowles. Her studies almost forgotten, she continued her progress through 1980s London, working for the jeweller Dinny Hall, the couturier Victor Edelstein – a favourite of Diana, Princess of Wales – and the milliner Philip Treacy. By the mid-1990s her list of contacts was almost as impressive as her depth of experience in the luxury sector. 'The only trouble was that I'd spent so long working for others that I still hadn't worked out what I wanted to do for myself.'

Toying with the idea of fashion design, she travelled to India to marvel at its rich resources of sumptuous textiles. But when she entered Jaipur's Gem Palace, her fate was sealed. The gem wholesaler is the most prestigious of the dealers and cutters that throng the city – the Antwerp of coloured gemstones. It is run by the Kasliwal family and once supplied jewellery to the maharajas. Taillac's eyes popped when she saw the number and quality of gems on display. 'I was like a child in a sweetshop,' she says. Her instinctive love of jewellery flooded her system – and with it the desire to design a collection of her own.

'Originally a friend from Japan had asked me to bring back some gems for her,' she recounts. 'I arrived at an opportune moment, because it was the middle of summer and extremely hot, with very few tourists. So I was able to stay for a few weeks soaking up the atmosphere. My first collection grew out of that experience.'

It's easy to see why Taillac found Jaipur inspiring. An extract from a 2006 article in *Time Style & Design* magazine perfectly captures the ambience: '[M]onkeys swinging in and out of dilapidated, baroque façades, sugarcane presses spewing smoke… Everywhere one hears the piercing shriek of cutting wheels' ('Passage to India', spring 2006). Taillac struck a deal with Munnu Kasliwal, one of the owners of Gem Palace, and today she buys the bulk of her stones through the firm. She even has her atelier next door: she lives in Jaipur for six months of the year with her son Edouard, designing her collections with a handful of loyal craftsmen.

Taillac's first collection in 1997 displayed all the hallmarks that have made her jewellery famous: sleek yet bohemian, with colourful gems, exquisitely cut, that seemed to burst from their discreet settings. She applied the teardrop-shaped *bricolette* cut usually reserved for diamonds to gems such as the pastel blue chalcedony or the bright orange fire opal. She shamelessly mixed precious and semi-precious stones. Necklaces were shimmering streams of colour. Taillac combined the bright light and vibrancy of India with her own fashion sense to heat up the frosty world of Parisian fine jewellery.

Thanks to the contacts she'd made throughout her career, she had plenty of people to show her first collection to. Before she knew it, Paris concept store Colette, influential London boutique Brown's and upmarket New York fashion retailer Barney's had snapped up pieces.

Soon, outlets in Japan began clamouring for her designs. The demand has barely faltered since. 'People remarked that my first collection was unusually mature and confident – but it had been in my head for about 20 years!' she remarks. 'In addition, I had a business side as well as a creative side. I understood very well the field I was entering. I was familiar with Barney's and I knew my target market.'

Not that the market for fashionable jewellery was particularly large at the time. Barney's had only one jewellery counter. 'But now they've had to move the cosmetics department to make way for jewellery and accessories. The business has developed incredibly over the last decade.'

Marie-Hélène de Taillac undoubtedly contributed to this new wave of interest in fine jewellery. She has a remarkable talent for communicating her particular form of luxury. She relies on word of mouth and press coverage rather than advertising – and her fascinating story attracts plenty of both. She has also created two boutiques that are the perfect expressions of her brand positioning.

The first, on the Left Bank of Paris, deliberately 'banished pre-conceived notions of what a jewellery store is supposed to look like'. Taillac believes that the traditional way of displaying jewellery actually detracts from the beauty and the colour of the stones. She called on Habitat chief designer Tom Dixon to transform a space inside a listed 19th century building into an uncluttered, light-filled salon. Mirrored walls and display cases reflect the pearlescent Paris light and the honey-toned wooden floorboards. Strange globular lighting hovers above, while bright red sofas, sky-blue walls and vivid paintings of gemstones recall the colours of India. Clients are treated as guests, invited to take a seat while jewellery is brought to them like delicious pastries on white trays. A visit to the boutique makes one feel pampered and privileged – which is all the connoisseur of luxury demands.

The second boutique is in Tokyo, a city that Taillac describes as 'futuristic and gracious at the same time'. The same could be said of her retail environment in the heart of Aoyama. This time Taillac called on Australian designer Marc Newson to help her conceive the space. She wanted the boutique to be as sleek as Tokyo itself, but also 'luxurious… easy, comforting and inviting'. The walls are decorated in blue lacquer, the floors with pliant taupe leather. Guests are served trays of jewellery as they relax on leather sofas. In Taillac's words, 'The overall effect is of an ultra-luxurious futuristic bubble, with clouds of glinting, rainbow-coloured gems floating past on screens or framed in glossy white trays. Place Vendôme feels like a million kilometres – and a whole different era – away.'

One thing that identifies Marie-Hélène de Taillac as a true purveyor of luxury is that rare component in the production and sale of consumer goods: passion. Taillac has a genuine feel for stones. She identifies with the Indians who place gemstones beneath their pillows at night to ward off bad dreams. Many of her designs allow the stones to come into contact with the skin of the wearer, because this is believed to be beneficial to the soul.

'It makes sense to me, because stones often change colour slightly after you've worn them for a while. They're nourished by the personality of the wearer. I've read lots about the mythology surrounding gemstones and I'm convinced that you never choose one by chance. It has a lot to do with your emotional state. If you're feeling fragile you might choose a pink stone, because it promotes self-confidence. If you're pregnant you might feel inexplicably drawn to bright orange, which is the colour of fertility. I've tested these theories many times – and they work.'

Marie-Hélène imparts all this not in the persuasive tones of a salesman, but with a hasty, almost innocent enthusiasm. She may be a skilled entrepreneur, but she has a romantic streak as wide as the Ganges.

With her collections and her boutiques, Marie-Hélène de Taillac has translated her aristocratic name and luxury industry experience into the sleek contemporary jewellery brand MHT. At the same time, however, she continues to write her own fairytale in an atelier perched above the dust and bustle of Jaipur. Although she has four craftsmen to help her, she selects the stones they work with, and each of the items she sells has passed through her own hands. Her brand will continue to grow, but the limits of its expansion will be defined by her artisanal approach. And that's just the way she wants it.

4

Watching the watchmakers

'It is a challenge to remain a true luxury brand.'

Just outside Geneva there is a light industrial district called Plan-les-Ouates. Locals jokingly refer to it as Plan-Les-Watches – the plain of watches. Driving around, it's easy to see why. Nearly every unit is the headquarters of a world famous watchmaker. In the space of a few moments I pass Rolex, Vacheron Constantin, Patek Philippe and Fréderique Constant. I'm on my way to see Piaget, which has agreed to divulge the secrets that have made Switzerland the leading producer of luxury timepieces, with annual exports worth in excess of 16 billion Swiss francs, or €10.3 billion, at the time of writing.

Piaget watches are assembled at La Manufacture, a factory constructed in 2001 to bring together workers previously scattered across numerous ateliers in Geneva. From the air, I'm informed, the layout of the factory mimics the shape of a wristwatch. Some 20,000 watches emerge from here every year, including 150 new models and a number of bespoke commissions. On a short tour, I see watchmakers painstakingly assembling timepieces by hand. Piaget also makes fine jewellery, which is designed and produced at the factory.

But La Manufacture is really only the face of Piaget. To glimpse the firm's soul, you need to get back into your car and point it towards the mountains of the Jura. The watches may be completed on the outskirts of Geneva, but their movements are made in a remote village called Côte-aux-Fées. The fairytale translation of this name is Hill of Fairies, but in fact it has a more prosaic etymology: in ancient local dialect, 'faye' meant 'sheep', so the village was originally named Côte-aux-Fayes. The newer version, it's true, is better for branding purposes.

Winding up into the Jura on an early autumn afternoon, the overriding impression is one of verdant hillsides: sloping grassland and pine forest broken here and there by pretty brick or wood-beamed cottages. But in a few months this area will become an impenetrable expanse of white. By mid-winter, conditions will be harsh enough to challenge even the nature-taming technology of the 21st century, and only the most determined motorists will attempt to battle their way through the drifting snow. In the 19th century, Côte-aux-Fayes and its neighbouring villages would have been entirely cut off.

And that, they say, is one of the factors that enabled the development of the Swiss watch industry. The original inhabitants of the Jura were mostly farmers, who tended their crops or their cattle throughout the warm months of the year. But when winter closed in, they were forced indoors. Staunch Protestants, they were allergic to idleness. And so while the women sat by the fireside making lace, the men constructed wooden puzzles and toys, and then complex clockwork mechanisms – and finally timepieces, which they would travel into town to sell as soon as the snow thawed.

There is a further explanation, also linked to Protestantism – or rather, to Calvinism. Under the church reforms implemented by theologian John Calvin in 1541, the wearing of jewels and finery was banned. This forced Swiss goldsmiths and jewellers to turn their hands to another trade: watchmaking. The Watchmakers' Guild of Geneva was established in 1601. Soon the city became so crowded with watch-makers that newcomers established themselves in the calm of the Jura, an area already known for its talented craftsmen. According to the Federation of the Swiss Watch Industry (http://www.fhc.ch), by 1790 Geneva was exporting 60,000 watches a year.

Born in Côte-aux-Fées in the Swiss Jura in the middle of the 19th century, Georges Edouard Piaget really only had two choices of career: farming or watch making. He chose the latter, becoming an apprentice to a local craftsman before setting up his own workshop in 1874. He was only 19 years old. For many years to come, Piaget would not be a brand owner but a supplier, providing movements to other watch companies. Following his marriage to Emma Bünzli in 1881, Piaget's business grew almost as fast as his family, forcing him to move to larger premises.

When your car mounts a final incline and rounds a bend into the small cluster of dwellings that form the village, you can see the tall grey building where Piaget lived, worked – and helped to raise no fewer than 14 children ('*Effet du froid*', in the words of Victor Hugo).

Piaget did not live to see his name of the face of a watch. He died in 1931, with the business now under the direction of his third son, Timothée. But it was the third generation that raised the House of Piaget to loftier heights. Timothée's sons Gérald and Valentin had specific talents that enabled them to transform this artisanal firm into a genuine luxury brand. Gérald was the entrepreneur, widely travelled, with a silver tongue and a head for figures. Valentin was the skilled watchmaker, whose creative flair drove him to make not mere movements but exquisite timepieces, slender marvels in elegant cases. In 1940, the name Piaget appeared on a watch for the first time. Two years later, the company had an advertising slogan: 'Luxury and precision.'

In 1945, Piaget moved out of the grey building and into a far bigger, whiter building across the street. The new factory – large enough to contain 200 workers – was an imposing sight in the tiny village. And it's here that Piaget's movements are still made today. Not only the movements, in fact: a team of specialist engineers also makes the tools that allow the watchmakers to assemble the delicate timepieces.

During my tour, I'm told that even the simplest movement comprises 163 parts. An automatic watch movement features some 200, a 'complication' (a watch with intriguing additions such as different time zones, moon phases and so forth) more than 300. And the whole thing begins with the 'platine', a disc of metal resembling an exotic coin engraved with runic indentations. This is the base on which the movement is constructed. As I follow the process, the accumulation of interlocking layers of miniscule wheels and cogs, I finally grasp the true purpose of the mysterious 'jewels' that each watch secretes. In fact they're tiny drilled rubies that act as bearings for components. Swiss scientist Nicolas Facio de Duillier developed this technology in the early 18th century and patented it in 1705 – although synthetic rubies are used today. A half-decent watch contains between 15 and 21 jewels.

There is something hypnotic about watching the watchmakers. It's like witnessing the assembly of a miniature universe – and of course Creationists have used the métier as an analogy, claiming that the intricacies of life argue for the existence of an intelligent designer. The debate would have been familiar to the Swiss-born poet Blaise Cendrars, whose early apprenticeship to a Swiss watchmaker in Russia left him with a constant itch to find out how the world ticked. His writings of the 1920s revelled in modernity and mechanization. He had, he said, an admiration for 'all these pretty factories, all these ingenious machines' ('The art of fiction', *Paris Review*, spring 1966). For the watchmakers, there must be something deeply satisfying about creating these little mechanical beating hearts from scratch.

As I move around the factory, I notice once again that the workforce is young and cosmopolitan. Some of the workers may be using the classic loupe that looks so much the part, but none of them has the accompanying stoop and snowy hair that I had imagined. Piaget's human resources director Yves Bornand – who conducts the tour – tells me that there is a considerable demand for young watchmakers. There are schools in Switzerland, France, Canada and the United States. Even Spain and Finland have a school each, in Barcelona and Espoo. Some of them barely have enough students to fill the available places. 'Not enough people are entering the profession, yet the demand for watches remains high,' says Bornand. 'It is not an object that is about to disappear.'

Or is it? I'm reminded of some of my friends, who no longer wear watches because they can check the time on their mobile phones. It may be that watches are destined to become purely luxury items – in the sense that they are not essential. The industry itself seems to know what time it is, luring collectors with ever more expensive and complicated timepieces. Take the infamous Opus 3, developed by Vianney Halter and Harry Winston. It's a mechanical watch with a digital display: the numbers pop into place in a row of six windows. When a prototype was first unveiled at the Baselworld watch fair in 2003, it did not even work. Another five years of development was required before a working model saw the light of day. It was expected to cost more than US $70,000 ('Make a splash, and then make it tick', *International Herald Tribune*, Saturday–Sunday, 14–15 December 2008).

In the economic downturn that struck at the end of 2008, the Swiss watch industry suffered like any other. In November of that year, exports declined for the first time since March 2005, falling by 15 per cent. The 'accessible luxury' segment was the hardest hit, with sales of watches costing between €300 and €2,000 shrinking by 30 per cent. Once again, however, the uppermost end of the market remained resilient. The market for watches costing more than €2,000 shrank by only 5 per cent (Reuters, 18 December 2008).

Switzerland had been through hard times before, threatened by the makers of quartz and LED watches in the United States and Japan in the 1970s. But it fought back then, as now, by insisting on authenticity, craftsmanship – and luxury. Piaget placed itself in this niche in the 1950s, when it deliberately set its prices high and strove for innovation. A major turning point was the launch in 1957 of its 9P calibre watch: the slimmest mechanical movement in the world. Particularly appealing to women – who naturally did not want thick cases bulging from their wrists – the design allowed for wafer-thin watches with larger, more extravagantly decorated faces. Piaget began to veer further away from the creation of purely functional timepieces and towards the universe of fine jewellery. The slogan adorning its 1957 catalogue was: 'Piaget, the watch of the international elite.'

The company's insistence on watches as jewellery enabled it to weather the crisis of the 1970s rather better than some of its rivals. Instead of resisting the quartz revolution, Piaget embraced it, using the technology to further develop its ultra-slim designs. The decade also saw the birth of one of its most successful models, the Piaget Polo. Watch faces were discreetly integrated into flat bands of gold, with no visible break in the line of the bracelet. Neither raised nor demarcated, the watch face became a constituent part of the piece rather than its focus. It was a watch–jewellery hybrid.

In that sense, it was a perfect fit when Cartier's parent company Richemont acquired Piaget during the great luxury brand consolidation at the turn of the millennium. Richemont also owns luxury watch companies Vacheron Constantin, Jaeger-LeCoultre, IWC and Panerai. But now Piaget is part of a big corporation, isn't it under pressure to take the 'mass luxury' route?

SELLING TIME

'It's a challenge to remain a genuine luxury brand,' admits Philippe Léopold-Metzger, CEO of Piaget. 'From time to time you wonder whether you're doing the right thing, when you look at the market share you could achieve by diversification and by moving towards a more mass market positioning. This might eventually affect the image of your products, but you could correct that by very sophisticated advertising. So the question is: what is the critical size for survival? Because it's all very well being small and exclusive, but in today's luxury market there's a danger that you might be forgotten.'

Léopold-Metzger believes Piaget is in privileged position, because it enjoys the protection of Richemont without any overt pressure to generate massive sales figures. 'They take a very long-term view of their brands. They wish us to be successful, of course – but not by doing anything that might damage the brand for future generations.'

A true luxury brand, says Léopold-Metzger, has a strong focus. 'We only do two things: we make watches and jewellery. We only use a handful of materials: gold, sometimes platinum, and precious stones. We deliberately have a very high entry price: we sell almost nothing for less than €2,500 for women and €6,500 for men. We keep levels of production fairly low. So, in short, we're about exclusivity and expertise. But at the same time, we can afford to invest in enough communications to give us visibility among our target market.'

Luxury watch advertising is tiresomely predictable. The brands tend to avoid TV advertising (too mass market) and concentrate on print ads in glossy magazines. In their most traditional form the ads make a star of the product, sitting the watch up front with its hands inevitably frozen at the ten-to-two position (so it appears as though the timepiece is 'smiling') above a wedge of blurb about the fine materials and precision engineering that have gone into its making.

A more costly option is to hire a celebrity. This is hardly a new strategy: Rolex has been at it since 1927, when it proudly boasted that a woman called Mercedes Gleitze had swum the English Channel wearing a Rolex Oyster. Pilot Chuck Yeager wore a Rolex when he broke the sound barrier; Sir Edmund Hilary checked the time on a Rolex when he conquered Mount Everest. Omega went a step further and assured potential customers that astronauts had worn its watches during the Apollo space flights.

More recently, as the online magazine *Haute Horlogerie* points out, the emphasis has shifted from stressing performance to generating glamour by association. 'Once a source of credibility, today these ambassadors bring the promise of notoriety. The accent is less on proving and more on seducing' ('Starmania meets haute horlogerie', http://journal. hautehorlogerie.org). Rolex has concentrated on figures from sport and the arts, with the occasional explorer thrown in. Breitling has parlayed its aviator-friendly positioning into a relationship with John Travolta, pilot and actor. Tag Heuer has turned its attention to the movies (stars of its ads have included Brad Pitt, Uma Thurman and a resurrected Steve McQueen); so has Omega (James Bond and Nicole Kidman). Incidentally, product placement is another marketing option for watch brands – Omega has been 'James Bond's choice' since 1995.

Piaget has certainly not been immune to the lure of celebrity. In 2005 it launched a poster campaign, devised by the advertising agency Saatchi & Saatchi, featuring the French actress Marie Gillain. There were a couple of differentiating factors, however: Gillain was not a major international star; and the art direction was by French artists Pierre and Gilles, giving the ad a lurid, surreal tinge that seemed out of step with a mature luxury brand. This was entirely deliberate, says Léopold-Metzger.

'We wanted to demonstrate that we are a creative brand. Luxury watch companies are in the business of status, so many of them stick to producing iconic models that are instantly recognizable. But innovation is part of our DNA, so we wanted to emphasize that.'

Léopold-Metzger says that although Piaget watches have been seen on the wrists of major stars, he feels this is not something a true luxury brand should over-emphasize. 'I like to think that our customers are aware of our history and our reputation. They don't need the reassurance factor that comes with knowing that a certain watch has been worn by Nicole Kidman.'

Similarly, while Piaget has an attractive website (www.piaget.com), it has not yet ventured into e-commerce. 'I don't know whether we'll get round to that, but it was clearly important that we should have a beautiful website. Our target market is fairly young, given the price of our products, especially in the emerging markets of Asia. So we must communicate in a way that is young and inspiring. And I don't think younger customers take a brand seriously unless it shows that it knows what it's doing online.'

However, Piaget is a fan of the bricks and mortar experience. It has 65 boutiques worldwide and Léopold-Metzger describes them as 'more powerful than any advertisement'. He explains: 'In the same way that you measure advertising by cost per thousand [views], you can measure how many thousand people enter the store. And I'm certain that the surroundings have a far greater affect on them than a page in a magazine. Take a magazine like *Vogue*: some editions contain 500 or so pages. Unless you buy a double page spread, there's a good chance your ad will be overlooked. But if you have a beautiful store, magnificently decorated, in one of the most elegant streets in the world, you are offering a much more accurate image of the brand.'

For an insight into how seriously Piaget takes the store environment as a component of branding, I returned the following morning to the centre of Geneva. I had an appointment in rue de la Rhone, the classiest street in the city. Here Piaget has established not a conventional boutique, but a 'brand experience'. For starters, behind a Perspex screen you can see two young watchmakers at work in a downscaled atelier, using similar tools to the ones I saw at Côte-aux-Fayes. Customers can bring their watches here for servicing, or simply come to get an insight into the watchmakers' art.

In addition, since 2008 the second floor of the boutique has been home to a Time Gallery (don't call it 'a museum') devoted to the history of the brand. This was established to take advantage of the 700 or so historic pieces that were languishing in the company's safe at Plan-les-Ouates. Today, there are two themed exhibitions per year, plus a permanent display detailing the history of the brand. For instance, you can see the 12P calibre watch – just 2.3 millimetres thick – that toppled the company's own record as creator of the world's thinnest automatic movement. Or the watch it designed in partnership with Salvador Dali. Watches of solid gold, watches studded with diamonds – they're all here for enthusiasts to drool over. Crucially, as well as playing the role of a giant three-dimensional billboard for Piaget, the Time Gallery – like the nearby Patek Philippe Museum – underlines the positioning of Geneva as a city of watch savants.

Switzerland does not have a monopoly on the production of luxury timepieces. Since the reunification of Germany, the small town of Glashütte, near Dresden, has emerged as an unlikely competitor, thanks to brands like A Lange & Söhne and Glashütte Original. (The former is owned by Richemont, like Piaget; the latter by the Swatch Group, like

Omega.) The watch industry survived there in a bubble, supplying the Communist East but sheltered from competition from the West. Now it competes in the international market and its timepieces are garnering critical acclaim from connoisseurs.

For the general public, however, Switzerland remains the home of luxury watch brands. And thanks to a serendipitous combination of geography and history, along with its own promotional efforts, it is unlikely to lose that status any time soon.

5

Auto attraction

'You can create an impression of luxury. Whether your brand has substance, validity and longevity is a different matter.'

The *Mondial de l'Automobile* – the Paris Motor Show – is spectacular. Several giant hangars in a vast exhibition space the size of a small airport are filled with the gleaming carapaces of motorcars. And as the auto industry has never fully embraced political correctness, many of these vehicles are draped with beautiful women. There are plenty of industry professionals here, identifiable by their suits and air of nervous energy. But this is also a family affair: the number of fathers and sons, each as wide-eyed as the other, is quite staggering. Held in October every two years, it is the most visited motor show in the world. It attracts almost 1.5 million visitors during its two-week run.

Personally, I've never been an automobile fanatic. I've owned a few cars, of course – particularly in my early 20s when I lived in the countryside. But city living makes car ownership irrelevant as well as impractical. In fact, I've always found city drivers to be the most arrogant of beasts. There they sit, alone in their polluting machines, only too willing to jump a light, ignore a pedestrian crossing, or hurl a curse at a cyclist. Let's face it, unless you have a large family or a job that requires extreme mobility, there's only one reason to own a car when you live in the city: status.

And yet, I am not immune to auto attraction. I love a movie with a good car chase. I always let out a sigh of envy when I see a classic car in the street – a Daimler V8, for instance, or a Citroën DS – and I occasionally regret that I've let my driving skills slip for so long that I'm a bundle of nerves behind the wheel of a hire car. I take comfort in the fact that, when you live in a big city, a car is a luxury.

Perhaps that's why, at the Paris Motor Show, I'm perversely drawn to the grandest, flashiest cars of them all. I make my way to Hall 5, the *Pôle Prestige*, the luxury car showroom. I can barely drag my gaze away from the latest Lamborghini, which looks – as ever – like a child's fantasy of a sports car. But I must move on, because I have an appointment with one of my favourite brands: Bentley.

THE BENTLEY BOYS

It began with James Bond. In the movie world, the immortal British agent is associated with Aston Martin. But he only drove an Aston in one of the books – *Goldfinger* – and it was a company car. Bond's real passion was for his '1930 4.5 litre Bentley coupé, supercharged, which he kept expertly tuned so that he could do a hundred when he wanted to' (*Moonraker*, 1955). Even as an adolescent I suspected that Bond's creator Ian Fleming was a true snob, and that only the very best was good enough for his agent. It therefore followed that Bentley had to make the most desirable and glamorous automobiles in the world.

Bentley sales and marketing chief Stuart McCullough is understandably pleased to hear this. 'As you know, "luxury" is a much-abused word. I mean, even chocolate can be described as luxurious. But I have a feeling that the idea is swinging back to its origins a little bit. As for Bentley, we aspire to being right up there – one of the ultimate luxuries. Prices start at £115,000, but the sky's the limit. At the factory in Crewe, we offer what amounts to a bespoke service. We can build you a car from scratch, to your specifications. We've built vehicles for clients in the Gulf that cost a million pounds each.'

Why choose a Bentley and not, say, a Rolls-Royce? A sensitive question, it transpires. Bentley has a dashing heritage, but its history is as chequered as a starting flag.

Walter Owen Bentley was a daredevil with a taste for speed. Born into a well-off London family in 1888, he apprenticed with the Great

Northern Railway before turning his attention to automobiles, with a post servicing taxicabs for the National Motor Cab Company. In his spare time he loved the thrill of racing motorcycles in the Isle of Man or at the new Brooklands circuit. By 1912 his ambitions had outgrown his job and he partnered with his brother H M Bentley to become the British agent for a French motor car called the Doriot, Flandrin et Parant. The vehicle was described as 'quick, robust, sporting in character and of the highest quality'. Inspired by an aluminium piston used as a paperweight by one of the DFP company directors in France, Bentley later kitted out his own cars with pistons made of this revolutionary light material. The adaptation allowed Bentley to outrace his competitors, who were still doubtful of aluminium's ability to resist heat.

During the Great War, Bentley put his expertise to military use, designing engines for the Sopwith Camel fighter plane. Finally, in 1919, he was able to turn his attention to the ultimate goal: the creation of his own automobile. The three-litre Bentley was unveiled in 1920, initially as a prototype. Appropriately enough, the first customer was a wealthy racing car driver and playboy named Noel Van Raalte, who took delivery of a three-litre Bentley on 21 September 1921.

The 1920s are considered Bentley's glory days. There were a series of racing triumphs: fourth place at the inaugural 24-hour race at Le Mans in 1923 became first place the following year, a feat that was to be repeated many times. Meanwhile, Bentley was refining his engines to adapt to a demand for heavier and more luxurious coachwork. This led to the 6.5-litre Bentley and its racing version, known as the Speed Six.

This was also the era of The Bentley Boys, a swashbuckling team of racing drivers who kept Bentley in pole position and had an indelible impact on the brand. Among them were the flying ace Glen Kidston, the automotive journalist S C H 'Sammy' Davis, the playboy Baron D'Erlanger and the Kimberley diamond heir Woolf 'Babe' Barnato. The heavily built Woolf's nickname was ironic. A former artillery officer and a first-class cricket player, he had inherited a multi-million pound fortune at just two years old. His love of racing was such that he became the majority shareholder and chairman of Bentley in 1925. He went on to win Le Mans three times in a row, starting in 1928.

But the Depression of the 1930s opened a dark period that was to cast a pall over the company for decades. Bentley had always considered Rolls-Royce an arch-rival, hence the bitterness when Rolls acquired the financially weakened Bentley in a hostile takeover – using the cover name British Equitable Trust to do so. Now considering himself little more than an employee, W O Bentley left the company. From the wartime period onwards, Bentley motor cars began to look like Rolls-Royce clones with a lower price tag, their racing heritage diluted. One of the few high points was the shift of production from Derby to Crewe, which had become an engineering hub during the war.

The 1970s may have been the bleakest period of all – with only 5 per cent of Rolls-Royce production bearing the Bentley badge. In 1973, the struggling Rolls-Royce Motors was spun off as a separate company, while the more successful aircraft and marine engine manufacturer briefly became a state-owned company, until it was privatized as Rolls-Royce plc by the Thatcher government. In 1980, the engineering company Vickers acquired Rolls-Royce Motors – and with it the Bentley name. With the creation of high-performance models like the 1982 Bentley Mulsanne Turbo, the brand began to recover some of its former élan. The critically acclaimed 1985 Bentley Turbo R reinforced the impression that Bentley was on its way back.

There was drama again in 1998, when Volkswagen acquired Rolls-Royce Motors. What it had not acquired, however, was the Rolls-Royce brand name. That still belonged to the aero engine giant, Rolls-Royce plc, which had merely licensed it to the motor company. Not only that, but the right to use the Rolls brand name would soon pass to BMW, which had a joint venture agreement with Rolls-Royce plc. There is no way of knowing what would have happened if VW had retained the right to use the Rolls-Royce badge, but the fact is that it committed to Bentley, pumping money into the brand and ensuring that it once again became a powerful name in its own right.

A number of events, Bentley will tell you, indicated that the brand was back on the right track. The first was the creation of a specially commissioned Bentley limousine for the Queen on the occasion of her Golden Jubilee in 2002. The second was the launch that same year of the Bentley Continental GT – here at the Paris Motor Show – which attracted 3,200 advance orders. The brand regained its pride on the racetrack a year later, when Bentley cars finished first and second at Le Mans. Other models were launched – the Continental GT and Azure convertibles, the Bentley Brooklands coupé – and sales continued to increase. In 2007 Bentley sold more than 10,000 cars in a single year for the first time.

MARKETING TO THE 'AUTOCRACY'

Genuine luxury purchasers, we know, are fussy. When they are buying a big-ticket item like an automobile, they are entitled to be fussier still. 'Ignore the people side of it at your own risk,' warns a report in *Admap* ('Luxury cars: different and purchased differently', issue 402, May 2006). 'People don't live in caves; they draw on associated luxury experiences. The laws of contiguity apply. The way they are treated in first class by British Airways, the greetings they receive at the Waldorf Astoria and the patience the salesman showed them when buying a Vacheron Constantin [watch] at Wempe are all used as reference points... Inconsistent behaviour, to the wealthier customer's eyes, does not build value, conviction or loyalty.'

Stuart McCullough would agree. 'You can always communicate an impression of luxury. Whether your brand has substance, validity and longevity is a different matter. You must truly be a part of the world you want to participate in. That requires authenticity and integrity. Your customers are extremely demanding. If the reality does not match the image, you're not going to fool them for very long.'

Bentley is confident that it can withstand close scrutiny. Tours of its factory – still located in Crewe – are known as The Bentley Experience. Don't worry if you are unable to go on one, because the desired impression is evocatively described on the brand's website (http://www.bentleymotors.com):

> Welcome to Pyms Lane, home of Bentley Motors, proud guardians of the Flying 'B'. You're struck, first of all, by the quiet. Then the scent of freshly cut leather mingling with hardwoods freshly sawn. So imperceptibly slow is its forward momentum you have to be told that this is the assembly line. Shapes emerge like sculptures partly formed. You make out the gracious lines of a new Arnage, the exciting thrust of a Continental body. Here and there in the cathedral-like spaces small clusters of green-clad engineers pore over the gleaming contours of a new Azure or a Continental GTC.

'The exciting thrust', indeed – who can deny that cars are symbols of virility? 'Gracious lines', meanwhile, are also the department of Mulliner, a legendary coachbuilder that worked with Bentley and

Rolls from their earliest days and was bought by the joint company in 1959. It was responsible for the bodywork of the original Bentley R-type Continental. Now called Bentley Mulliner, it is the bespoke arm of the company, staffed with coachbuilders, coppersmiths, electronics wizards and cabinetmakers. Craftspeople, in other words, who are on hand to personalize your motor and provide the artisanal touches that genuine luxury requires.

'Some might suggest that the interior fitting of a car is even more important that the exterior,' says McCullough, 'particularly for people who don't want to be too overtly ostentatious about their wealth. They can retain a classic exterior while investing on the inside of the car: marquetry, gold fittings, initials... we can do most things.'

Interestingly, McCullough admits that instantly identifiable luxury automobiles like Bentley don't always appeal to the world's richest people, the 'ultra high net worth consumers'. 'It's one of the challenges the luxury car industry faces. Let's imagine a guy who's just bought himself a $500 million vineyard in California. He has his Gulfstream sitting at Monterey Jet Center, but the trip from the vineyard to the jet is done in something as anonymous as a black S-Class Mercedes. In fact, at the uppermost end of the market the S-Class is practically the default option.'

The immensely rich and famous prefer to keep a low profile: behind the smoked glass windows of the blandly sleek Mercedes, they could be anybody. But where does that leave the likes of Bentley? 'It depends on the client, of course, but for some people they are a private indulgence. They are also highly collectible: I'm talking about people with their own car museums, filled with 400 or so vehicles. For example, the American chat show host Jay Leno is well known for his huge collection of cars from every era of motoring history.'

For a classic car overdose, you just have to go along to the Concours d'Elegance at Pebble Beach, California, in August. These are people who are truly passionate about cars – and presumably more attracted by the prospect of driving a Bentley than riding in the back of a limousine.

'The one does not necessarily cancel out the other,' observes McCullough. 'You may have a Bentley at home, but if you're the head of a corporation, especially right now, you don't want to be chauffeured to the airport in it. After all, to be on the road is to be in the middle of society. You are cocooned in your automobile, but the cocoon speaks volumes.'

It goes without saying that Bentley lives without mainstream advertising. Its marketing is centred on press coverage, its racing triumphs and, of course, word of mouth. For some customers, the Bentley legend is a driver of desire. And although buying a Bentley is an indulgence, it's not necessarily a frivolity. 'People aspire to owning a car like a Bentley. They tend to make the leap when they've reached a milestone in their lives, or a certain level of experience. It's not whether you can afford one – it's whether you *deserve* one.'

At this point, I couldn't resist asking whether Bentley customers had developed a conscience, and were now demanding environmentally friendly vehicles. Would we be seeing a hybrid Bentley? In fact, Bentley was poised to reveal details of a biofuels strategy that would, it hoped, reduce CO_2 emissions from its cars by 40 per cent within three years. There was even a hint that the Royal household might acquire Bentleys fuelled by ethanol. 'The total emissions of all the cars ever built by Bentley amount to a can of Coke in an Olympic swimming pool,' stresses McCullough, 'but we want to do our bit.'

He acknowledges that this opens up a debate about the moral integrity of plant-based fuels (does their production, for instance, result in deforestation, soil erosion or the use of land that might be needed for food?), but says that Bentley will stand by them as a means of reducing CO_2 emissions.

Many car fanatics no doubt reach for their metaphorical revolvers when they hear the word 'environment'. But perhaps they need not feel so victimized. After all, it's not as though they own an aircraft.

6

Fractional high-flyers

'Live like a millionaire on a more modest budget.'

An acquaintance of mine, the founder of a large textile company, is the owner of a private jet. I would say 'proud owner' – but actually he seems a little embarrassed about it. 'The fact is,' he tells me, apologetically, 'sometimes you need to be at a meeting a long way from your office, very quickly, with a minimum of fuss.'

He stresses that his jet is a small, rather elderly affair that he bought second hand. The more obvious step when you're in the market for a plane is to go to a company like Gulfstream, which makes the desirable Gulfstream G550: a long-range business jet (it could whisk you from New York to Tokyo in style) that costs around US $48 million.

The Gulfstream brand was created in the late 1950s by Grumman Aircraft Engineering Co, which made military planes. It named its first civil aircraft after the Gulf Stream: 'the current that flows along the coast of Florida, a favoured vacation spot for Grumman executives' (www. gulfstream.com). In the 1960s Grumman spun off the civil aviation arm of the company and relocated it in Savannah, Georgia, where it remains to this day. In 1978, an aviation entrepreneur named Allen Paulson acquired the Savannah operation and renamed the business after its planes. Today, Gulfstream is owned by General Dynamics, 'a giant in the defence industry', which bought the business at the end of the 1990s.

The current flagship of the Gulfstream fleet is the 'ultra-long-range' Gulfstream 650. When it was unveiled in 2008, it was described as the world's 'largest, fastest and most expensive private jet'. Capable of flying at 700 mph ('faster than a Boeing 747'), it seats 18, has a full kitchen and bar, individual entertainment screens, satellite phone service and wireless internet access during the flight. Passengers can sip cocktails at 51,000 feet, its maximum altitude. The plane costs US$58 million. And don't worry about lack of customers. Aerospace analyst Richard Aboulafia of the Teal Group explained, 'Gulfstream is staking out the top end. There's always a part of the market that is willing to pay for the best and the biggest' ('What flies 700 mph and costs $58 million?', *USA Today*, 24 March 2008).

In the same article, Gulfstream spokesman Robert Baugniet said that 80 per cent of Gulfstream's clients were companies, 12 per cent were governments and 7 per cent were high net worth individuals.

Tucked away in the section about the history of Gulfstream on the company's website is a line that points to a new direction for luxury jet ownership – and for the acquisition of other fabulously expensive items, too. It mentions that, in 1994, Gulfstream signed a five-year contract with a company called NetJets. Despite its name, NetJets has little to do with the internet. But it has everything to do with a recent trend in luxury: fractional ownership.

A SLICE OF THE GOOD LIFE

Fractional ownership means exactly that: the chance to own a part of something. The concept is usually sold on its practicality, but in fact it has parallels with mass luxury. If you are wealthy – but not *immensely* wealthy – you can still afford a villa, a vineyard, a yacht or a plane, as long as you don't mind sharing it with a bunch of other people. In the property market, such asset sharing makes more sense than the more familiar 'timeshare' arrangement, because you have an equity stake in the building – meaning that you could eventually sell your share for a profit.

The fractional ownership of property emerged in the United States in the 1990s before crossing over to Europe. The *International Herald Tribune* ran an article about the trend in 2008. 'The hottest segment of the market in Europe, as in the United States, is the so-called private residence club, a fancy term to designate high-end properties that come with luxury amenities and services. The clubs have limited membership and generous use policies, and because they are in premiere locations, they are often viewed as investments that can appreciate' ('Fractional property ownership heads to Europe', 10 August 2008).

Less than US$350,000 buys you membership of a residence club that has properties all over Europe. Obviously you have to negotiate the dates of your stay with the other members, but apart from that small inconvenience you're effectively getting access to a network of villas in some of the world's most desirable locations, free of worries about staffing and maintenance.

Soon, the fractional ownership bug had spread to almost every corner of the luxury market. An article in *The Independent* at the beginning of 2009 confirmed that the trend had caught on with aspiring yacht owners, linking it to the economic downturn. 'For gilded millionaires struggling to manage declining fortunes and bruised egos, it is the prudent way to keep up appearances,' the piece began. Martin Gray, the founder of 'fractional sailing' company Pure Latitude, commented: 'Everybody recognizes that boats are extremely expensive and underutilized assets. You need to have a tremendous amount of money to keep a boat all year round, and most people prepared to do so recognize how little time they spend on them. A lot of people who want to try sailing but can't afford that outlay think fractional ownership is a smart use of money' ('Now even the have-nots can have yachts, too', 12 January 2009).

A website called Fractional Life (www.fractionallife.com) offers shares in just about everything: not only cars, boats, planes and helicopters, but also racehorses, works of art – and even handbags. A chirpy bit of editorial on the site explains the dilemma:

> As you are reading this piece, you will no doubt be aware of the opportunities offered by fractional ownership for you to live like a millionaire on a rather more modest budget… One just wouldn't feel right sporting an uncoordinated high-street bag when stepping out of a £150k sports car at the latest London hotspot. But what if you don't already own the correct arm jewellery to match your outfit/car/occasion?

What indeed? The solution is simple: you borrow the appropriate bag. The site explains that the basic premise works along the same lines as a DVD rental library. 'You pay a monthly fee, you borrow a number of items at a time (determined by your membership level) and each time you return an item, you can select another.' Say goodbye to accessory insecurity, hello unlimited 'arm jewellery'.

While renting a handbag is an amusing proposition, buying a chunk of jet requires a more hefty commitment. NetJets is one of the best-known brands in the market.

JETS FOR LESS

Although it sounds like a perfectly contemporary concept, the fractional ownership of planes dates as far back as 1986. That year, the man who became the founder of NetJets, Richard Santulli, was thinking of buying a plane. But as the NetJets website (www.netjets.com) explains, 'while the convenience and flexibility made sense, the finances didn't.'

Santulli understood fractions. He was a mathematics wizard, whose head for numbers had taken him from the Brooklyn Polytechnic Institute – where he was a maths teacher – to Shell Oil and then to Goldman Sachs. According to a profile in the magazine *Wired*, Santulli was hired to develop a computer program for Goldman's leasing department. 'But because no one but him knew how to crunch the numbers, pretty soon Santulli was running the whole department, selling and closing the big contracts himself – which often involved the financing of airplanes' ('Hey, you're worth it – even now', June 2001). He later left to set up his own leasing company, specializing in aircraft deals.

In 1984, Santulli came across a struggling but colourful private jet charter service called Executive Jet Aviation. It had been started in the 1960s by a couple of retired air force types (including General Paul Tibbetts, captain of the *Enola Gay*) and the actor James Stewart. Santulli acquired it as a side business. It was around this point that he began hankering to buy his own aircraft. He told *Wired*: 'In terms of the amount of time I fly, it made no sense to own a plane... But when I divided the numbers by four, it started to make sense.'

After juggling the figures – it took a while to come up with the ideal balance of planes and customers that would result in a seamless service – Santulli re-launched Executive Jet as NetJets in 1986. And here Robert Dranitzke, COO of NetJets Europe, takes up the story. 'When the service was first launched, people thought it was crazy. They'd ask,

"So what am I getting for my money?" But in fact it made perfect sense. When you own an aircraft, it sits on the ground for two months of the year for maintenance. And of course you have to pay for a hangar, for a crew and so on. NetJets gives you access to a private jet 365 days a year – and when you've finished with it, you can forget about it.'

Investor Warren Buffett certainly recognized a good idea when he saw one. Having come across NetJets in 1995, he bought the company three years later. Buffett's arrival helped to position the company as exactly what it is: an exclusive club of private jet owners. It also sent out a subtler message to potential customers. If the richest man in the world is a fan of fractional ownership, there must be something to it.

NetJets Europe was established in 1996, with two aircraft and only 10 employees. Arguably, the concept was an even tougher sell in Europe, where private jet travel remained less acceptable than it did in the United States. Today the European arm has more than 160 aircraft and 1,600 'owners'. The company can fly them hassle-free to almost 900 airports in Europe – and 5,000 around the world.

For anybody who flies regularly for business, NetJets sounds like a kind of paradise. Not only can you reserve your own jet within 10 hours' notice, but you can also stock it with your favourite magazines and choose your meals from menus devised by the world's greatest restaurants: Nobu and Hakkasan in London, L'Arpège and Ladurée in Paris, the Hotel de Principe de Savoia in Milan, La Réserve in Geneva and Sumosan in Russia. Simply consult the menu online and make your choice before your flight. As for the wine, NetJets' own sommelier has created a list worthy of any of the establishments mentioned above.

All of that, to a certain extent, is the icing on the cake – the 'going way beyond the basic' that separates a luxury brand from a workaday one. But it's the sheer convenience that NetJets customers are really after. Imagine: no more queues at check-in or waiting for luggage. You fly to your own schedule. And you choose who travels with you, so you can squeeze in a business meeting while you're airborne.

'Our clients are not, in general, the kind of people who think it's cool to sip champagne at 40,000 feet,' says Dranitzke. 'In fact, they are more likely to regard a plane as a utilitarian tool – something that gets them from A to B. Rather than a lifestyle choice, this is something that enables them to work better, travel more efficiently and be where they need to be, on time, with no unexpected delays. Time is extremely important to these people.'

And safety is extremely important to NetJets Europe. The company boasts that it is the first dedicated business jet operator to have obtained the internationally recognized IOSA (IATA Operational Safety Audit) certificate from the International Air Transport Association – the highest safety accreditation in the world. Its pilots are highly experienced, frequently evaluated and well rested. In terms of the planes themselves, the company has one of the newest fleets in the sky, serviced by a full team of technicians at its own maintenance facility. In 2004, this became the first facility of its type to receive full approval from the European Aviation Safety Agency (EASA). All this is highly important given what happens when – God forbid – a private aircraft crashes with a well-known personality aboard. 'Safety,' stresses Robert Dranitzke, 'is not a commodity.'

There are several different levels of programme on offer at NetJets Europe. The least you can pay, at the time of writing, is €131,000 for a Private Jet Card, which entitles you to 25 hours of flight time a year – and a jet within 24 hours' notice. The Owner Programme allows customers to buy a share of an aircraft – as little as 1/16th of a plane, or 50 hours of flying time – in proportion to their anticipated needs. Half a million euros would get you a pretty decent slice.

So how do you reach out to the kind of people who may be in the market for what amounts to their own private airline? NetJets has run conventional print advertising, featuring happy customers like Warren Buffett, Tiger Woods and Bill Gates. These tend to appear, as you might expect, in quality broadsheet newspapers. But – as we've heard time and time again – the luxury business is a people business.

'More than 70 per cent of our new customers come to us via owner referral,' says Dranitzke. 'Our customers talk about us because we look after them. More than that, we spoil them. We deliver on our promises, and then we go beyond their expectations. Being a luxury brand is about taking care of every single detail, from the voice and attitude of the person who answers when a customer calls, to the tiny details that make them more comfortable. For instance, we've devised a signature scent for our planes, which is barely perceptible but extremely agreeable.'

He points out that the NetJets service is aimed at society's elite. 'And that elite is small. They are on the boards of the same companies, they play golf together and they find themselves at similar social events. This is the most efficient marketing channel for us.'

So what about the future? With environmental issues at the top of the menu, isn't there a danger that owning a portion of a jet could be considered wildly irresponsible? 'Well, fractional ownership is certainly preferable to everyone owning a whole plane,' he replies, not unreasonably.

Of course, NetJets is aware that it operates in a tricky sector and is going out of its way to deflect criticism. For a start, since October 2007 the company has included the cost of a carbon offset scheme in its prices – with not a murmur of dissent from its customers. It has also bought fuel-efficient aircraft. More radically, it is investing in research at Princeton University that should lead to the development of an ultra-low-emission jet fuel. As trends that begin within the luxury sector often trickle down to the mainstream, this is good news for all of us.

NetJets Europe says that 60 per cent of its clients are individuals and the rest are corporations. But the corporations do far more flying – 70 per cent of the airline's total. While few of us will ever be in a position to regard private air travel as a business tool, we can all appreciate its attraction. Like many other luxury products or services, it makes us dream a little. It's perhaps not so surprising to discover that the executive chairman of NetJets Europe is Mark Booth, who was previously founding chief executive of MTV Europe. For the lucky few, private aviation is very rock and roll.

7

Super yachts

'Pure objects of desire.'

In the harbour at Monte Carlo, the only sounds first thing in the morning are the ping of cables against aluminium masts and the hiss of water as somebody hoses down a deck. It all seems very calm after the short but crowded train ride from Nice and the bustling exit of passengers from the station. Not very many ordinary people live in Monte Carlo, but quite a few work here. They clip hedges and barber lawns, tend bars and wait in restaurants, or work in sleek offices managing other people's money. And they commute every morning on the train from Nice.

Like commuters all over the world, they are mostly buried in magazines and newspapers, or cocooned by their headphones. They are numb to the view beyond the windows. And yet it is a splendid train ride, with big villas on one side and sparkling blue water on the other. At a little station called Cap d'Ail – which happens to serve one of the most desirable seaside towns on earth – there is a sign that reads, 'It is forbidden to cross the tracks.' Clearly, they've seen my bank statement.

The uncomfortable feeling of being an interloper stays with me in Monte Carlo. The harbour is guarded by ranks of smooth 1960s high-rise buildings hugging a rocky crag. The Hotel Hermitage rears grandiosely over them like a queen among courtiers, a charming reminder of the Belle Époque. Everything seems dreadfully clean – the harbour appears to lack the oil sheen and flotsam that usually snag at the edges of such places. Beside it are a line of waterfront cafés and a public swimming pool. I sip a coffee and gaze out at the jumble of boats, which range from stubby Bombard dinghies to giant vintage yachts with funnels. I'm reminded of Tony Curtis playing a fake playboy in *Some Like it Hot*: 'They raise a flag when it's time for cocktails.' Still, I like these nostalgic cruisers rather better than their modern descendants, which are a glaring blend of stealth bomber and yoghurt pot.

I've seen boats like this before, many times. I did part of my growing up in a town called Poole, in Dorset, where there is another harbour – larger but far less glamorous than this one. (Just beyond Poole harbour, by the way, there is an island called Brownsea, which was once owned by the family of 'Bentley Boy' Noel Van Raalte.) The town is the headquarters of Sunseeker, a boatyard founded in the 1970s as Poole Power Boats. It makes dramatic motor yachts with names like Predator 130 or Superhawk 43. It doesn't take too much imagination to picture them: they have featured in four Bond movies.

Today, though, I'm not looking for Sunseeker boats. In keeping with my search for genuine luxury, I'm here to find a breed of yacht that combines ultimate comfort with a kind of aesthetic perfection. When I was a kid, the word 'wally' was a slang term for somebody ignorant and without taste – the kind of person who hangs furry dice from their driving mirror and completes the look with a green windscreen strip that reads 'Dave and Shirley'. Wally yachts could not be further from this image. With their knifing carbon-skinned hulls and teak-laid decking, seemingly dwarfed by glorious swathes of white sail, they are objects that capture the romance of the sea, even (or especially) for a landlubber like me.

At this point, with my unfinished coffee in front of me, I have yet to set eyes on a Wally sailing yacht in real life. But I know there's one in this harbour. It should be easy to find. Luca Bassani, the founder of Wally, instructed me: 'Just look for the black mast.'

A PASSION FOR THE SEA

Roughly around the time I was a small boy eating fish and chips on the quay at Poole Harbour, Luca Bassani was a teenager sailing off Portofino. Born into a wealthy Milanese family, he spent all his vacations at their holiday home, developing an intense passion for sailing and the sea. Today, his boatbuilding business occupies an office suite tagged discreetly onto the end of a luxury condominium in Monte Carlo. He is tanned and craggy, with a bristle of graphite hair, matching stubble, a white grin and a piercing gaze. He looks, in other words, like a sailor.

'Although I was born in Milan, I spent four or five months a year in Portofino,' he relates. 'To a certain extent, I feel as though I grew up there. That was where I got my feeling for the sea.'

Bassani also has a feeling for business – he managed to combine a nascent career as a sailboat racer with an excellent education, leaving Bocconi University in Milan with a PhD in economics. Boats were the real buzz, though.

'I had some success in my racing career, but I'd never found a yacht that really impressed me. At a certain point, I realized that I would have to build one for myself. The boatbuilding industry was very conservative and old-fashioned at the time. It was mired in tradition. I couldn't understand why people weren't using modern technologies to build bigger, faster, more comfortable and yet simpler yachts. Nobody was using carbon fibre, for example.'

Having drafted a concept for his ultimate yacht, Bassani went looking for a marine architect. Most of them, he says, were 'scared off' by the project. However, a young yacht designer called Luca Brenta was happy to take it on. The result was the *Wallygator* – which Bassani named after a cartoon featuring an animated alligator. Despite its light-hearted name, the vessel was no joke. It was a game-changing, 25-metre, 30-tonne yacht with a vertical bow, a hull swathed in carbon-Kevlar and a carbon mast whose aerodynamically swept-back spreaders (the horizontal spars extending from the mast) gave it the purposeful look of a fighter jet. It took to the waves in 1991 and set a template for the Wally look.

Everything about a Wally sailboat is stripped down and streamlined. The anchor retracts seamlessly into the hull. The winches and cables that do all the heavy lifting are concealed below the tan expanse of teak-laid deck. Hoisting the sail, tacking or reefing can be done at the touch of a button from the helm station. Cleats, stanchions and the other clutter of yachting have been dispensed with or smoothed down to such an extent that they are barely visible. This not only leaves the deck safe and unobstructed, but also provides room for luxurious living quarters. The signature black or gunmetal Wally hull adds a final unconventional touch. Bassani was clear from the start that he wanted to combine comfort, performance and jaw-dropping looks to create 'a pure object of desire'.

'I was pretty pleased by the first boat, even though it attracted a few raised eyebrows. But I got some publicity, and I was confident enough to start a business to develop my ideas. I commissioned another version of the *Wallygator* and a third boat called *Genie of the Lamp*.'

Finally, in 1997, he made his first sale – to Sir Lindsay Owen-Jones, then the CEO of L'Oreal. Owen-Jones had been a motor racing enthusiast before turning his attention to yachting. According to an interview in French journal *Les Echos*, this was partly at the request of his wife, who had grown increasingly nervous about his exploits on the racing circuit. Owen-Jones said he initially found yachting 'a bit granddad' – which is perhaps why the dagger-like form of Wally yachts appealed to him. He named his new pride and joy *Magic Carpet* ('Lindsay Owen-Jones, *40 ans de passion*', *Les Echos Serie Limitée*, 11 July 2008).

The decision certainly meant a lot to Luca Bassani – and to the future of Wally. 'One of the peculiarities of this business is that you can't simply explain your ideas to people. If you want to innovate in yacht design, the only way forward is to build yachts.' Similarly, he says, advertising alone is not going to drive custom. 'You need ambassadors. Sir Lindsay Owen-Jones was important for this company because he enthused about us. His yacht was a beautiful, three-dimensional commercial. This is all the more important for Wally because our boats are so different – they look like nothing else on the sea. It's a cultural challenge to get people to understand what we're doing.'

Bassani hints that some members of the yacht-racing community regard Wally with disdain. 'There's a reverse snobbery about their attitude. For them, everything has to be about performance. But I wanted to design an object that people could enjoy. I want you to be able to see one of our boats from the dock and gasp. For me this was always going to be a luxury brand as well as a shipyard.'

Wally yachts are literally in a class of their own. The International Maxi Association – which organizes races and regattas for yachts and sailing cruisers of over 24.08 metres – has a separate Wally Class that allows the owners of Bassani's boats to compete amongst themselves. 'It was obvious that my clients would want to race,' he says, with a smile. 'They tend to be very competitive people. I created Wally Class so they could race against those who shared their passions and values. It also emphasizes the uniqueness of our products. When you see photographs of all these Wally yachts in the harbour together – well, it's not a bad marketing tool!'

Inevitably, the success of Wally sailboats has led Bassani to expand into other areas. Today, as well as sailing yachts of anything from 10 to 85 metres in length, it makes a range of seven motor yachts that are just as rakish and desirable as their sailing cousins. The 118 Wallypower has become a design icon. Once again, clutter like winches and radar antenna have been magically vanished into the smooth shell, while the vertical bow and side air inlets give the boat a coolly predatory look. It is so futuristic that it featured in Michael Bay's science fiction film *The Island* (2005).

Talking of islands, Bassani's most ambitious project to date is a 110-metre 'gigayacht' called WallyIsland. Resembling a designer super-tanker, it has a huge 1,000-square-metre forward deck area that could easily contain a tennis court, a garden with a swimming pool and maybe a helipad or two. With a price tag of €90 million, the boat had yet to be built at the time of our interview – but Bassani was confident that it would find not one, but several buyers. Customers for Wally motor yachts, which usually come in at a more modest US $25 million or so, are vaccinated against even the most virulent economic upsets.

Indeed, the giant yacht sector generally feels little more than a swell when the markets get stormy. The magazine *Men's Vogue* compared the situation to 'an arms race' in which the stupendously wealthy try to outdo one another with ever-larger vessels ('Sword in the water', November 2008). It reported that the largest yacht in the world was a '531.5-foot colossus fittingly called the *Eclipse*' commissioned by Russian oil oligarch Roman Abramovich. It also mentioned the 'state-owned yacht' *Dubai*, which is 525 feet long. The shipyard behind these giants is Germany's Lürssen, a 125-year-old business that also builds vessels for the German navy. Its website (www.luerssen.de) includes videos of super yachts carving through the briny.

All of which leads me to ask Bassani what methods he uses to tempt the unreasonably rich to choose Wally and not its rivals.

HOW TO SHOW BOATS

'The products themselves choose the clients,' he begins. 'They are clearly wealthy people, but there is more to it than that. They are unconventional. They see themselves as leaders and trendsetters. They also, I would argue, have taste.'

The supposed vulgarity of super yachts is a touchy area, and one that the designer Philippe Starck has addressed in his characteristically outspoken style. Starck was asked to create a yacht at the beginning of this decade. 'They are not designed for their owners' comfort or pleasure, but only exist to show off money's vulgarity and money's power... On top of that, as the market grows, more of these boats pollute the landscape,' he said in an interview (www.luxuryculture.com, 22 May 2008). Starck relented when his client insisted that a yacht need not be vulgar, especially with the right designer at the helm. The result was an elegant, almost classical vessel called *Wedge Too* (2001). Starck has since taken on other maritime design projects.

Bassani, too, feels that the aesthetic quality of his boats is a defence against accusations of vulgarity. He also believes that they move the industry forward. 'One of our roles is to innovate – and our clients see themselves as innovators with us.'

His potential customers do not live in a bubble, he says. Yachting enthusiasts read yachting magazines. 'When I first became interested in sailing I bought every magazine available. At about 15 years old I was subscribing to 20 or 30 magazines. I pored over every image. Pictures of boats filled my dreams. So as well as learning a lot about boats, I learned how to *show* boats in a way that was seductive.'

Wally has run a series of advertisements in yachting magazines using the slogan 'Thinking Wally'. The images are not conventional side-on shots of boats, but close-ups of different aspects of the vessels, often repeated in a collage effect so that they resemble eccentric, alien craft. Bassani likes to confound readers by providing teasing images: he might simply show the stern of a boat and the foaming white trail behind it. Even standard shots have a hidden message. One shows Bassani, alone at the helm of a 24-metre yacht, sailing it at full power just five metres from some rocks. To an enthusiast, this is a clear demonstration of the boat's easy handling.

Bassani maintains a close relationship with the yachting press and often invites journalists aboard new boats for sea trials. He also ensures that Wally is present at international boat shows, although he adds that 'there are too many of them.' The biggest and most influential in the world is the Monaco Yacht Show, held every September. It is not just the relaxed tax regime that has lured Wally to the principality. 'Monte Carlo has become the capital of big yachting. Here I am close to my customers.'

Wally's offices look out onto a small harbour and are almost opposite the heliport where well-heeled visitors arrive from Nice.

But Bassani sees Wally as a global brand, and for that he needs the internet. 'The very wealthy have different attitudes to the web. There are some who don't like writing e-mails and say that they don't have time to surf the internet. But our younger clients, obviously, appreciate the web a great deal. Luxury brands can be dismissive of the internet because it is a mass communications tool. But that's what gives us a global presence. It puts us on stage and lets people admire and aspire to our products. Today, I can't imagine a marketing strategy without the web.'

I suggest that luxury brands are wary of the web because they believe it makes their designs too accessible to counterfeiters, adding that it would be pretty difficult to forge a Wally boat. Bassani shrugs, 'Of course people have borrowed some of our ideas, which is very flattering. But it's difficult to copy when you don't own the soul of the concept. And I believe that's what separates Wally boats from many others – they have a soul.'

Place Vendôme: a Parisian hub of traditional luxury

Bespoke shoemaker Pierre Corthay hard at work in his atelier

Photo: Stéphanie Fraisse

Pattern making at the Corthay atelier

Photo: Géraldine Bruneel

Photos reproduced by kind permission of Corthay Bottiers

Moulds at the Corthay atelier

Photo: Géraldine Bruneel

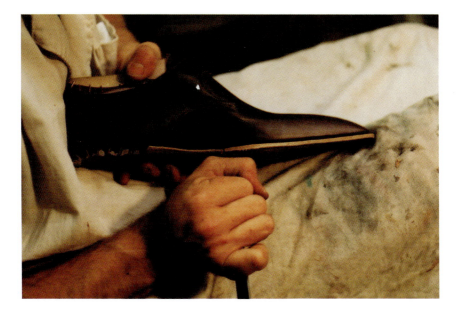

Bespoke shoemaking

Photo: Stéphanie Fraisse

Photos reproduced by kind permission of Corthay Bottiers

Independent jeweller Lorenz Bäumer…

Photo: Takao Oshima, reproduced by kind permission of Lorenz Bäumer

…and one of the rings he designed, the 'urchin'

Image provided by Lorenz Bäumer

The founders of Piaget

Image provided by Piaget Time Gallery

The Piaget workshops today

Photo: Mark Tungate

The Mark: after a revamp by French architect Jacques Grange, an iconic New York address has been repositioned as an example of innovative luxury.

Image kindly provided by The Mark press office

Restored stained glass at Paris department store Printemps

Long-lost mosaics were uncovered during the restoration work

Photos: Christophe Lemaître, reproduced by kind permission of Printemps

Waterborne luxury: the Wally yacht Saudade

Photo by: Carlo Borlenghi. Reproduced by kind permission of Wally

Interiors of the Saudade

Photos: Toni Meneguzzo. Reproduced by kind permission of Wally

In champagne country

The grapes that dreams are made of

Images provided by Louis Roederer

Inside the cellars

'Turning' the champagne bottles

Images provided by Louis Roederer

The Bentley icon

Bentley Brooklands

Images provided by Bentley

Recreating the Bentley Boys spirit on a heritage drive

Celebrating the Bentley factory at Crewe

Fractional luxury: own a slice of a NetJets plane

The future of luxury? Tesla's electric roadster

8

Haute property

'Luxury becomes beautiful and almost real under the sun.'

When Philip Weiser first came to the Côte d'Azur, he thought he would stay for three years. That was 30 years ago. Like many Brits who venture west of Nice, Weiser had found a little slice of paradise. And more to the point, he found that he was skilled at selling it to others. His company, Carlton International, sells luxury property 'at the highest end of the market'. These are not just retirement homes for baby-boomers. They are also oases on the Riviera for the super rich.

It's true that the market for hot property cooled dramatically as the recession took hold. Manhattan was hit particularly hard. The former masters of Wall Street were humbled. Even though bricks and mortar are far more secure than the stock market, investing in property was no longer an option, at least for the time being. The very word 'property' caused hackles to rise, because the economic downturn had been blamed on the sub-prime mortgage catastrophe – in short, the granting of hefty bank loans to those who could not afford to repay them – and the manipulation of highly complex financial instruments linked to the insurance of those mortgages. As the economy collapsed like a punctured soufflé, sellers of penthouses on Central Park West were forced to slash their asking prices by millions of dollars.

But it was difficult to feel the chill when you stood in Antibes looking out at the Mediterranean.

The Côte d'Azur benefits from what one French journalist called *'la rançon du prestige'* – the ransom of prestige. It is so desirable that, while prices may fluctuate, they are unlikely to collapse. Philip Weiser explains: 'The Côte is a very limited area in terms of size. It's bordered on the one hand by the sea, and on the other by the mountains. Development is almost at a standstill – and there are strict regulations to ensure that it stays that way. This means that, whenever a property becomes available, it is very quickly acquired.'

What lies behind the almost mystical allure of the Riviera? Weiser cites the culture, the climate, stability, security and easy access from major European capitals. Nowhere on the Côte is more than 45 minutes from an airport – and yet it seems the perfect escape. The writer Somerset Maugham famously described it as 'a sunny place for shady people'. Jim Ring uses the phrase to kick off his marvellously entertaining study *Riviera: The rise and rise of the Côte d'Azur* (2004). It was, he writes, 'the world's first major tourist destination'. This sun-baked ribbon of coast, which had been an outpost of the Roman Empire, fascinated 18th-century travellers. They came on a cultural pilgrimage to La Turbie, where they sought the remains of a monument to the military might of Augustus. 'They were… fascinated by this ruined emblem of imperial Rome, because they saw their country as Rome's successor. Insular, presumptuous, ignorant of foreign languages and, above all, rich, they were, of course, English.'

The Brits have enjoyed a long romance with the Côte d'Azur. At first merely a way station on the Grand Tour, it was popularized as a destination in its own right by the former Lord Chancellor, Lord Brougham. Detained on his way to Rome in December 1834 by a cholera outbreak – which had forced the Italians to shut the border – Brougham settled in for the duration at Cannes. At that time it was 'a fishing village of no more than 300 inhabitants, with two streets of the most humble Provençal houses'. But the sunlight, warmth, sea views and good food – Brougham particularly appreciated the bouillabaisse – soon wove their spell. He bought a plot of land, had a villa built on it, and almost single-handedly turned Cannes into a fashionable resort.

The number of pale migrants from the British Isles rose steadily each winter, but their number increased sharply with the arrival in the 1860s of the Paris–Lyon–Méditerranée railway. This was the train that in 1922 was to be given a new, achingly romantic sobriquet: *Le Train Bleu*. Jim Ring writes: 'At 1 pm sharp, with all the ceremony of an ocean liner, the express would draw out of the grey windswept Gare Maritime… To draw up the blind the following morning was to experience deliverance. The spectral cold, the gloom, the damp, the fog, the grey had vanished, to be replaced by a sunlit world of terracotta roofs, white houses, blue Mediterranean bays, high green hills with a glint of Alpine snow, and vegetation reminiscent of the tropics.'

The photographer Jacques Lartigue was seduced, writing in 1923 that 'luxury becomes beautiful and almost real under the sun'. He thought of the Riviera as a place where you could shrug off your stiff city personality and the clothes that went with it, 'where you could walk soundlessly in tennis shoes or espadrilles, where every boutique offers joyous futilities' (*Lartigue's Riviera*, 1997).

These elements, then, were what they all came for: the artists and the writers, the models and the photographers, the wealthy settlers and finally the package holidaymakers. The formula remained unchanged for over a century. Even Parisians, who had regarded the whole hot, savage, mosquito-ridden coast with disdain, eventually warmed to it. Although Ring suggests that the Riviera was brutalized by post-war architecture – particularly the hideous high-rise creations of the 1960s – he admits that visitors can still experience its old charms. 'The coast, the sun, the arc of the shore, headland after headland running out into the blue water, sails gleaming against the purple sea, these will remain.' As with a great many luxuries, however, what the hoteliers and property developers are really selling is a dream. 'Much more powerful than the reality of the Riviera is the whole idea of perpetual human happiness that it promises.'

THE BUSINESS OF VILLAS

France largely avoided the sub-prime mortgage debacle because its banks had historically based loans on the capacity of the borrower to repay, rather than on property values. Nevertheless, French property prices plummeted at the beginning of 2009. Some mentioned a figure of 12 per cent – others went as far as 20. This was seen as a heavy correction to an over-inflated market, where prices had risen by 140 per cent in little more than a decade, according to French real estate agents' association FNAIM. For buyers eyeing the Côte d'Azur, it was a chance to pick up a bargain.

The term 'bargain' is relative, of course. Philip Weiser's portfolio of properties starts at about €1 million, rising to as much as €250 million, with the average price coming in at around €6 million. 'The vastly wealthy are easier to deal with than the merely well-off,' says Weiser. 'When you're incredibly rich, you can afford to tick nine out of 10 boxes on the list of what you want from a property. You can almost afford perfection. But others cannot – and that's when the negotiations start.'

For those with an eye on the future, he advised investing in one of the limited number of new developments on the Riviera. Construction companies were obliged under French law to complete the building work, even if sales had slowed. Not wishing to be left with an empty building on their hands, they were likely to sell the units at highly advantageous prices. Investors were counselled to snap up these cut-price apartments, rent them out to people who wanted to experience the Riviera touch, and then sell them when the economy recovered.

As you may have surmised, Weiser was a marketing man before he became a property dealer. For a long time, he was international marketing director of the hotel chain Trust House Forte. Later, he ran a chain of stylish serviced apartments for visitors to London. He says he 'stumbled into' real estate when he was asked to help out a struggling estate agency here in the South of France. He nursed the business back to health, acquiring half of it along the way. This he then sold to create Carlton International.

At the time of writing, the company has 17 negotiators with wide-ranging linguistic abilities: along with French and English there are Russian, Arabic, Dutch and German speakers. Between 80 and 90 per cent of Weiser's clients are 'non-French'. He brushes aside the familiar accusation that foreigners have pillaged the coast and pushed prices out of reach of potential French buyers. 'The property has always been available to whomsoever can afford to buy it. You could just as easily say that the French decided to cash in. And if you take the entire market in the region – not just the very top end – French transactions probably exceed foreign transactions.'

Carlton International, of course, specializes in overseas clients. In this respect, the internet is a vital marketing tool. 'It's the ultimate brochure. You can place links on other property sites all over the world, you can create a coherent brand identity, and you can build mini-sites that deal with specific projects or properties. Looking back, it's hard to see how the real estate industry managed without it.'

But Weiser has by no means turned his back on traditional print. Working with local contract publishing company Luxarro, he created a tri-annual English-language lifestyle and interiors magazine called *Carpe Diem*, which aims to capture the zest of life on the Riviera. Typical articles might include an interview with a local chef, a piece on the connection between Saint Tropez and the cinema, and a handful of discreetly promotional tours of some the properties on Carlton's books. Printed on thick, matt paper, with ravishing colour photography, it is less a throwaway item than a collectible coffee table book. The magazine is sent directly to the names on Carlton's database and has about 50,000 readers. At first the scheme seems counter-intuitive: it's a good idea to constantly remind consumers of your brand values when you're in the fashion business, but is it really worth adopting the same tactic when you're selling houses? Weiser replies, 'You have to remember that most of our clients buy these properties as second homes. And on average, they change them every five years.'

Really? Why? 'Changing desires, changing circumstances. Their children are getting a bit older so they want to be nearer the coast. Their business is doing well so they want to upgrade. Or vice versa, of course.'

The need to retain clients who chop and change villas the way others might upgrade their motor cars gives rise to another crucial element of Weiser's operation: after sales. 'The ironic thing about this business is that you can't really sell somebody a property – they can only buy it from you. You can show them around, explain all the features, handle the meeting professionally and politely – but at the end of the day, if the property doesn't tick all their boxes, or they just don't feel right about it, they won't buy. Once they've committed, however, our real job begins.'

Carlton's renovation and decoration department can liaise with clients to ensure that the property lives up to their dreams. The company's services include interior design, purchase and installation of materials and supervision of the work. It has used the same qualified contractors for years. The company can also handle garden design, landscaping, planting, the installation of sprinklers and the construction of swimming pools and tennis courts.

And once the property is shipshape, Carlton makes sure it stays that way. Its property management department 'takes the worry out of home ownership' by ensuring that the house, gardens and pool look their best at all times. There are weekly garden and pool maintenance visits, mail is collected and administrative tasks like paying bills, insurance and staff are all taken care of. There are regular security visits and Carlton oversees repairs 'in the unlikely event' of a break-in. Owners need not fuss about dripping taps, storm leaks or even shorted light bulbs.

'For me, that's the real difference between luxury and any other industry. The sale is only a small part of it – what really matters is what happens afterwards. These consumers want to be loyal to you. All you have to do in return is give them the very best.'

Another thing they admire – indeed, demand – is expertise. Luxury consumers, it turns out, are suspicious of dilettantes. 'I once made the mistake of thinking I could charter yachts at the same time. But the people who were into yachts said 'What does a property company know about yachts?' and the people who were interested in property became confused about the brand. I now believe that the secret of building a successful business at the high end is to specialize. In this business, experience and credibility are everything.'

9

Deluxe nomads

'I know what guests want from a luxury hotel – and it's not vanilla.'

My second visit to Monte Carlo within the space of a few months is far more glamorous than the first. It begins at a heliport whose tiny departure lounge is discreetly tucked away behind a large fish tank in a remote corner of the Nice Côte d'Azur airport. Today, at least, I am the sole passenger. Out on the pad, a disconcertingly small helicopter winds up. At a signal from one of the ground crew I walk out to the machine, stooping instinctively in the downdraft from the blades. The crewmember stashes my bag in the back and I take a seat next to the pilot. Seconds later, my stomach swoops as we lift up and scythe out over the bay.

Rotor blades are often described as 'clattering', but the sound in the cockpit is a high whine accompanied by a bass judder that I can feel in my shoes. Below us, the deep blue waves are flecked with whitecaps. To my left a toy-town Nice glides by; I catch a glimpse of the bright yellow Corsica ferry and the war memorial in its rocky niche below the cliff. Then we point our nose at the misty horizon, moving fast now over a sea dappled with patches of silver.

From the air, the pinkish beige towers of Monte Carlo resemble the work of maniacal termites. At touchdown, a black mini-van is on hand to meet me. Within 15 minutes I am standing on the balcony of my room at the Hotel de Paris, looking out over the harbour. The big white yachts are still anchored there, exactly where I left them.

So this is how the other half lives, I think to myself. Welcome to the world of the deluxe nomads.

MONTE CARLO: THE BRAND

Monte Carlo is one those destinations that will be forever labelled 'playground of the rich', along with a handful of others like St Tropez, Mustique, the Hamptons, Capri and St Moritz. One can easily imagine the colourful labels on the steamer trunk. But Monte Carlo is unique in that it is, quite literally, a luxury brand. A large chunk of it is owned by a company called Monte-Carlo SBM, which is currently expanding worldwide in the form of branded hotel and leisure properties.

To understand how this came about, we need to take a trip back in time. Like other destinations along this strip of coast, Monaco (of which Monte Carlo is the commercial centre) was settled by the Romans, who appreciated its protected harbour and used it as a port of call on the way to Gaul. With the collapse of the Roman Empire, the little settlement receded into the mists of time, only to emerge in the 13th century when it became an outpost of Genoa.

On 8 January 1297, Francesco Grimaldi, leader of a Genoese clan embroiled in power struggles with rival factions throughout the region, led a daring night raid on the fortress of Monaco. Known as *Il Malizia* ('The Cunning'), Grimaldi is said to have approached the fortress disguised as a Franciscan monk. Having thus gained entry, Grimaldi and his men took the fortress. Grimaldi established himself as de facto ruler, succeeded by his stepson Rainier I. The Genoese did not acknowledge either of them as legitimate monarchs; that honour went to Rainier's son Charles I of Monaco, who is considered the founder of the dynasty that continues to rule today.

For the early part of its history, Monaco was a rather unimpressive city-state, living on the duty it was able to levy on the wine, tobacco and lemons that passed through its port. And when in 1848 the nearby communities of Roquebrune and Menton declared their independence from the tiny empire, the future of the principality looked bleak. Having noted that spas were all the rage along the Côte d'Azur, Prince Florestan envisaged a resort that would comprise a hotel, villas and entertainment – notably gaming. Gambling was illegal in France and this represented a considerable opportunity for Monaco.

When Charles III came to power in 1856 he launched himself into the task of turning his father's vision into reality. The 'Société des Bains de Mer et du Cercle des Etrangers à Monaco' was founded as a bathing establishment and casino operator. Construction of the Casino de Monaco began on 13 May 1858, on a stretch of land called the Plateau de Spélugues that had previously been planted with olive bushes and lemon and orange trees. The metamorphosis of Monaco had begun. Progress was halting, however. When the casino opened on 18 February 1863, it attracted few customers. As Jim Ring observes in his book *Riviera* (see previous chapter, 'Haute property'), Monaco was still four hours from Nice by carriage or choppy boat ride across the bay. Why make the effort when there were plenty of glittering diversions close at hand?

A solution arrived in the form of a man of experience: François Blanc. The casino and spa at Monaco were based on the German model, with which Blanc was extremely familiar. The son of an impoverished Provençal tax collector, he was a former card sharp, stock market speculator and casino owner who had made a fortune transforming the tiny Germanic principality of Bad Homburg into a gambling and leisure destination. His nickname was 'The Magician'.

François Blanc and his twin brother Louis – from whom he was inseparable – had become fascinated by card tricks during their childhood after watching a magician at a circus. Quitting the family home to join the circus, they became expert prestidigitators in their own right, while making money from gambling on the side. The pair led a picaresque existence, heading a gambling house in Marseille and later becoming stock market speculators in Bordeaux. After being fined for what amounted to insider trading (a contact would tip them off in advance about fluctuating share prices on the Paris bourse) they turned up in Paris, where they headed a gaming room under the bustling arcades of the Palais Royal. An 1836 proclamation outlawing gambling in France hustled them on to Luxembourg, where they opened yet another establishment. It was here that they attracted the attention of the ruler of Homburg, who asked them to help him turn his impoverished principality into a gaming centre. The pair accepted the concession and pretty soon Bad (as in 'bath') Homburg was flourishing thanks to a spa, a casino, luxury hotels and restaurants.

François Blanc's twin brother died in 1852. François had lost his wife earlier that year. In order to shake himself out of depression, he began to cast around for a means of boosting his income in winter, as Bad Homburg was essentially a summer gambling destination. His avid gaze inevitably fell on Monaco. After a little research, he learned that the railway that was shortly to reach Nice might eventually be extended to the principality. With a little promotion, Monaco could be transformed into a winter gambling destination par excellence.

A meeting between Charles III of Monaco and François Blanc appears to have been engineered by the prince's lawyer, a smooth-sounding gentleman named Monsieur Eynaud. According to Jim Ring, he advised the prince that 'Blanc is colossally rich... he is a past master of the art of dissimulating the green cloth of the gambling tables behind a veil of elegance and pleasure.' Accompanied by his young second wife, Marie, François Blanc arrived in Monaco to take up its gambling and leisure concession in 1863.

Soon the Plateau de Spélugues had been renamed after the ruler of the principality – 'Mont Charles' translates into 'Monte Carlo' – and Blanc was following the strategy he had adopted in Bad Homburg. He oversaw improvements to landscaping and lighting. He launched a newspaper, *Le Journal de Monaco*, and arranged to have it distributed with *Le Figaro*. He invited journalists to the resort by the score. Rather than waiting for the railway to arrive, he started a regular steamer ferry service from Nice, as well as stagecoaches for those who wished to arrive by road. He engaged the architect Dutrou to build the Hotel de Paris, 'the most beautiful hotel in Europe'. (Alexandre Dumas of *Three Musketeers* fame was one of its first guests.) Just across the street, the Café Divan – later the Café de Paris – opened its doors in 1868. In the casino, Blanc dropped one of the two zeros (one red, one black) from its roulette wheels, thus improving clients' chances of winning. By 1870, Monte Carlo was attracting 170,000 visitors a year. At the time of Blanc's death, in 1877, this had increased to more than 300,000. 'The Magician' had bewitched Riviera tourists with a heady brew of risk, pleasure and opulence – and conjured up a country founded almost entirely on hedonism.

Today, as I mentioned earlier, the Société des Bains de Mer operates under the brand name Monte-Carlo SBM. Majority owned by the Monegasque state, it has around 3,000 employees and an annual income of more than €450 million. Alongside the original Casino de

Monte-Carlo it owns four other casinos, four hotels – including the magnificent Hotel de Paris and Hotel Hermitage – the Thermes Marins spa, the jet set nightclub Jimmy'z and no less than 32 restaurants, as well as a clutch of other bars and nightspots. Its conference venues provide space for hundreds of seminars every year. And it is expanding abroad. In 2003 it entered into a strategic alliance with the US casino operator Wynn Resorts, acquiring a 3.6 per cent share for US $45 million. The alliance includes 'an exchange of management expertise and the development of cross-marketing initiatives' ('Wynn Resorts and SBM of Monaco enter into strategic alliance', *Business Wire*, 20 June 2003).

More recently, Monte-Carlo SBM announced the opening of a branded hotel, the Jawhar ('jewel') in Marrakech. The 80-room establishment incorporates a spa and banqueting rooms. The company is also looking at locations around Europe.

The repositioning of Monte Carlo as a luxury brand really began in 2002, with the arrival of director general Bernard Lambert. He considered that although the Société des Bains de Mer functioned perfectly well as a business, it was not fully exploiting its potential. With the resort's clientele becoming younger and more international – hailing from Russia, Central Europe and China – he felt that the name 'Monte Carlo' had an increasing global resonance. More than a mere location, Monte Carlo was a spirit, a state of mind. In order to explore this idea further, Lambert hired the company's first marketing director, Axel Hoppenot, in 2004.

Hoppenot says: 'When I arrived, it seemed obvious to me that Monte Carlo was not just in the business of selling gambling chips, hotel rooms, food and drink and conference spaces. There was an emotional element to the brand that attracted people above and beyond its various facilities. It's the "fairy tale" of Monte Carlo. And I thought this element could be strengthened within the resort as well as exported to other markets.'

Asked to define the values of the Monte Carlo brand, Hoppenot lists five key elements: 'The first is the thrill. We're a place that makes the pulse race, whether you're talking about casinos, the Monaco Grand Prix or the Monte Carlo Masters tennis tournament. The second is the sense of liberty we engender. Since the early days, when people came here to gamble because it was banned in France, Monte Carlo has been associated with freedom. Thirdly – and this may seem contradictory

– Monte Carlo offers a sense of security. It's extremely stable, with very little crime. And allied with that is the sense that this is a place where you feel good. It is blessed with an extremely pleasant climate and there are many facilities devoted to health and well-being.'

Fourth on Hoppenot's list is *l'art de vivre* – the French concept of 'the art of living' – by which he means the pleasurable lifestyle that Monte Carlo offers to those with the means to enjoy it: the boutiques, the bars, the gourmet restaurants and the nightlife. He adds that Monte Carlo has a reputation for glamorous social events, such as the annual *Bal de la Rose* ('Rose Ball') in aid of the Princess Grace Foundation, which raises money for children in need.

Hoppenot is keen to stress another kind of art, too. You'd be wrong, he says, to assume that Monaco is a philistine place. The Opéra de Monte Carlo was inaugurated in 1879. Diaghilev came here with his Ballets Russes in 1911, with scenery designed by Jean Cocteau. The opera house still has a varied and innovative programme, specializing in staging little-known operas. Monte Carlo has its own symphony orchestra and ballet corps, as well as a 25-year-old spring programme of classical music recitals. Meanwhile, the concert halls at the Sporting Monte Carlo entertainment complex feature headline names like Eric Clapton, Grace Jones and Leonard Cohen. 'The power of the Monte Carlo brand means that we can attract the world's most famous performers,' says Hoppenot.

The final element is, of course, aspiration. The fabulously wealthy could vacation anywhere – but many of them choose to come to Monte Carlo. 'I believe there's a sort of "wow factor" that attracts them. When you tell people you're going to Monaco for a vacation, you can expect a certain reaction. We underline this by constantly striving to surprise our guests with new events and innovations.'

As an example he cities the Monte Carlo Jazz Festival, created in autumn 2006 as a way of spicing up the low season. In a similar vein, the Moods Studio & Music Bar – located below the Café de Paris – is a new live music venue for jazz, blues and rock artists.

Having rebranded as Monte-Carlo SBM, Hoppenot and his team deployed a number of tactics to promote the brand in a more concrete manner. An internet portal, montecarloreseort.com, brought the group's offerings together under one digital roof. A new logo was designed to emphasize the name 'Monte Carlo' in the company's communications. And in 2007 it worked with a Paris advertising agency to create a campaign using the slogan 'Be Monte Carlo'. It spent more than €2 million on media placement in the upmarket international press (including the *Financial Times*, *Forbes* and *Fortune*), on the internet and on TV, notably CNN and CNBC. In addition, Monte-Carlo SBM also launched its own glossy lifestyle magazine, *Monte Carlo Society*, distributed throughout its various properties.

Monte Carlo's clear positioning as a brand has given it the legitimacy to embark on projects like the hotel in Marrakech. In the future, there seems no reason why it shouldn't expand into areas such as cosmetics – related to its spa offering – souvenir gifts and premium online gambling sites.

Axel Hoppenot says: 'François Blanc said that it was not the prospect of winning that attracted people to Monte Carlo, but the sense that they could throw off their troubles and devote themselves, even for a short time, to the pursuit of pleasure. In that sense, when you come to Monte Carlo, you can't lose.'

HOTEL WORLD

I've been staring at the view from my balcony at the Hotel de Paris for long enough – it's time to go down to the lobby and do some work. With 182 rooms, 74 suites, three restaurants and a bar, the hotel is one of those dauntingly grand edifices that feel like miniature cities. You could get lost in its lobby – a vast marble-floored piazza whose domed ceiling swirls with plaster representations of turtles, stingrays, octopuses and giant gape-mouthed fish. Its supporting columns are crowned with seahorses.

I move through to the American Bar for a meeting with Luca Allegri, the hotel's general manager. Allegri is a genial yet suitably suave gentleman whose trim salt-and-pepper goatee beard goes perfectly with his dapper suit. The hotel trade is in Allegri's genes: his father was the head concierge at the Splendido in Portofino, part of the Orient Express group and one of the world's most glamorous hotels. 'I worked there during school holidays, carrying bags and helping out in the kitchen,' Allegri recalls.

There is not enough room here to list all the famous hotels at which Allegri subsequently worked. They include the Mayfair Regent in New York, the Connaught in London, the Palazzo Sasso in Ravello and Il

Pellicano in Porto Ercole. Midway through his career, Allegri decided that he wanted to learn more about the restaurant business, so he went to France and back to basics, working once again in a kitchen. During this period he made the acquaintance of the great French chef Alain Ducasse (see Chapter 16), with whom he developed an informal working partnership. When Ducasse signed a contract to open a restaurant at the Hotel Plaza Athénée in Paris, Allegri joined him as food and beverage director – later rising to executive assistant manager.

'The hotel had very strong brand. For instance, the bar at the Plaza Athénée was a popular socializing spot for fashionable young women, so we were able to sign a merchandizing deal with Lancôme to produce a branded lip-gloss range based on the flavours of our cocktails.'

Branding is important, says Allegri, because luxury travellers often regard hotels as destinations in their own right, rather than just beds for the night. 'There should be nothing standard about the hotel. Everything should say: "This is different, this is why you come here." For instance, the George V in Paris [where Allegri worked during its pre-opening period] is famous for the beautiful flower arrangements in the lobby.'

This sense of detail comes right down to the products in the bathroom. When Allegri arrived at the Hotel de Paris, he negotiated a deal with La Prairie, the Swiss skincare and cosmetics brand, because he wanted something that was 'at the same time premium and trendy'. These arrangements are considered mutually beneficial as they express messages about both the hotel and the brand. And because the young rich have grown addicted to spa experiences, they devote more time to bathing rituals and are apt to judge a hotel by the luxuriousness of its bathroom – including the quality of the brands on display.

Allegri confirms that the first duty of a manger when he arrives at a hotel is to ensure that every square metre of the property is being capitalized on. Are the rooms priced correctly? Is the mix of accommodation varied enough to appeal to different tastes, or should some new concepts be introduced? Are the bars and restaurants of a high enough quality? Have they been successfully marketed to non-guests?

But all this, he says, is basic management. At the ultra-luxury level, it's the human dimension that makes the real difference. 'For instance, I learned from my father that the concierge is the most important person in the hotel – certainly as far as the guests are concerned. A good concierge is a guide, a diplomat and counsellor; they smooth over problems and book restaurant tables. They arrange theatre tickets and excursions. A concierge can actually make the difference between an excellent vacation and an average one.'

He adds, however, that every single member of a hotel's staff should consider themselves a brand ambassador. 'They should be elegant in their manners and formal in their approach. Sometimes there is an opportunity to adopt a more relaxed manner with a client, but in my view you should always keep a certain distance. It's a tricky balance: provide excellent service without being overwhelming; be friendly without being familiar. These are the talents of the true professional.'

Allegri's words bring to mind the motto of Horst Schulze, who helped to found the Ritz-Carlton group: 'We are ladies and gentlemen serving ladies and gentlemen.' This was accompanied by an entire customer service credo that Ritz-Carlton staff are still expected to carry on their person. It includes such gems as 'I build strong relationships and create Ritz-Carlton guests for life,' 'I am empowered to create unique, memorable and personal experiences for our guests' and 'I own and immediately resolve guest problems.'

The latter is not just an empty phrase: even the most junior members of staff are allowed to spend up to US $2,000 to take care of a guest's problem without having to seek permission at a higher level. Like many hotel groups, Ritz-Carlton has used technology to refine its approach to customer relations. The requirements and preferences of each guest – from specific requests to the type of fruit they selected from the basket in their room – are entered into a database, so their room can be personalized for their next stay. Employees are encouraged to remember names and use them.

With so many grand hotels dotted around the world – run, it seems, by groups who have raised customer service to an art form – new luxury establishments must work hard to compete. Some do so by offering a smaller 'boutique' format that provides guests with the quirky charm of a family-run hotel. Others package the hotel as 'an experience' that goes far beyond mere shelter. Often the result is an overblown 'theme' hotel of the sort that has long been familiar in Las Vegas. Until the recession put a brake on development, the Gulf was becoming a prime location for these sorts of projects. The Burj al Arab in Dubai led the trend: the sail-shaped profile of this 321-metre-tall hotel is familiar to architecture buffs everywhere. The hotel considers itself to be a 'seven-star' establishment due to touches like butlers appointed to every guest room. A more recent addition is the Emirates Palace in Abu Dhabi, a blend of Arabian Nights fantasy and European grand hotel. The sand on its private beach was imported from Algeria, the local desert sand being too coarse.

There are plans for luxury underwater hotels (the Hydropolis, in Dubai, looks the closest to opening at the time of writing) and even a luxury airship hotel called 'Manned Cloud', envisioned by French designer Jean-Marie Massaud. '[His] plans foresee the 20-room sight-seeing hotel accommodating 40 guests and 15 employees. A restaurant, bookstore, fitness studio and bar will provide entertainment, should watching the world go by through the enormous panorama windows... become boring' ('Luxury airship lets tourists enjoy the high life', Spiegel Online International Edition, 7 February 2008).

These examples veer dangerously close to gimmickry. But what do you do if you plan to open a subtly smart hotel in a city with a genuine history and plenty of competing establishments? This was the challenge facing The Mark Hotel in New York as it prepared to reopen in the summer of 2009 after a top-to-toe overhaul. (In fact The Mark is a hybrid – the elegant building on Madison Avenue at 77th Street comprises 42 apartments and 118 hotel rooms.)

The solution was to blend French chic with zingy Manhattan hipness and a dash of whimsy. Izak Senbahar and Simon Elias of real estate developer Alexico Group have a track record of working with renowned designers and artists to give their properties a cultural touch. For The Mark, they called upon the services of Paris-based interior designer Jacques Grange.

The choice was unusual enough not to stumble into cliché, while elitist enough to appeal to a discerning target market. Grange made his name designing apartments for private clients like Valentino Garavani, Yves Saint Laurent and François Pinault. His style combines an haute couture sensibility with a bric-a-brac eccentricity, the edges rounded off by faultless sophistication. (If you don't know what I mean, take a look at The Mark's black-and-white striped marble lobby, which manages to be both startling and classic.) Grange's American adventures began when Louise Sunshine, 'a New York real estate marketing strategist', visited his office on the rue du Faubourg St-Honoré in 1999. She persuaded him to work on an apartment complex called One Beacon Court, opposite Bloomingdale's. And in 2006 she introduced him to Alexico and The Mark ('A French star reinvents a New York classic', *The New York Post*, 1 November 2007).

Grange designed all of the hotel's 118 hotel rooms and 32 of its apartments (the remainder come unfurnished), along with its bar and lobby. His partner, Pierre Passebon, whose gallery in Paris exhibits the work of leading contemporary designers, also came on board as 'curator' of the project. Passebon commissioned star furniture designers like Ron Arad and Vladimir Kagan to create exclusive pieces for the hotel. The French duo and their collaborators have spearheaded the marketing of The Mark: approving articles appeared in the US press months before the hotel was due to open. Writers enthused about the cloud-shaped bar, the oversized beds and sofas, the ivory taffeta curtains and the carpets whose design was based on Iznik lace.

To add to the stylish buzz around the hotel, French cartoonist and illustrator Jean-Philippe Delhomme was commissioned to create a lavish press kit and brochure, as well as to provide images for the website. The multimedia package was peppered with teasing 'franglais' slogans such as 'l'adresse plus chic de New York' and 'c'est un landmark de l'Upper East Side'. These created the ambience of whimsical elegance that the developers and branding agency Pandiscio Co hoped to evoke.

But The Mark also had a secret weapon. Having blended Paris with Manhattan, the developers added British stiff upper lip in the form of the hotel's general manager, James Sherwin. With ironic humour bubbling gently under his steely accent, Sherwin must go down a storm in New York. Having worked for the Savoy Group for many years, he has lived in the city since 1991 after 'falling for the excitement and buzz of the place'. But his British sense of correctness remains intact: his staff will wear Turnbull & Asser tailoring and shoes by John Lobb. The hotel's private car is a Bentley.

'I believe I know what guests want from a luxury hotel – and it's not vanilla,' Sherwin says. 'People are bored of corporate blandness. When they stay with us, they will be staying at a hotel with an identity.'

The hotel's unique design may also tempt potential customers to abandon their usual choice of accommodation when they're in town. Wealthy consumers – especially of the more mature variety – are notoriously set in their ways and may be loath to let go of a place where everyone knows their name. Sherwin himself has played an ambassadorial role by telling his own contacts and regular clients about The Mark.

As well as enthusing about the hotel's more obviously extravagant touches – the restaurant headed by Jean-Georges Vongerichten, the hairdressing salon overseen by Frédéric Fekkai – Sherwin puts himself in his guests' shoes. 'For example, at many hotels the mini bar is simply a disgrace. Here, every single room is equipped with a 1930s-style cocktail bar that opens up to reveal full bottles – not just miniatures – and a refrigerator that provides plenty of ice. It's all about going that extra distance. We are the first hotel in New York to be fully equipped with Bang & Olufsen equipment, for instance.'

Details count when it comes to service, Sherwin notes. For example, the hotel can provide 'black tie emergency kits' containing a pressed shirt, bow tie and cufflinks, for guests who find that they are required to attend a formal event.

And finally, of course, there is the personal touch. 'American hotel groups are fond of the idea that you should address every guest by their name, but staff sometimes apply this rule rather unthinkingly. There may be certain circumstances – in the hotel lobby, for example, with others looking on – in which guests may not want to be addressed by name. In those cases, "sir" or "madam" will do quite nicely.'

LUXURY TRAVEL SERVICES

How do the rich travel? Not light, that's for sure. One expert at dealing with the fabulously wealthy is Roshan Pillai, general manager of the Al Mousim Travel Group based in Riyadh, Saudi Arabia. In 2007 Roshan founded the group's luxury travel department, which specializes in organizing vacations for prominent Saudi families. It is a concierge-style service with a password-protected website and a very exclusive clientele. Only those who have received a personal invitation from the agency are granted access to the service. The average price of a vacation arranged through the department is between US $150,000 and US $200,000. Pillai and his team of six consultants regularly organize family vacations for groups of 15 or 20 people: mother, father, up to six children, friends and members of staff.

'The key is engagement,' says Pillai. 'This is a bespoke service and the client gets one-to-one advice from their personal consultant.'

Once a client has contacted the service, a consultant is dispatched to their home to discuss their ideas and desires. He takes notes and then returns at a later date with suggestions. 'We have to be creative because our customers always want something new. We try to come up with an entirely different package for every single inquiry. Having said that, there are trends: recently South America has become a more popular destination. We have organized a cruise on the Amazon, for example.'

Naturally, travel is fast track and hotel rooms are the very best. An Al Mousim consultant flies to the destination a day or two in advance to check that the accommodation is up to scratch and to greet the travellers. The manager of the hotel or resort is usually on hand to welcome the party when it arrives. Just as some clients provide their own jet, others vacation in cities where they own a property. In that case, Pillai's team organizes just about everything else: transfer, excursions, shopping trips, visits to exhibitions and access to the trendiest boutiques, restaurants and shows. 'Of course, we build plenty of flexibility into the schedule, so we don't put any pressure on our clients,' he adds.

The team has also expanded into corporate trips, generally to glitzy international events like the Monaco Grand Prix. Pillai adds that Europe remains a beloved destination among Saudi travellers, many of whom have second homes in France. Indeed, Pillai is on the advisory board of the Maison de la France – the French tourist board – to help it cater to the needs of visitors from Saudi Arabia.

Al Mousim's luxury service attracts new customers by word of mouth, as well as the occasional envious article in a premium magazine. Economic tremors have had little impact on the business. 'We're planning to expand our infrastructure because right now we're actually having to turn down business. We don't want to take on more assignments than we can handle and undermine the service for our existing clients.'

Central and Eastern Europe is another source of wealthy travellers. A young Slovak entrepreneur named Radoslav Radosa hopes to capture that market with the Radosa Luxury Travel Group. Founded in 2008, it specializes in hotel reservations and concierge services. An invitation-only, password-protected website gives clients access to some of the world's most luxurious hotels. The hotels pay a subscription to become part of the service. 'In return, they gain access to the clients of the future. Many services like this exist already, but they are English-language and Western-oriented. If hotels wish to develop their businesses, they need to look to emerging markets, which include Romania, Bulgaria, Poland, Kazakhstan and Armenia as well as Russia and the Gulf.'

Luxury hotels are familiar with the concept of joining forces under an umbrella brand for marketing purposes: examples include The Leading

Hotels of the World, Five Star Alliance, Relais & Châteaux and Design Hotels. Many alliances were formed to tackle the challenges presented by central reservation systems (CRS). Forerunners of the internet, CRS enabled travel agents to book hotel rooms by computer rather than over the phone. The cost of appearing on these systems was prohibitive, which gave big hotel chains a major marketing advantage. And so independent hotels banded together to share the cost and raise their profiles. Today, members of these groups pay annual fees in order to benefit from joint websites, a presence in glossy annual directories and shared advertising campaigns. This is particularly useful to 'boutique' hotels that appeal to wealthy travellers but lack marketing dollars.

Meanwhile, after a hard day's interviewing, I am back on my balcony at the distinctly un-boutique Hotel de Paris. Night has fallen and gold and silver reflections shimmer on the satin waters of the harbour. Pop music and snatches of laughter drift up from a big yacht strung with lights from prow to stern. I'm off duty for the evening, but Monte Carlo is still working. It's busy living up to its image.

10

Art brands

'Artists incarnate the idea of the unique and the rare, which is the very foundation of luxury.'

FIAC may not be the most prestigious contemporary art fair on the calendar, but it has one of the loveliest settings. *La Foire Internationale de l'Art Contemporaine* is held in the nave of the Grand Palais, a giant secular cathedral with a curvilinear glass and steel roof that soars above the trees lining the nearby Champs Elysées. Opened in time for the Universal Exhibition of 1900, the edifice took three years to build. Inside, the arcing steel girders are painted a particularly French shade of light green known as 'mignonette', which gives the structure the look of a retro-futuristic city in a Jules Verne novel. The central dome is suspended 45 metres over our heads at its highest point. Rather like the Eiffel Tower, this is gratuitous architecture, useful for little other than being gawped at. It is, therefore, the perfect space for a contemporary art exhibition. Standing in the middle of it as light cascades down onto the first visitors of the day, it is difficult not to feel a surge of excitement.

Despite the fact that this edition of FIAC has attracted more than 180 modern and contemporary art galleries – two-thirds of them from outside France – and has erected a secondary exhibition space in the courtyard of the Louvre, most people involved in the fair tell me that it is a rather modest event. The landmark gatherings of the year for the art crowd are TEFAF, The European Fine Art Foundation Fair (held in

Maastricht in March), Frieze in London (held just before FIAC every October) and Art Basel (held in June) along with its sister event Art Basel Miami (in December).

FIAC is more relaxed and accessible than these events, and it is a more comfortable environment for members of the public. Some dealers consider this an advantage. '*La FIAC* plays a vital educational role,' says legendary Parisian gallerist Denise René, whose gallery has been specializing in abstract art since 1944. 'Future collectors are born here.'

Frieze and Art Basel are big brands. There is a great deal of branding in the art world. Just as the fairs are branded, so are many of the artists showing work there. The galleries are certainly branded. A handful of collectors are branded, too. All this is purely logical. Like it or not, works of art are luxury goods. 'Artists incarnate the idea of the unique and the rare, which is the very foundation of luxury,' the French artist Fabrice Hyber told *Madame Figaro* magazine ('*L'art, c'est du luxe*', 26–27 October 2008).

He added: 'The world of luxury needs us.'

BRANDED COLLECTORS

To confirm the parallel between artworks and luxury goods, one only has to take a closer look at the 'branded collectors', as Don Thompson calls them in his excellent (2008) book *The $12 Million Stuffed Shark*. Perhaps the most famous of them all is Charles Saatchi, who helped to fund the artist Damien Hirst's titular shark – which hovers in a tank of formaldehyde with its jaws agape – and later sold it for US $12 million, or US $8 million, depending on who you talk to.

As a former advertising man, Saatchi is no doubt highly aware of the importance of branding. He is famous for exhibiting challenging or 'shock' art that provokes media buzz and pulls in the crowds, turning his chosen artists into celebrities. Saatchi has a knack for discovering artists who stir the imaginations of the press and the general public. He spotted Damien Hirst, for example, when this most famous of British artists was still a student a Goldsmith's College in London. Hirst was to become the ultimate branded artist, effacing the boundaries between art and commerce in a way that far eclipsed similar efforts by Andy Warhol.

Saatchi is dismissive of critics who feel uncomfortable with this clash of art and celebrity. 'Better to be a celebrity because people talk about your art, rather than your wedding pictures in *Hello!*', he told *The Sunday Times* ('The revolution continues at the new Saatchi Gallery', 5 October 2008).

I first came across Saatchi's take on art in 1997, at a now-notorious exhibition called *Sensation*, held at the Royal Academy in London. It featured more than 120 Saatchi-owned works by 42 young British artists. Among the pieces on show were Marcus Harvey's portrait of the child murderer Myra Hindley – her pixelated features formed by children's tiny handprints – and Jake and Dinos Chapman's sculptures of children whose noses and mouths had been replaced by penises and anuses. There were public demonstrations outside the gallery and the media had a thoroughly good time getting steamed up over the 'scandalous' artworks. Inevitably, the exhibition achieved international press coverage ('Art that tweaks the British propriety', said a headline in *The New York Times* on 20 September 2007) and attracted around 300,000 visitors during its three-month run.

I remember being dismayed by the child sculptures, but other exhibits seemed teasing and fun. Hirst's shark was on show (its correct name is 'The Physical Impossibility of Death in the Mind of Someone Living') along with an infamous piece by Tracey Emin. Entitled 'Everyone I Have Ever Slept With 1963–1995', it was a tent decorated with the names of all those who had shared her bed, from sexual partners to a teddy bear. (When the tent was destroyed in a warehouse fire in 2004, several tabloid newspapers offered to replace it for considerably less than the £1 million it was reportedly insured for.) And there was something queasily fascinating about Mark Quinn's 'Self', a frozen cast of the artist's head made with eight pints of his own blood. Whatever else *Sensation* achieved, it opened my eyes to the infinite possibilities of contemporary art – and established Charles Saatchi as the ultimate branded collector.

In October 2008, almost exactly 11 years after my first brush with Saatchi's art, I visited his new gallery in a former army barracks just off the King's Road in London. The highlight of the inaugural exhibition, devoted to Chinese artists, was a basement room containing Sun Yuan and Pen Yu's lifelike sculptures of elderly ex-military types in robotic wheelchairs. The chairs collided, reversed and set off again in new directions, performing a grotesque ballet. The work seemed to suggest that these men – with their waxen features, dusty uniforms and chinking medals – could not avoid waging war, without rhyme or reason, even on the brink of death. Like much of Saatchi's art, it was disturbing and provocative. Yet the gallery is highly accessible – free to visit and next to a busy shopping street. Saatchi is not just in the business of buying and selling: his brand name has enabled him to bring 'difficult' contemporary art to the attention of a wider public. The contemporary art boom and the popularity of museums like London's Tate Modern and New York's MoMA can at least partly be attributed to the taste-making instincts of Charles Saatchi.

Saatchi's brand has an impact on the art market because less visionary collectors follow his lead. Anybody who has spent any time looking at contemporary art will know that it is almost impossible to fathom why one artist is 'hot' and another is not. Reading the art critics does not help, as most of what they have to say is impenetrable or, at the very least, hyperbolic. And yet here you are, a shiny new billionaire, and you want to invest in the sexy world of contemporary art. As Don Thompson writes: 'Even if you are only moderately rich, there is almost nothing you can buy for £1 million that will generate as much status and recognition as a branded work of contemporary art.'

So if you can't crack the code, what do you do? You buy what Saatchi buys.

Two other branded collectors have direct links to the luxury goods industry. They are also rivals – in the art world as in the luxury world. The individual best known to the general public is Bernard Arnault, chairman and CEO of LVMH (Moët Hennessy, Louis Vuitton), who is said to possess one of the most important collections of modern and contemporary pieces in France. Louis Vuitton has an art gallery on the top floor of its flagship store in Paris; cynics say this was added to help the store circumvent France's ban on Sunday trading, as it could legitimately claim to be a cultural attraction.

In 1999, LVMH bought the 200-year-old auction house Phillips for US $100 million, merging it with the gallery of private art dealers Simon de Pury and Daniela Luxembourg. But it seems that the house did not perform as well as LVMH had hoped. In 2002, LVMH sold the bulk of its shares to De Pury and Luxembourg. A year later, it pulled out altogether ('LVMH to sell Phillips stake to auction house executives', *The New York Times*, 28 January 2003). Simon de Pury moved the operation to trendy new headquarters in New York's Meatpacking District and announced that it would focus on 'contemporary art, design, jewellery and photography'. In 2008, Russian luxury and retail company the Mercury Group acquired control of Phillips de Pury & Company. Mercury owns the TSUM department store in Moscow, as well as the Barvikha Luxury Village just outside the city.

Back at Louis Vuitton, luxury goods themselves are fusing with works of art. In 2001 the company produced bags and other items featuring designs by the graffiti artist Stephen Sprouse – a line it resurrected in 2009. It has also collaborated with Takashi Murakami and Richard Prince. Like Murakami and Sprouse, Prince reworked Vuitton's monogram logo – but the brand's spring/summer 2008 fashion show went a step further by sending out models dressed as the 'sexy nurses' who feature in some of Prince's paintings.

Vuitton is not the only luxury brand to have made a grab for cultural legitimacy by joining forces with the art world. The French brand Longchamp, for example, recruited Tracey Emin to design a successful collection of bags. The White Cube gallery in London sold a limited edition range of the bags via its online shop.

On a far larger scale, at the beginning of March 2008 Chanel sponsored a mobile art exhibition of works loosely inspired by the shape of its quilted '2.55' handbag. Some 20 artists – including Daniel Buren, Sophie Calle, Fabrice Hyber and Yoko Ono – exhibited works in a futuristic collapsible structure designed by the fashionable architect Zaha Hadid. Launched on the rooftop of a skyscraper in Hong Kong, the nomadic 'art pavilion' was due to embark on a worldwide tour that would take it to New York, London, Moscow and Paris. Touching down like a computer mouse-shaped UFO in the middle of a recession, the structure and its contents could hardly have looked more out of place. The tour was quietly cut short in New York.

Another well-known collector from the luxury industry is also a Frenchman: François Pinault, who runs the PPR group. As mentioned earlier, this owns a raft of famous luxury brands, including Gucci, Yves Saint Laurent and Bottega Veneta. For a while, it looked as though Pinault's ventures into the art world had been more successful than those of Bernard Arnault, his great business rival. Pinault remains the owner of the prestigious auction house Christie's. In 2004 he established a private art foundation at the Palazzo Grassi in Venice, having abandoned plans to build a museum in his homeland when French bureaucracy prevented him from getting his hands on his preferred site – a giant former Renault plant.

Bernard Arnault was not to be outdone, however. In 2006 he announced the creation of a US$100 million centre for contemporary art in the Bois de Boulogne, just outside Paris. And as the steel cherry on the undulating cake, the structure would be designed by Frank Gehry, the architect famous for creating 'branded buildings' like the spectacular Guggenheim Museum in Bilbao.

It's interesting to note that, at various times, both collectors have relied on outside advisors. Three names have been associated with Monsieur Arnault of LVMH: Patricia Marechal, Hervé Mikaeloff and Jean-Claude Claverie. The daily newspaper published at Art Basel teasingly called them 'Team Arnault' ('European collectors on their annual shopping spree', *Art Basel Daily Edition*, 14 June 2006). A couple of years later, referring to Arnault's plans for an art foundation, Claverie told Bloomberg.com, 'It's a way of showing that luxury, which often has an arrogant, elitist, egotistical image, can be generous' ('LVMH plans museum as companies review arts spending', 2 October 2008).

Meanwhile, Monsieur Pinault's advisor is Philippe Ségalot, a colourful figure who features prominently in Sarah Thornton's entertaining (2008) book *Seven Days in the Art World*. Thornton reveals that Ségalot did not formally study art – in fact he started out in the marketing department of L'Oréal in Paris. 'It is not by chance I went from cosmetics to art,' Ségalot tells the author. 'We are dealing with beauty here. We are dealing in things that are unnecessary, dealing with abstractions.' He adds that, of all the people he advises, Pinault is his favourite collector. 'He has a true passion for contemporary art and a unique instinct for masterworks. He understands quality. He has an incredible eye.'

Nevertheless, it seems that even the most passionate collectors like to get a second opinion before making an investment.

For an outsider, it's difficult to tell whether the collectors are attracted to the investment or the art. Are they simply looking for impressive trinkets to fill their homes? Do they get a thrill from buying and selling artworks – just as they do from playing the stock market? Do they enjoy the social aspect of rubbing shoulders with their own kind at auctions and art fairs? Or are they seeking immortality through collections housed in museums that bear their names? Commenting in the Bloomberg article mentioned above, art historian Didier Rykner said: 'If French billionaires want to make museums, even if it's for their own glory, I'm all in favour, especially if the public benefits.'

But there is probably more to it than that. One art world insider told me that by comparing the collections of Pinault and Arnault, he could tell that they had specific and informed tastes. 'They are genuinely clued-up about the art world,' he insisted. 'They often find themselves at social events surrounded by people who know a great deal about art. If they could not hold their own, they would soon be exposed. These men and others like them are not casual collectors: I am convinced that they care about contemporary art.'

BRANDED ARTISTS

Not so long ago, shortly before Christmas, I found myself enjoying a meal at a trendy London restaurant called St Alban. The large, streamlined space was decorated like a fantasy 1970s airport lounge, complete with colourful sofas. But the most eye-catching thing in this already striking room was the large artwork on the back wall. Had I not been aware of its provenance, I might have assumed that it was a 20-foot-long stained glass window in which the predominant colours were turquoise and mauve. But I knew for a fact that the kaleidoscopic picture was made of hundreds of real butterfly wings. Despite its cruelty, I found the work breathtakingly beautiful. It was created by Damien Hirst, one of the most successful branded artists of all time.

When I asked a waiter about the piece, he told me that it was called 'Jubilation' and that it was on loan from Hirst to the restaurant's owners, Chris Corbin and Jeremy King. The artist had been happy to get involved in the project because his former art school tutor, Michael Craig-Martin, had designed the restaurant's interior. The waiter added that, only a few months before my visit, a customer had offered £1.5 million for the work. The inquiry was forwarded to Hirst, who declined to sell. The story quickly found its way into the press. It is exactly the sort of tale of metropolitan glamour that has made Damien Hirst such a powerful brand.

There are a number of ways in which an emerging artist can become a brand. One is to be bought by a branded collector like Charles Saatchi, which legitimizes your work. Another is to attract media coverage that adds value to your brand. And yet another is to gain marketing support from a branded dealer or gallery owner. Perhaps the ultimate is to have your work acquired by a museum: dealers use the term 'museum quality' to describe particularly expensive pieces.

Museums partly drove the contemporary art boom: more than 100 new museums have opened in the past 25 years, all hungrily buying up stocks of the best-known names. And with a new generation of wealthy collectors coming onto the market during roughly the same period, demand outstripped supply.

'Every year art schools spit out thousands of groomed-for-success graduates, whose job it is to supply galleries and auction houses with desirable retail,' explains an article in the *International Herald Tribune*. 'They are backed up by cadres of public relations specialists – critics, curators, editors, publishers and career theorists – who provide updates on what desirable means' ('Does the downturn carry a silver lining for the art world?', 18 February 2009).

Even those with only a vague knowledge of the contemporary art scene are aware of some its best-known brands. The late Andy Warhol felt that his own celebrity was an art form. Jeff Koons – who once worked as a Wall Street commodities broker – gained notoriety with, among other things, a series of sculptures and paintings featuring himself and his wife, the former porn star known as La Cicciolina, in various sexual positions. (Don Thompson observes that Koons once defined his target market as 'really rich collectors'. The artist also excels at coming up with catchy slogans, such as 'abstraction and luxury are the guard dogs of the upper class'.) Tracey Emin has a 'sexy bad girl' brand positioning and once turned her own unmade bed into art.

But with his combination of dark humour, marketing savvy, industry clout and sheer *chutzpah*, Damien Hirst towers over them all. His work sells for far more than the sums Andy Warhol was able to command in his lifetime.

Born in Bristol and brought up in Leeds, Hirst attended Goldsmiths College in London. Part of the University of London, Goldsmiths prides itself on looking at subjects in 'creative and unconventional ways' (www.gold.ac.uk). Graduates include the artist Bridget Riley and the godfather of punk, Malcolm McLaren. In 1988, while still at Goldsmiths, Hirst exhibited the work of 17 of the school's art students alongside some of his own pieces in a now-legendary show called Freeze.

Hirst already knew how to turn art into an event. Don Thompson writes: 'Freeze was Hirst's personal creation. He chose the art, commissioned a catalogue and planned the opening party,' in an abandoned building in London's docklands. The show did not escape the attention of Charles Saatchi, who would soon endorse and package the Young British Art movement. In 1990 Hirst curated another exhibition, called Gambler – and Saatchi dropped by. The collector bought a Hirst installation: a piece called 'A Thousand Years', in which newly hatched flies were killed by a fizzing electric zapper as they tried to get to a rotting cow's head on the other side of a glass partition. (Hirst says his obsession with death sprang partly from a work placement in a mortuary.)

The following year, according to Thompson, Saatchi commissioned 'The Physical Impossibility of Death in the Mind of Someone Living' – the shark. (It is said to have cost £50,000 and was sold just under 15 years later for £6.5 million.) Also in 1991, Hirst met another person who was to have a significant impact on his career: Jay Jopling, founder of the influential White Cube gallery. Originally located on the traditional gallery circuit in Duke Street St James's, the space moved in 2000 to Hoxton Square in the East End, contributing to the formerly down-at-heel area's regeneration as one of the hippest quarters of the city.

Hirst's shark is one of a series of meditations on death, along with embalmed sheep and severed cows in glass cabinets. The 'butterfly paintings' address a similar theme, as do the 'cabinet' works, which are medicine cabinets filled with bottles of pills or surgical tools. (Hirst and some friends briefly ran a London restaurant called Pharmacy – its fixtures and fittings were later auctioned off as works of art.) All these have attracted disapproving newspaper articles, as have Hirst's 'spot paintings'. These multicoloured dots on white backgrounds would be entirely inoffensive were it not for the means of their production. Hirst doesn't paint them – his assistants do. Just like Rubens in 17th century Antwerp, Hirst now has a 'school' to help him produce his artworks. In fact, he has four production facilities – two in London and two in Gloucestershire – and around 180 full-time members of staff. Although he directs operations, he happily admits that he does not apply the paint. Once you accept that Hirst is a global luxury brand, however, this seems perfectly reasonable. Would you be shocked to learn that Miuccia Prada had never laid a finger on your suit?

Hirst is also proof that a powerful brand name affords some protection against recession. On 15 September 2008, with newspapers full of doom-laden reports about the credit crunch, Sotheby's kicked off a two-day auction of 223 brand new works by Damien Hirst. This was unusual because pieces sold at auction are usually sourced from existing collections rather than fresh from an artist's atelier. Hirst treated the sale itself like a work of art, giving it one of the evocative names he is so good at dreaming up: 'Beautiful Inside My Head, Forever'. The most striking piece was 'The Golden Calf', a bull preserved in formaldehyde, with golden hooves, golden horns and a jaunty golden crown. Staging an auction of new work rather than going through a dealer – especially at a time like this – was an act of sheer bravado. If the work failed to sell for a decent sum, Hirst's reputation would have been damaged. Predictably, the media bought in to the suspense and the sale generated headlines worldwide.

The auction was a triumph. It raised US $198 million, simultaneously defying the economic gloom, giving Hirst's critics the gilded finger and breaking a record. The previous record for an auction of works by a single artist at Sotheby's was US $20 million, set in 1993 by a sale of 88 works by Pablo Picasso. Hirst's 'Golden Calf' alone fetched US $18.5 million. And a preserved tiger shark netted US $17 million, making its distant cousin seem like a minnow in comparison. 'The market is bigger than anyone knows,' commented Hirst. His brand had emerged not just untarnished, but with a new gleam of invincibility.

GALLERIES, AUCTIONS AND FAIRS

Jay Jopling's White Cube gallery is well named. A typical contemporary art gallery is exactly that: a blank box. 'This featureless environment,' writes Don Thompson, 'is meant to reinforce the idea that what is being viewed is "art" and that galleries are elitist.'

The Spartan décor is also designed to intimidate casual visitors, as is the buzzer one is invariably required to push in order to gain access. Although this is essentially a retail environment, 'just looking' is even less encouraged here than it is in luxury fashion boutiques. There are many similarities, however, including the pretty young women – known as 'gallerinas' – who cast an uninterested eye in your direction as you enter. One always fights the urge to quote Edina (played by Jennifer Saunders) in the BBC sitcom *Absolutely Fabulous*, who snaps at an aloof gallery assistant: 'Get over it, darling – this is just a shop.'

In fact, branded galleries like White Cube and renowned dealers like Mr Jopling – and the art world titan Larry Gagosian on the other side of the pond – are the highest rung on a ladder that begins at the artist's atelier, where artists are often obliged to stage their first shows. With any luck, they are then discovered by a 'mainstream dealer', which gives them access to serious collectors. Only if their work begins selling to branded collectors for elevated prices – and attracting press buzz – do they stand a chance of being lured away by a branded gallery. Most artists remain with mainstream galleries or smaller 'high street' galleries – if they even make it that far.

Very occasionally, galleries become global brands. During my research I came across one such operation in the form of Opera Gallery. In fact, it is an international luxury retail chain. Gilles Dyan opened his first gallery in Singapore in 1994, followed by Paris that same year. It now has additional branches in Dubai, Geneva, Hong Kong, London, Miami, Monaco, New York, Seoul and Venice – with more due to open at the time of writing, possibly in the Middle East.

Didier Viltart, the amiable director of the London branch of the gallery, says: 'Successful art dealers sometimes have galleries in perhaps two or three locations – but it's pretty unique to find one with a presence in 10 or more cities. We open in places where there is a clear demand from clients. We opened in Singapore because we could see that there were a lot of new collectors in Asia. Now there is a great deal of interest from the Middle East. There are new collectors and also some very talented artists, especially from Iran.'

The galleries show a mixture of 'modern and contemporary' art in spaces with similar grey, black and white colour schemes. As well as emerging contemporary artists, they sell the heavyweights: 'masters' whose works are available at Opera galleries around the world include Bonnard, Chagall, Dufy, Matisse, Modigliani, Monet, Picasso, Renoir and Rodin (see www.operagallery.com for the full line-up).

I wonder aloud what might induce somebody to sell a piece by a legendary artist once they have it in their collection.

'There are almost as many reasons as there are styles of art,' says Viltart. 'A collection may come onto the market as the result of a divorce or a death in the family. There might have been a change in the financial circumstances of the owner. Or it may simply be that their tastes are not the same as they were 20 years ago. What you must also understand is that, for some people, collecting is more than a passion

– it is a vice. And they may be forced to sell in order to feed their desire to collect art.'

Modern collectors, says Viltart, tend to be more daring than their counterparts from the 19th and early 20th centuries. 'It used to be that people would collect a certain style of art – or even a certain artist. But now there is a sort of "cabinet of curiosities" approach. Collectors are not afraid to combine different styles and eras.'

And carefully chosen art keeps its value. One Russian collector who lost a considerable amount of money on the stock exchange at the end of 2008 was grateful that he had invested in a Picasso a year earlier.

But where do these artworks come from? And how do clients find out about them? In other words, how does one choose an art dealer?

'We place advertisements in appropriate media like the *Financial Times*,' says Viltart. 'The location of the galleries also helps: we are present in districts known for art galleries. And you must also remember that an art gallery is a very sociable place. We organize gallery openings and charity events so people can come along and meet us. Thanks to our worldwide network, we have many excellent contacts. Clients recommend us to their friends.'

With a handful of the right connections it is not so difficult to build up a database of wealthy and influential people. Then it is simply a case of sending them smart, attractive invitations on thick card, or glossy exhibition catalogues resembling hefty coffee table books. The Opera Gallery in Monaco, for instance, is in touch with a company that owns many of the hotels and casinos in Monte Carlo (see Chapter 9, 'Deluxe nomads'). Because of this relationship, the gallery is able to invite the hotel group's most valued customers to the cocktail evenings it holds every three weeks or so. At events like this, logos and strategically placed catalogues form a subtle but insistent marketing presence. And even if the guests are unlikely to snap up a painting there and then, they might be impressed enough to browse the gallery's website at their leisure. With a quick click of a mouse, they can ask for more information about any of the paintings displayed on the site.

Not all of the work on show at Opera Gallery is accessible only to the immensely rich. For an outlay of a few thousand pounds, you might be able to pick up a lovely vintage print by a Japanese photographer, for example. 'You don't fall in love with something because of its price,' Viltart points out. 'The most sympathetic collectors buy not to invest, but for their own pleasure.'

And if funds are short, some galleries may allow you to pay in instalments. You won't receive the artwork until the last payment has been made, however. Now that money is tighter everywhere, this arrangement may become more common. Viltart says: 'We are still doing plenty of business, but there are fewer traders than before. What you're seeing now are the genuine collectors – those for whom art is a passion rather than a business.'

Dealers in the gallery district of the Marais in Paris confirm that collectors continued to buy as the recession took hold. In fact, the more accessible galleries benefited from the downturn, because seriously addicted collectors fed their need by investing in smaller pieces by little-known artists, costing anything from €500 to €15,000.

My last question turns out to be the most controversial one: if you have a painting to sell, why do so through a gallery rather than at an auction? 'Partly because if you go to an auction house you have to wait until the date of the next auction,' Viltart says. 'And while an auction is designed to drive up the price, the seller pays more commission: there's a big difference between the hammer price and the amount that finds its way into your pocket. There is also the little matter of discretion: you may not want the world to know that you are selling your painting.'

In fact auction houses can arrange 'private' sales, involving a limited number of potential buyers – but that is beside the point. It transpires that there is intense rivalry between galleries and auction houses. The advantage of galleries is that they have built up personal relationships with artists and clients (Viltart tells me he has visited the homes of 95 per cent of his clients and considers many of them friends). Galleries nurture artists' careers and act as educators for collectors. Auction houses, on the other hand, excel at creating buzz around sales. Websites, full-page advertisements in art magazines and newspapers, stunning catalogues sent in advance to key collectors, expertly hung pre-sale shows, cocktail parties and private viewing sessions for the happy few – these are some of the weapons in their arsenal. They have also developed bespoke services for their 'mega clients' and think nothing of hopping on a plane with a picture in order to give a potential buyer a one-to-one viewing. And then there is the suspenseful sale itself, a complex piece of theatre designed to ensure that the work sells for the highest possible price.

Dealers – or 'gallerists', as they prefer – look upon all this with distaste, viewing big auction houses like Sotheby's and Christie's as behemoths who are out to crush the smaller, more humane galleries. It does not help that the borders are blurring. As we've seen, auction houses are beginning to sell new works rather than concentrating on the 'secondary' market of pieces that have already been owned. They are also starting to buy art galleries: Christie's is the owner of Haunch of Venison, a gallery with branches in London and New York.

Art fairs are the dealers' combined response to the threat of the auction houses. Only galleries are allowed to take part in art fairs. The events are attractive to collectors because they offer the chance to see a large volume of work from the world's leading dealers in one place and over a short space of time. And the leading dealers are there to greet them, their best work dusted off and ready for its close-up. The competitiveness between collectors and the air of excitement can provoke high prices.

The 40-year-old Art Basel is considered the most powerful art fair. It is sponsored by the Swiss bank UBS. Although galleries from around the world are desperate to pay around €200 per square metre for a stand at the event, Art Basel prides itself on its high standards. Any gallery taking part must have been trading for at least three years – and a seven-member committee of leading dealers vets all demands. Like other fairs, Art Basel is open to the public, but those of a low net worth can expect a frosty reception. The genuine collectors descend from on high: upstairs at Art Basel there is a maze of VIP lounges to which the milling throngs below will never gain access. This concentration of wealth inevitably attracts luxury brands. Associate sponsors of Art Basel 40 included Cartier and NetJets Europe. Among the 'lounge hosts' were Davidoff and Moët Hennessy. The champagne came courtesy of Moët & Chandon.

Didier Viltart of Opera Gallery told me that collectors could be surprisingly nationalistic: British buyers preferred to collect the Young British Artists, while Asian collectors tended to buy the work of artists from their region, and so on. Because Art Basel was viewed as a European fair, in 2002 its organizers created Art Basel Miami Beach to target the American market. The Miami edition is glitzier and more fashionable than its Swiss counterpart, attracting a slew of celebrities and, naturally, luxury brand sponsors. NetJets provides its owners with admission to the show, exclusive access to the invitation-only private preview and, of course, its own lounge. In 2008 Cartier flew in a crystal dome to shelter its guests during a party at the city's botanical gardens.

London's Frieze is the youngest of the 'must see' fairs, having been launched in 2003 by Amanda Sharp and Matthew Slotover. It started as a brand extension of their art magazine, also called *Frieze*, which they started in 1991 after graduating from Oxford. Their contacts in the art world enabled them to attract 135 galleries for the very first show. The number of exhibitors has more than tripled since then. 'Frieze Week' in mid-October is an annual rendezvous, with auction houses staging parties and sales to lure the collectors who descend on London for a few precious days.

In keeping with its London setting, Frieze has a hipper, edgier flavour to it than the other art fairs. It is just as much a part of the luxury world, though. A line from *The Daily Telegraph* newspaper sums up the ambience: 'At the Cartier Frieze Dinner, guests including Charles Saatchi and Roman Abramovich's girlfriend Daria "Dasha" Zukhova will discuss a blockbuster year which has seen records tumble at auction for works by the likes of Francis Bacon, Lucian Freud, Claude Monet and of course Damien Hirst' ('Frieze art fair: super-rich to cast economic crisis aside', 16 October 2008).

THE SALE OF THE CENTURY

When viewed from the perspective of Basle or Frieze, FIAC is indeed a far more humble affair, with barely a superstar collector in evidence. But many of the dealers told me that the Paris show is growing in importance and prestige. Among them was Neil Wenman of White Cube, which was making its debut at the fair. The gallery's stand was devoted to a new body of work by Jake and Dinos Chapman. Actually, 'body' is not quite the right word: the painted bronze sculptures reduced humankind to ramshackle constructions of cogs, pistons and oozing organs. The malfunctioning machines looked as though they'd emerged from some grim Gothic horror tale.

Looking on were a series of stern Victorian portraits. Except that the portraits had been defaced by plastic surgery, scarification and mutilation. 'It's all about ageing and decay,' Wenman explained, cheerfully. 'We felt a solo presentation would have more impact than pieces by several different artists,' he added. He said he was pleased with the show's brisk first day, which compared favourably to the recent Frieze. 'We did very well in London. The difference there is that all the real selling is done privately, behind the scenes. But of course we don't have showrooms here in Paris.'

Almost everyone I met claimed that although the free-falling economy had deterred speculators, 'real' collectors continued to buy. The problem was that estimates of the number of these committed collectors ranged from a couple of thousand worldwide to just 200 individuals.

Some months after FIAC, the atmosphere at the Grand Palais was rather different. Now it was evening, and the magnificent glass-domed building was the setting for what the French press had dubbed 'The Sale of the Century'. Christie's was auctioning the entire art collection of the late fashion designer Yves Saint Laurent and his partner Pierre Bergé. The amount fetched by the sale – estimated at more than €300 million – would be donated to charity.

Modern art was the first category in the three-day sale. And as the names involved were colossal brands – Matisse, Picasso, Mondrian, not to mention Yves Saint Laurent himself – the event had attracted fervent interest from the media and the public. Almost 35,000 people had filed through the two-day preview exhibition. Now some of them stood outside the building as if hoping that the atmosphere would leach through the walls. Inside, more than 1,200 collectors, dealers and art enthusiasts were seated in rows before the podium. These were the visible potential bidders: others were waiting at the end of 100 telephone lines. The domed roof high above was suffused with a bluish twilight. Disc-shaped chandeliers the size of flying saucers hung in the immense space, warming the crowds along with the rows of spotlights that added to the sense that this was a blend of theatre and fashion show. The air was thick with anticipation and expensive fragrance.

In the end, François de Ricqlès, the chairman of Christie's France, conducted the auction with a suave self-possession that – despite the enormous sums of money in play – made the event seem civilized and even gracious. When a fabulous piece sold for an astronomical amount, there was polite applause. No fewer than five world records were set that night. The first was for a wooden Brancusi sculpture called 'Portrait de Madame LR'. Its value had been estimated at between €15 million and €20 million – in the end the hammer came down at €29.17

million. About 15 minutes later, Piet Mondrian's 'Composition in Red, Yellow and Black' sold for €21.56 million – double the estimated price. A gloriously colourful 1911 Matisse, 'The Cuckoos, a Blue and Pink Rug', went for €35.9 million, while Giorgio de Chirico's 'The Returning Ghost' fetched a comparatively modest €11.04 million. Marcel Duchamp, one of the leaders of the absurdist Dada movement, must have been smiling wryly on high when a fake perfume bottle whose label featured a photograph of him in drag sold for €8.91 million.

At the end of the three-day auction, the grand total fetched by the collection was a staggering €373.5 million. And this in the middle of one of the worst downturns the art market had ever known.

The auction's success was due to the convergence of several luxury brands. First there were the artists themselves. Second there was Christie's: a major art world brand owned, as we know, by luxury tycoon François Pinault. And finally, Pinault's group also owns Yves Saint Laurent – the brand that really drove the success of the sale. That's why the Christie's website prominently featured an image of the late designer. It's why people who might not normally have been interested in art pressed into the Grand Palais for the preview show. And ultimately it's why the sale broke records. Everyone knows that it's cool to own a Matisse. But it's even cooler to own a Matisse that once belonged to Yves Saint Laurent.

The sums fetched at the sale prompted some observers to suggest that the art market was more resistant to the economic crisis than had at first been feared. For a few years, the market had been lofted into the stratosphere by a bubble of new wealth from Asia, Russia and central and eastern Europe. The bursting of that bubble precipitated a sudden plunge to earth. This was not necessarily a bad thing. When the US economy entered the doldrums in the 1970s, artists in New York began colonizing the post-industrial wasteland that later became known as SoHo. Similarly, the Young British Art movement – led by Damien Hirst – emerged in the thick of recession at the beginning of the 1990s. Just as SoHo artists had squatted decaying industrial spaces, so the Young Brits invaded warehouses in imitation of the illegal 'raves' that were transforming dance music. Today, empty retail spaces are being targeted by artists in search of new venues.

Like the Damien Hirst auction shortly before it, the Yves Saint Laurent extravaganza proved that art is driven by branding.

11

Upscale retail

'The first attribute of luxury is quality. The second is emotional reward.'

The retail space is a crucial communications vector for many luxury brands. As we've heard time and time again, one of the key differences between a luxury product and a humdrum one is the element of fantasy. 'Nobody needs another handbag,' admitted Robert Polet, CEO of the Gucci Group, in an interview with *The Wall Street Journal*. 'So you have to create what I call the "need to have it" factor, when the customer says "I need to have that $2,000 bag, and my only worry is that it be in stock. I want it now." This is the emotional desire of the brand, the power of the dream' ('Gucci chief peddles power of the dream', 24 September 2007).

So far so predictable – but Polet went on to say that he had experienced this power as a young man while sitting in his father's brand new Austin Westminster car. 'It had leather seats, and sitting in the car smelling the leather made a tremendous impact on me.'

This is exactly the kind of visceral response that luxury brands strive to provoke with their retail spaces. They want to seduce the shopper with lavish surroundings – to create a Disneyland of desire. If luxury brands have taken a hesitant approach to online retail (see next chapter, 'Digital luxury') it is because they are afraid that, when stripped of fancy framing in the form of these awe-inspiring stores, their expensive gewgaws might appear banal. The power of context has driven Prada to design stores with hip architects like Rem Koolhaas and Herzog & de Meuron, and Louis Vuitton to open flagships in emerging markets at the rate that other brands erect billboards.

Aldo Gucci defined the appeal of authentic luxury goods in 1938, when he hung a sign in the brand's first store in via Condotti, Rome. It read: 'Quality is remembered long after price is forgotten.' Ironically, few people can remember what the store's original interior looked like, because it has been redesigned to reflect each incoming designer's interpretation of the Gucci brand. The latest transformation was overseen by Frida Giannini, who took over from Tom Ford as Gucci's chief designer in 2005. Working her way through the chain of stores, she has banished Ford's black-and-chrome aesthetic and replaced it with her own lighter, more gently nostalgic vision. In the world of luxury fashion, the retail space must correctly evoke the 'codes' of the brand, with no disconnect from what is going on in the advertising or on the runway, otherwise it risks the consumer becoming disenchanted. As each successive designer tweaks the codes of the brand, its original values disappear under layers of artifice.

Luxury brands tend not to attempt to weave their magic alone, however. Upscale stores are invariably located in elegant districts that transport strollers to a parallel, more sophisticated, world. One example is London's Regent Street, the gently curving boulevard designed by John Nash in 1811. Despite being redeveloped by numerous architects in the early 20th century, it retains a beauty and symmetry that can compete with any of Europe's finest thoroughfares.

Regent Street has a single owner, Crown Estates, which embarked on a £500 million renovation in 2002 in order to reinforce the street's positioning as an upscale retail hub. 'We knew from the very beginning that Regent Street had fantastic architecture but that it was lacking in brand or style in retailing terms,' said David Shaw, head of Regent Street strategy and development. 'We've been... focusing on bringing flagship stores to the street that can provide something above what can be found in other retail areas' ('London's retailers look beyond today's bad news', *International Herald Tribune*, 17 September 2008).

The efforts have borne fruit in the form of 60 new stores since 2002, including Britain's first Ferrari store. Meanwhile, Israel's Alrov Group has leased the 150-year-old Café Royal at the end of the street and will turn it into a luxury hotel. As it is the sole landlord of Regent Street, Crown Estates can 'curate' the avenue to provide a coherent environment for brands and visitors. 'What we are doing is looking at the whole of the street, not just at individual buildings,' said Shaw. 'You [shouldn't] just think about retail space but also about restaurants and hotels and offices.'

Another example of a 'curated' district is Marylebone High Street, one of London's most attractive shopping destinations. Once again, a single landlord, the Howard de Walden Estate, manages the street's almost seamless brand identity. It wanted to develop a 'village within a city' that would set Marylebone apart from other neighbourhoods and deliver a nostalgic yet upscale experience. Its strategy was driven by the insight that customers are increasingly seeking an alternative to global brands and homogenized environments. The landlord discourages multinational chains and welcomes independent shopkeepers with unique concepts. Those who stroll down the street today can indulge in the archaic pleasures of visiting a traditional butcher and fishmonger, browsing in a quaint wood-panelled bookstore, or enjoying a cup of tea and a cake in a genteel café. Like Regent Street, the district also has its own website, solidifying its existence as a brand.

New developments confirm the theory that luxury brands like company. When the 46-acre (19-hectare) Westfield shopping centre opened in the west of London at the end of 2008, it instantly became one of Europe's biggest luxury shopping complexes, offering brands such as Dior, Gucci, Louis Vuitton, Miu Miu, Prada and Valentino.

In the article mentioned earlier, the designer Amanda Wakeley – who was poised to open a site at Westfield – said she intended to distinguish her brand with superior service. 'The customer has to feel assisted but not intimidated,' she said. Although some customers may get the feeling that vendors in luxury boutiques take lessons in glacial snootiness, service is a primary concern – especially when it comes to targeting high net worth individuals.

SERVING VIP CUSTOMERS

The personal touch is part of Louis Vuitton's marketing strategy. The company has a department called Private Client Relations, whose mission is to target the fabulously wealthy. The company estimates that there are around 8 million people worldwide with immediate access to a million dollars or more. Many of them are already Louis Vuitton customers – but it is very keen to attract those who are not. In order to seduce this elusive market, Louis Vuitton uses a combination of 'ambassadors' and 'in-store private shoppers'.

Each ambassador has a defined territory. Their job is to attract newcomers to the brand via special events and social occasions. An insight into how this might work is provided by the following snippet from a blog called Fresh Mess:

> Anette Stai, early supermodel, brand ambassador and marketing chief of Louis Vuitton Norway, greeted the well-heeled guests. Flutes of Moët & Chandon were served while everyone admired the stunning display of Special Order creations flown in for the event from France. In exhibition were a beauty case in leather from 1927, a violin case in natural cowhide leather from 1895, and a picnic trunk in monogram canvas from 1926, all encased in vitrines. Guests were also treated to a demonstration of Louis Vuitton's eminent craftsmanship by artisans from France (19 June 2008).

Once the ambassadors have lured high net worth individuals to the stores, the private shoppers can take over to look after them. Home or hotel visits can also be arranged. If all goes according to plan, the target will join Vuitton's existing database of around 5,000 VVIC (Very Very Important Clients) around the world.

But even the average salesperson in a luxury store is supposed to be slicker than his or her downmarket equivalent. According to Chevalier and Mazzalovo in *Luxury Brand Management*: 'The way luxury store sales staff engage with, talk to and deal with potential customers is very particular... The aim is to establish a relationship that goes beyond a mere commercial transaction. Many personal relationships between sales personnel and their clients are born this way.'

Elsewhere in the book the authors note that the jewellery-case-style displays of the typical luxury boutique – which almost dare consumers to touch the goods – serve partially to encourage interaction with the staff. If you want to handle an item, you have to ask.

In order to get a view from the sales floor, I set up an interview with an acquaintance of mine who'd done a stint as a vendor at Louis

Vuitton in Paris. Let's call him Samuel. I wanted to know what traits separated super-rich clients from idle browsers like me. 'One thing is certain: everybody knows when an important customer is in the store,' he says. 'Louis Vuitton has a heightened sense of client relations and the store managers are fully briefed on who is who.'

Samuel's flair for languages – particularly Arabic – meant that he was often asked to help wealthy visitors from the Middle East. He notes that they preferred to deal with the same vendor each time: 'These people feel special and like to be treated as such. After that, there are cultural variations. When visitors from the Gulf come to the flagship store in Paris, they are only interested in exclusive and limited edition products. They want the items that are not available in their home market. Customers from emerging markets tend to go for the flashiest and most expensive items. Very few of them leave with just one piece; some of them want to be branded from head to toe. Louis Vuitton is popular with nouveau riche consumers because the brand is internationally recognizable – so they can communicate their status anywhere.'

As far as the very rich are concerned, the client–vendor relationship is inversed. 'They basically see you as domestic servants,' says Samuel. 'When you approach them, their initial facial expression is one of disinterest, arrogance or even contempt. But once you've shown you've got a brain, a bit of charm and sense of humour, they usually warm to you. Speaking the language obviously helps – but quite often they prefer you to address them in English or French, because they want to demonstrate their worldliness to their companions. I've been in situations where I'm speaking English and the customer will be replying in Arabic.'

He's also dealt with Russian customers, of whom he has mixed memories. 'They're very blunt: they don't mess you around. But they have an adoration of luxury that's quite touching.'

For consumers like myself, who buy luxury products very occasionally, good service is one of the things that make the expense worthwhile. After all, we consider ourselves VIPs too. High on my personal 'good service' list is J M Weston on the Boulevard de la Madeleine, where I have been known to buy pricey footwear. Not only do the vendors have a reassuringly avuncular air, they also spend hours shunting shoeboxes back and forth without complaint and are mines of arcane footwear lore. But here's the best part. About three months after I bought my last pair of shoes, somebody left a message on my mobile phone. It turned out to be the sales assistant from J M Weston. 'Monsieur, I just want to check if everything is well with your shoes. If you have any problems with them, or if they need to be polished, please do not hesitate to contact me.'

Naturally, I need suits to go with my shiny shoes. At the Dior boutique in Rue Royale one Saturday, I found the staff a little distracted, to say the least. One male assistant was occupied by a trio of flashy-looking tourists and didn't so much as glance in my direction. His blonde colleague was searching for something under the counter. When I finally got their attention for long enough to try on a suit, it wasn't right: the sleeves were too long, the vent didn't fall correctly and the trousers were slightly loose at the waist. I mentioned this to the saleswoman, who told me that the alterations person was at lunch. I shrugged, as if to say: 'No problem – I'll take my hard-earned cash elsewhere.'

As I was about to change back into my jeans, a voice outside the fitting room told me that the seamstress had returned. I emerged to see a diminutive dark-haired woman of a certain age dressed in a white lab coat and wearing a large pincushion on her arm like a spiky wristwatch. She took one look at me said: 'I see exactly what's wrong.' Then she began deftly pinning and tucking. By the time she'd finished, the suit was transformed. The alterations were so extensive that the garment would practically have to be remodelled – a service for which I paid nothing. It emerged that Bianca had trained as a couturière 30 years ago. She had been with Dior for over a decade. Her reassuring professionalism changed my impression of the store.

And here I must add a word of praise for Elisabeth at Le Comptoir de l'Homme in Saint Germain. Is this male grooming emporium a luxury store? Since nobody really *needs* to spend money on fragrances and skincare products, I think it fits into the category. Go there on a quiet Saturday morning and Elisabeth will fix you an espresso as she chats to you about all the wonderful things you can buy. Did you know, for example, that Hammam Bouquet by Penhaligon's was the favourite fragrance of the film director Franco Zeffirelli? He personally saved the firm from ruin when he heard it might be going out of business. Or that Winston Churchill wore another Penhaligon's fragrance, Bleinheim Bouquet? Like Scheherazade, Elisabeth spins enchanting tales.

People like Bianca and Elisabeth make the real difference between the luxurious and the banal. If the human touch is absent, no amount of glossy marketing can fill the void.

SPRINGTIME FOR PRINTEMPS

Printemps is not just a department store – it is a listed monument. In fact, with more than 80,000 visitors a day, it is one of the most visited historic sites in France. But Printemps has a problem. Although it is an iconic destination, having been part of the Paris retail landscape since 1865, it is located right next door to another famous department store: Galeries Lafayette. For more than a century these retail mastodons have battled one another for the attentions of the shoppers and tourists who swarm down the Boulevard Haussmann.

At the beginning of 2008, Printemps announced a dramatic change of direction. While Galeries Lafayette had an accessible, family-oriented identity, Printemps had for some time positioned itself as a little more chic, a little more coquettishly Parisian than its rival. Now it decided that half measures were no longer enough – it would differentiate itself from its neighbour by lofting itself upmarket and becoming a luxury emporium. When the well-heeled came to Paris, it reasoned, Printemps should be their first port of call. Plans were drawn up for a four-year, €280 million refurbishment that would restore the building's 19th-century façade and establish a glittering new atrium inside.

The project was prompted by the €1.1 billion purchase in 2006 of Printemps by the Italian Borletti Group – which also owns Italian department store La Rinascente – in partnership with an investment fund. Like La Rinascente itself, Printemps had found itself caught in the middle of two trends: the emergence of low-cost 'fast fashion' chains (Zara, H&M, Primark) at one end and the rise of mass luxury at the other. Middle-market retailers found themselves in a widening chasm between the two. It made sense to follow in the footsteps of Selfridges in London or Bergdorf Goodman in New York and establish Printemps as a home of premium brands.

The store's CEO is Paolo de Cesare, a former Procter & Gamble beauty products executive. Having worked in Japan for three years, de Cesare knows what makes luxury consumers tick. Even so, he says, his first task when considering the repositioning was to get the concept of luxury straight in his mind: 'To me this was the fundamental question: what are we trying to deliver? So with my marketing background I naturally went to the customers and asked them to define luxury. It emerged that the first attribute of luxury is quality. The second is emotional reward. Only the third area is about price, exclusivity or status. Now, we know that customers from developing markets are interested in status, but in the Western world it is becoming less important – perhaps even undesirable. So we decided that our objective was to provide quality and emotional reward.'

The job of Printemps, as de Cesare sees it, is to ensure that customers have access to these elements across many different price points and categories. The store stocks something like 3,000 brands and is constantly reviewing the selection to ensure that the quality requirement is being met at every level. 'Fashion, elegance and sophistication are within the store's DNA – elitism is not. Our interpretation of luxury is not to say: "Show me your wallet or you're not getting in." It is to invite customers to enjoy a luxurious experience.'

De Cesare saw the potential of Printemps from the moment he first arrived, two years before our interview. 'It has always been a popular store, but it felt like it was on autopilot. My ambition was to return it to its rightful status as one of the world's flagship department stores.'

The physical transformation of Printemps has attracted considerable media attention. In a section of the store devoted to fashion and accessories, interior architects Yabu Pushelberg ripped out three gloomy, low-ceilinged floors and replaced them with a spectacular atrium filled with air and light. The design is typical of George Yabu and Glenn Pushelberg's work, which is minimalist without being frosty. 'They've done a great job for department stores like Lane Crawford in Hong Kong, but they've also worked on hotels,' says de Cesare. 'The hospitality and entertainment elements come through.'

Yabu and Pushelberg's work was overseen by the store's director of architecture, Patrizia Pressimone, a dynamic Italian woman who has worked for brands like Benetton, Celine, Versace and Escada. 'If a house is a machine for living, to quote Le Corbusier, a store is a machine for spending,' she says. 'Nobody *has* to visit a luxury department store, so the trick is to make them *want* to visit it. And once they're inside, you want them to stay for a long time – preferably a couple of hours

– and hopefully spend some money. And there are various techniques for making sure that happens.'

Architecture can have a mood-altering effect, she explains. The wide, symmetrical, artfully arranged windows and broad entrances invite you to step inside the store – just for a quick look. Once inside, the air temperature, the lighting and the noble materials that surround you combine to instil a feeling of well-being. The street you've just left behind suddenly seems like a more hostile place. In the store, low ceilings and enclosed spaces are a no-no, says Pressimone. 'What you're looking for is a sensation of space. The floors above should be visible so the customer can see the rest of the stock, which is just out of their reach. And here's a handy escalator to sweep them towards it.'

The unabashed modernism of Printemps' reconfigured interior contrasts with the façade, which has been restored to its Belle Epoque glory. At 45,000 square metres, with no less than eight cupolas swathed in gold leaf, the palatial store appears to be trying to steal the baroque thunder of the Opéra Garnier just around the corner. Over the years, though, its façade had become grimy and its domes dull. A team of artisans was brought in to put this right. The interior of one of the cupolas was turned into a workshop where the half-forgotten skills of another era became suddenly vital and relevant.

Paolo de Cesare says: 'As this is a listed building, we had to use the same material and techniques that the original craftspeople employed. For instance, beneath the gold leaf that covers the cupolas are zinc tiles, which one cannot purchase any more – so we had to produce our own. Similarly, we went to the original supplier in Murano for the stained glass. And we've painstakingly uncovered and restored the mosaics that had been painted over or obscured.'

The contrast between the new atrium and the restored 19th-century façade should have 'the impact of seeing the glass pyramid outside the Louvre', says de Cesare.

He also wanted to indulge an obsession with service that he developed while living in Japan. 'I became really spoiled there,' he recalls. 'There are certain places I go back to now and they still remember my name – it's phenomenal. For me it was an absolute priority that the customers should feel welcome.'

This meant introducing a valet parking service, a revamped loyalty card scheme and a team of personal shoppers, as well as a series of

VIP lounges where customers can discuss their retail therapy needs in private. More radically, Printemps became the first department store in France to introduce a concierge service. French residents pay an annual fee of €1,500 for the privilege – but on the presentation of their passports, overseas customers get free-of-charge access to a personal assistant and a 24/7 telephone service. In the style of a grand hotel, the concierge can do everything from reserving restaurant tables and booking theatre seats to getting you on the VIP list of a nightclub or finding a babysitter.

As de Cesare observes, however, good service is not just about innovations like the concierge service – or even about inviting the holders of loyalty cards to exclusive soirées. The everyday sales staff must be on the ball, too. 'We discovered that some of the staff were nervous about dealing with demanding customers, so we've developed a training programme to put that right. We stage role-playing sessions and give them advice on appearance and make-up. We also put a great deal of emphasis on product knowledge. Being a good salesperson is all about having absolute confidence in yourself and the products you are selling.'

In Japan, he had always been impressed by the way in-store beauty advisors were the perfect ambassadors for brands, even though they weren't on commission. 'They felt that representing their brand to the best of their ability was the minimum requirement of the job.'

Speaking of brands, Printemps also tweaked its external image. A few months after his arrival, de Cesare asked Stephen Gan – the co-founder of the influential *Visionaire* magazine – to devise a new advertising look for the store. Working with the photographer David Sims, Gan created a series of double-panel print and poster ads. Each execution featured a close-up of a model's face, next to a long shot of the same model in a cutting-edge outfit. If the images resemble glossy magazine spreads, this is no coincidence: Printemps is actively seeking a fashion-oriented brand positioning. The look was carried over to the store's website and a customer magazine. 'The previous image had a fairytale feel about it,' says de Cesare. 'I believe we've updated it by about 50 years.'

If the repositioning of Printemps succeeds, its new owners will have synthesized the glamorous retail landscape of the 19th century with an experiential, contemporary take on luxury. And in an age when window shopping can be done with the click of a mouse, that may be what it takes to persuade customers to come and see what's in store.

12

Digital luxury

'We have deluded ourselves that online is not relevant to our customers.'

Toss a crystal goblet in Paris and the chances are you'll hit a luxury conference. The organization and hosting of these events is a minor industry here, supported by legions of 'luxury consultants' who pad out the lists of attendees. At a certain point *la crise* – as the French press called the economic crisis – distracted the luxury brands from their other great concern: what to do about the internet? It seemed not to have occurred to them that the two subjects were intimately linked.

In late 2006, long before there was any wisp of a cloud on the luxury horizon, I attended the World Luxury Congress at the Hotel George V. While the rest of the retail world buzzed with the possibilities of Web 2.0, the luxury giants were still struggling to get to grips with its first iteration. Brands like Swarovski and Theo Fennell – a London jeweller – spoke of many different ways of enhancing their image, from product placement in movies to unequalled customer service. But nobody mentioned the benefits of going online.

Significantly, the web first reared its head in a discussion about counterfeit goods. Journalist Tim Philips, author of the book *Knock-Off: The true story of the world's fastest growing crime wave*, published the previous year, pointed out that by not having a strong presence online, luxury brands were unwittingly encouraging consumers to buy fakes from other websites. 'You are effectively franchising out your brands,' he stated, to dark mutterings from his audience.

Of course, there were means of buying luxury goods online. Net-A-Porter, to name one, was an outstanding success. Created in June 2000 by Natalie Massenet, a former fashion editor of the UK magazine *Tatler*, it had been voted retail space of the year during the British Fashion Awards a couple of years previously. Since then it had achieved cult status among tech-savvy fashionistas.

But the luxury brands had largely shied away the idea of setting up transactional websites, preferring to use the web as a shop window – and often not a very exciting one. Louis Vuitton had only recently allowed consumers to buy a selection of items online. Others insisted that, to get the full luxury experience, consumers must visit their stores.

In a conversation shortly after the conference, Marie Laver, a senior strategist at the media planning and buying agency Initiative, told me: 'Selling luxury goods online is a huge challenge. Luxury purchases are highly sensory in nature, which is clearly difficult to replicate in the online world.' She added that a successful e-retail environment needed to incorporate three key elements: strong visual and aural clues, personal service, and interactivity.

Back at the event, luxury industry commentator Carol Brodie, who gloried in the exquisite title of 'chief luxury officer' at the magazine *The Robb Report*, presented herself as a typical example of a new kind of luxury shopper. 'I'm a shopaholic – but now I have children and I'm time poor, I shop online,' she told congress attendees. 'And I'm addicted to Net-A-Porter. For me, receiving one of those boxes is a luxury experience in itself.'

Popular fashion website Style.com, the online home of *Vogue* and *W*, among others, had forged a series of advertising partnerships with luxury brands, allowing visitors to click through to their websites. But that did not necessarily lead to a buying experience. Dee Salomon, Style.com's managing director, said, 'There is… the feeling that customers are much more likely to transact at the point of sale, where they have a chance to really look at the product.'

Upscale retailers agreed. Michael Ward, CEO of Harrods, felt that a website could never replicate 'the emotional experience' of picking up a trinket in his store. Joseph Wan, CEO of Harvey Nichols, a ritzy chain of department stores, was of a similar opinion. 'I don't think an online brand that doesn't have any bricks and mortar presence will ever be able to challenge a luxury retailer.'

It was a familiar viewpoint. Despite the increasing prominence of digital tools in the everyday lives of consumers, luxury goods manufacturers felt that the internet removed the exclusivity and personal touch of the physical environment. Ironically, though, offering a uniquely personal service is something websites excel at – who hasn't looked at their 'personal recommendations' on Amazon.com? Instead of viewing the internet as a poor cousin to the shop window, it seemed clear that luxury companies needed to start experimenting with enriched content like video clips, interactivity and one-to-one dialogue with customers.

At the end of that 2006 event Guy Salter, the deputy chairman of British luxury goods association Walpole, sounded a warning. He was convinced, he said, that there was 'a new generation of high net worth individuals who don't want the hassle of going to a store'. He added: 'We have deluded ourselves that online is not relevant to our customers. But the specialist online retailers who have stepped into the breach have shown us how wrong we were.'

LUXE MEETS WEB: A HESITANT ROMANCE

Flash forward six months, to another conference in another hotel. June 2007 saw a select group of luxury industry professionals gathering at The Ritz in Paris. This time they had come together specifically to address the challenge of the web. Appropriately, speakers who attempted to demonstrate their theories by connecting to the internet live onstage discovered that the grand old hotel had a distinctly sluggish connection.

While the luxury sector appeared to have made little progress in its tentative rapprochement with the online world, the conference was studded with useful sound bites. Marketing consultant Evelyne Resnick, who specializes in working with French wine producers, admonished elite brands for hugging the idea that their consumers – notionally older and less adventurous than regular shoppers – were still not online. 'In France alone, research shows that 85 per cent of consumers earning more than €55,000 a year regularly surf the web. The figure is even higher than in the United States.'

Despite this, said Resnick, a handful of French luxury brands had no online presence whatsoever. She cited the example of Pétrus, the legendary Bordeaux wine, whose lack of online presence had led an outside company to hijack the brand, resulting in a dreary unofficial site. 'Luxury companies fear loss of control of their brands if they go online,' said Resnick. 'In fact, the opposite is the case. If you don't establish an online presence, your consumers will do it for you.'

Mainstream advertisers agree that, when it comes to brands and the web, consumers run the show. Blogs, forums, chat rooms and virtual networking sites crackle with conversations about consumption and service. This, of course, is exactly the kind of loss of control that luxury brands fear: the carefully polished facade must not be besmirched by the sticky finger marks of interlopers. But Syrine Fehri, a researcher specializing in the emerging area of 'nethnography' – the study of human behaviour online – said that there was little evidence of 'aggressive or abusive behaviour' within online communities, which tended to be 'self-censoring'. Alexandre Wehrlin, who heads multimedia and interactive projects at luxury watch company Piaget, supported this view. He observed that a simple password system formed a natural psychological barrier, so that 'only those who are committed to the brand make an effort to join the debate'. He added that the people who take part in such forums are 'passionate consumers' rather than those who seek to criticize or undermine the host brands.

There were plenty of reasons why luxury brands should embrace online communities. One was that upmarket consumers were getting younger and felt far more comfortable in the digital environment. Pam Danziger, president of Unity Marketing, said as much on the firm's website the very month the conference took place:

> Young affluents – roughly corresponding to the Generation X
> and Millennial generations – will play an increasingly important
> role in the target market for global luxury marketers over the
> next 10 to 20 years. This is true not just in the United States
> (with a median age of 36.5 years) or in the European countries
> (where the median age ranges around 40 years old), but in the
> developing luxury markets like Brazil (median age 28.2 years),
> India (24.9 years) and China (32.7 years), where the population
> as a whole is more youthful… Global luxury marketers have
> gotten used to the passions and nuances of the maturing Baby

> Boomers after so many years of targeting this generation…
> Now they have a new challenge to appeal to the young affluents
> who have different ideas about luxury and different priorities
> in how they spend their wealth. (Unitymarketingonline.com,
> June 25 2007.)

Proof of the existence of this young, net-savvy generation of high-end
consumers was readily available in the form of ASmallWorld.com.
Launched in 2004 by former banker Erik Wachtmeister, the invitation-
only networking site works much like a private members' club for the
elite. Once you're 'in', you can be thrown out again for contacting
members you don't know, stalking the site's celebrities or targeting
members with aggressive sales pitches. Spamming, posting semi-porno-
graphic movies and requesting friendships with beautiful strangers – all
regular occurrences on other sites – are unknown. While the site isn't
quite as elite as it purports to be (even yours truly is a member), its
users tend to be youngish, educated, wealthy and/or well connected.

In terms of its attraction for luxury advertisers, ASW claims to offer
access to 'the world's most valuable demographic'. Two years after
its launch, the magazine *Advertising Age* stated that 85 per cent of the
site's members had a bachelor's degree (40 per cent had a master's),
more than 30 per cent worked in banking and consulting, and 97 per
cent lived in the world's major cities ('For this social-media net, it's
quality, not quantity of members', 6 June 2006).

At the time of writing, the site has more than 300,000 members in 200
countries (compared to the 140 million-odd global users of the highly
egalitarian social networking site Facebook). Wachtmeister told *The
Guardian* that he expected membership to grow 'very, very carefully'
to a million members. To grow too large too fast would alienate
members and, crucially, advertisers. While the owners of fast-moving
consumer goods are interested in big numbers, luxury advertisers seek
small yet relevant audiences. 'If we employ the right methodology, we
can grow to a million people and still be as exclusive as we are today,'
Wachtmeister insisted ('Small world that may be getting too big', 1
September 2008).

For the time being, the site's members still look pretty rich. This very
day, items being offered for sale by members include a Porsche 997
GT3 (€97,000), a beachfront property (US$3.6 million) and a Falcon
900 jet (US$38.5 million), along with a trove of designer furniture,

watches, clothes and handbags. Online discussions range from the serious (conflict in the Middle East) to the hedonist (seeking tips for the perfect weekend in Rio de Janeiro) to the practical (the best gym in Barcelona). Watch brand Tudor is advertising on the home page.

And luxury brands are interested in ASW. In 2007, Rémy Martin advertised its Louis XIII cognac (some bottles of which sell for US$1,500) by placing banner ads, a microsite and sponsored editorial features on the site over a period of three months. It also created an exclusive tasting opportunity at a private gallery opening, spreading the word through members. 'The campaign is an example of how advertisers are taking niche brands that once might not have garnered much in the way of marketing support into new digital channels,' commented *AdWeek* ('High end cognac gets social to woo jet set', 14 August 2007).

In March 2008, Mercedes Benz signed a partnership deal with ASW. The deal included a branded automotive forum, blogs and inclusion in the site's events calendar. Mercedes would also sponsor the site's fledgling internet TV channel – ASW TV – and become the first of the site's brand partners to broadcast on it. Dr Olaf Göttgens, vice-president of brand communications for Mercedes, said that the partnership made 'direct dialogue' with consumers possible, as well as enabling the company to reach 'a young, influential target group'. In May that same year, Cartier advertised its 'Love by Cartier' collection of products by creating interactive content for ASW.

Back in June 2007, all this was some way off. As we stepped out to sip champagne on the terrace at the end of that early summer afternoon, I looked around. Bearing in mind that it took place in what was supposed to be the heart of the luxury industry, the digital branding event was nowhere near as crowded as it should have been. The message to elite brands was clear – but few of them had taken the time to listen to it.

THE VUITTON CASE

In the end, progress came from an unexpected quarter: Louis Vuitton. For years, the most visible face of the brand (apart, of course, from its increasingly extravagant flagship stores) had been advertising images of models and actresses dressed from head to toe in its products and sprawled across the pages of glossy magazines. While cost-effective, this was the most traditional of all luxury branding strategies. Suddenly, though, Vuitton engaged with the 21st century.

Its first step, in January 2007, was to hire the global advertising agency Ogilvy & Mather. Luxury brands have traditionally fought shy of traditional advertising agencies, which are looked down on as the pedlars of fast-moving consumer goods. Instead, luxury firms tend to use internal 'creative directors' (in fashion circles, it's usually the designer) who hand pick freelance photographers, stylists and makeup artists to interpret their vision. For Louis Vuitton, appointing a big advertising network like O&M – founded in the United States during the consumer boom of the 1950s – was an almost radical move.

The first offspring of the union was rather disappointing: a print advertising campaign. Granted, it was a departure from the previous print work. The 'star' of the most talked-about ad was Mikhail Gorbachev, a Vuitton bag placed casually by his side as his limousine cruised past the remains of the Berlin Wall. Shot by Annie Liebowitz, the image was designed to remind consumers that Louis Vuitton was, above all, a maker of stylish luggage. 'Journeys' would be the theme of the new campaign. But while the choice of Gorbachev was startling, the ad was basically an interpretation of a strategy that was as old as the hills: celebrity endorsement. Other executions in the series showed Andre Agassi and Steffi Graf relaxing in a New York hotel room, a Vuitton bag lying nearby, and Catherine Deneuve sitting daintily on a Vuitton trunk in what appeared to be a movie-set railway station.

The press liked the idea, though. The *International Herald Tribune* felt that the campaign reflected 'a move by some luxury companies to connect with consumers on a more human level. In the past, many fashion houses and other luxury brands relied primarily on the so-called product-as-hero approach, featuring their products, perhaps accompanied by a model, in a stylized, static way.' It pointed out that the participation of Gorbachev was designed to attract the attention of the growing Russian market. In the same piece, Ogilvy's chief executive for Europe, the Middle East and Africa, Daniel Sicouri, said: 'The product is just part of the story, a companion on the journey, not the hero' ('Luxury gets less flashy', 29 July 2007).

Louis Vuitton had accentuated its heritage and garnered a bit of press buzz. Its next step was far more interesting. O&M's web arm, Ogilvy Interactive in Paris, asked celebrities to describe their favourite places. These narrations were illustrated with photography, sound and video on a new website called 'Journeys', accessed from the main Louis Vuitton site. Warm, emotional and stylishly executed, these online 'collages' were genuinely entertaining. They injected the sought-for 'human factor' into the Vuitton brand and made the consumer feel connected to the VIPs concerned. Who could resist travelling to Edinburgh with Sean Connery, San Francisco with Francis Ford Coppola or London with Keith Richards? The web execution of the 'journeys' campaign won a number of awards.

Louis Vuitton now appears to be committed to building its brand in the digital world. As mentioned earlier, one of the trickiest challenges facing luxury companies is the power that has been conferred on consumers by the internet. We are all citizen journalists now. Whether brands want to engage in a dialogue with their potential clients or not, they can rest assured that consumers are already chatting and blogging about them – and not always in flattering terms. Rather than trying to shut out this background hum, Vuitton has decided to actively engage with the net generation – or 'digital natives' if you prefer. A full-time employee at its Paris headquarters is tasked with building relationships with virtual communities via blogs, Facebook, Twitter and other applications. The company is concerned that, although there are hundreds of 'fan pages' devoted to the brand on the net, not one of them is official.

In June 2008, Vuitton harnessed the power of blogs to help launch its 'soundwalk' offering – which was an innovative idea in its own right. Sticking to the 'journeys' theme, Vuitton had asked three actresses to narrate a walk around their favourite cities. Users could then download the resulting MP3 files from the Vuitton site onto their iPods or similar devices and follow in the footsteps of the actresses. The first three 'soundwalks' were recorded by Gong Li (Beijing), Joan Chen (Shanghai) and Shu Qi (Hong Kong). Vuitton flew six of the world's most influential bloggers to Hong Kong to test the soundwalk, equipping them with free iPods. There was a tacit agreement that the bloggers would post articles about the experience.

Louis Vuitton is not the only luxury brand to have reached out to bloggers. In September 2007, Chanel invited 14 bloggers from around the world to visit Coco Chanel's former apartment in Paris and its perfume laboratories in Neuilly. British participant Susanna Lau of the blog Style Bubble wrote approvingly: 'This is an age old French brand who are moving forward with the times not just in their presence online (their websites, viral activity and multimedia footage) but by connecting with the people who start that dialogue online.'

Taking bloggers on what was essentially a press trip was something of a gamble. Unlike glossy magazines, most bloggers do not live on luxury brands' advertising dollars, so they are under no pressure to write glowing reports about them. In the luxury sector, bloggers now perform the inquiring, critical role that magazine journalists – who are in chains to their advertising departments – long ago relinquished. Luxury brands had wondered whether blogs – erratic, unpredictable and frequently amateurish – were the right environment for them. But they seemed to have accepted that the replacements for their ageing client base were all reading and/or writing these online journals.

Cartier made another unexpected leap into the digital breach in the middle of 2008, following its earlier experiment with ASmallWorld. com. Once again promoting its Love by Cartier collection – which was aimed at younger consumers – it created its own profile page on the social networking site MySpace, which has a strong user base of music fans. The page included downloadable songs that had been composed specifically for Cartier by artists such as Lou Reed and Marion Cotillard. Given the luxury brands' previously standoffish attitude towards the web, the statement from Cartier International's communications director, Corinne Delattre, was positively jaw-dropping. 'Today, the world is connected by a network. Blogs, group or individual websites are no longer the signs of a new era, but are an established reality for a whole new generation. As a large brand, we must be able to communicate to this new generation of adepts of the digital world – the MySpace community makes that possible' (Brandrepublic.com, 27 June 2008).

The digital space is changing fashion marketing, too. Rather than staging the traditional – and expensive – runway shows that play the role of live advertising spots before an audience of journalists and buyers, some fashion brands have chosen to show their collections in the form of slickly produced videos. These can often be accessed through their websites. The buyers and the press are then encouraged to go and look at the collections close up in the brands' showrooms.

They may be at the back of the crowd, but luxury brands have finally joined the digital revolution.

13

By royal appointment

'International customers see our Royal Warrant as a stamp of authentic British quality.'

It's not often that you read the word 'marmalade' in a book about luxury brands. But it was a jar of Frank Cooper's Original Oxford Marmalade on a breakfast table that inspired this chapter. Being a voracious reader, I am the kind of person who might, in the absence of a newspaper, idly scan the text on the back of a cereal packet. Or, in this case, on the back of a jar of marmalade – which was when I was reminded that Frank Cooper's is the holder of a Royal Warrant. At first it simply amused me to imagine the Queen eating toast and marmalade at roughly the same hour as myself. Did she spoon it directly on to the toast, or onto the side of her plate first? Or was she one of those people who just stuck her knife directly into the jar?

Then I started to think about Royal Warrants in a broader sense. How did one get a warrant? How many companies had them? And what did the possession of one mean to the holders?

A quick internet search turned up the telephone number of the Royal Warrant Holders' Association in London, which led to a conversation with its secretary, Richard Peck. Along with only three other members of staff, working in a small office in Buckingham Place (that's *place*, not *palace*), Richard coordinates the relationship between the Royal Family and the warrant holders. For the time being, there are about 850

Royal Warrant Holders working in many areas of trade and industry. My first question, then, is obvious: how do I join them?

'You can't,' says Peck, crushingly. 'Warrants are only granted to tradesmen. So that counts out bankers, chartered accountants, lawyers, architects and – I'm afraid – journalists.' So while The Carphone Warehouse is allowed to sport the Queen's coat of arms and the words 'By Appointment to…' on its stationery, I will never be able to do so.

The warrants are a mark of recognition to those who have provided goods and services to the Queen, the Duke of Edinburgh or the Prince of Wales for more than five years. Warrants are reviewed every five years and can be revoked. 'The grantor signs off each application personally and they take a very personal interest in the process,' underlines Peck.

I wonder aloud who received the very first Royal Warrant, half-expecting the system to date back to the industrial revolution, when mass production and therefore the need for branding was born.

'Warrants have existed since at least the 12th century,' says Peck. 'The first recorded relationship between royalty and business was the granting by Henry II of the British Royal Charter to the Weavers' Company in 1155. There are also official records from the 18th century. But it was under Queen Victoria's reign that the royal tradesmen got together to form the Royal Tradesmen's Association, which was the start of the organization that is still in place today.'

It turned out that my original presumption was half right, because Victoria dished out warrants like toffees. At the start of her reign, there were some 200 Royal Warrant Holders. By the time she died, there were around 2,000. (It's worth noting that, when a member of the Royal Family dies, the warrant they have granted remains in effect for a further five years.) At that time, the Lord Chamberlain's office was responsible for litigating against the fraudulent use of the royal coat of arms, but in 1907 this power passed to the association.

The benefits of holding a Royal Warrant are obvious. On the one hand, as Peck puts it, the warrant is 'a recognition of a satisfactory trading arrangement and a mark of personal approval from a member of the Royal Family'. On the other, he continues, 'it is something far more than that: it is a statement about the company and the level of quality and service it provides, which obviously appeals to a wider clientele. These companies stand at the highest echelon of British trade and industry'. There is occasional speculation, he adds, that 'normal customers' are unlikely to enjoy the level of service enjoyed by, say, the Queen. 'But I can assure you that is not the case.'

As many Brits are fairly cynical – or at the very least blasé – about the Royal Family, a Royal Warrant often has more impact abroad. 'It is held in huge esteem in Asia and the United States. It may be something of a cliché, but these are the companies that make Britain great.'

Ian Eastwood, managing director of luxury leather goods maker Swaine Adeney Brigg, wholeheartedly concurs. 'We have a large proportion of international customers, from Japanese to American, from Italian to Russian, and they all see our Royal Warrant as providing a stamp of authentic British quality. Our customers buy in to the fact that we have a 250-year history and they appreciate that we provide something very different from the high street.' He adds that possession of the warrant is also highly motivating to those in the firm's Cambridge workshops who handcraft its products. 'The knowledge and care that goes into the creation of our pieces and the individual service that each customer receives all support our status as a Royal Warrant Holder.'

To a certain extent, it seems strange that consumers should be reassured – impressed, even – by the fact that a member of the royal family uses a product. Is being 'a royal' necessarily a guarantee of superior taste, or even of exigency? In fact, the Royal Warrant is one of those 'immaterial elements' – a mixture of storytelling, mythology and heritage – that swirl around premium brands. David Atkinson is general manager of spreads at Premier Foods, the owner of Frank Cooper. He says, 'Founded in 1874, Frank Cooper has always stood for quality and tradition. The Royal Warrant reinforces this for consumers... The Royal Warrant remains as a prominent feature of the design, because for Frank Cooper's core consumers – typically older men – it is a very positive reinforcement of the brand equity.'

ROYAL WARRANTS WORLDWIDE

The United Kingdom is not the only country in which tradesmen are allowed to publicize their relationships with the court. Sweden has one of the most elaborate systems, as well as one of the most engaging websites (www.hovlev.se). Swedish royal warrants date back to the 17th century, when the title 'merchant to the king' was used. Early recipients of the royal blessing included cabinet- and casket-maker Georg Haupt, watchmaker Johan Fredman and pastry cook Hans Georg Düben, who had a shop in Stockholm's Old Town. This mixture of artisanal activities suggests, once again, that 'luxury' is more a question of quality than of price: those who could not afford one of Fredman's watches might, one imagines, have occasionally treated themselves to a cake baked by the royal pastry chef.

Royal warrants almost disappeared in Sweden in 1973, when Carl XVI Gustaf came to the throne and considered throwing them out in a burst of modernizing zeal. Instead, he tightened up the system, so that today only 130 companies hold the title of Purveyor to HM King Carl XVI Gustaf. They include shoemaker Lundhag and bicycle manufacturer Albert Samuelsson & Co, as well as eyewear company Polaris Optic and Victoria Scandinavian Soap. Denmark also has a royal warrant system – brewer Carlsberg and clothing company Ecco are among the grantees – as does Holland.

None of these markets are as intriguing as Japan, however. Japanese consumers are extremely partial to British products that bear the royal seal of approval. But the country also had its own system – Purveyors to the Japanese Imperial Household Agency – until just after the Second World War, when it was abandoned. Curiously, though, the title still exists and is held in great esteem. Purveyors to the imperial family are known as *goyotashi* and have enjoyed a privileged position since medieval times. Even products that are 'unofficially' linked to the royal family have a huge marketing advantage.

'Critics see the phenomenon as a textbook example of the blind faith Japanese place in brand-name products,' states an article on the website of the country's leading newspaper *Asahi Shimbun* ('Royal allure', 1 June 2006, Asahi.com). As an example, it offers the German stuffed toy manufacturer Stieff, which gained a crucial foothold in the country after a member of the imperial family literally embraced one of its products. 'Steiff's high-priced products had underperformed for years. All that changed in 1994 when TV viewers glimpsed Steiff's trademark yellow tag on a teddy bear owned by Princess Mako, the eldest daughter of Prince Fumihito, younger brother of Crown Prince Naruhito. TV broadcasters were inundated with calls from parents and grandparents about the unfamiliar toy. In the twinkling of an eye, shoppers descended on Steiff's flagship store in Tokyo's Ginza district, snatching up the bear, known as Molly.'

Now known as 'Princess Molly', the bear remains a popular toy, according to the article. Parents also showed great interest in products and services favoured by Princess Aiko, the daughter of Crown Princess Masako. Books, slippers and even callisthenics classes benefited from the association. 'These classes became de rigueur for many moms after the toddler princess was seen dancing in video footage aired by news-variety shows,' says *Asahi Shimbun*.

Predictably, the lack of an official system causes problems. An association representing kimono makers in the Nishijin district of Kyoto was forced to take action following confusion over which manufacturers were genuine suppliers of kimonos to the imperial family. In 2004 the Nishijin Textile Industrial Association decreed that its members could no longer use the word *goyotashi* in advertising.

Some European brands insist on royal or imperial connections that date back to a distant past. One only has to think of Courvoisier: 'the cognac of Napoleon'. The legend recounted by the brand is that Napoleon visited the warehouses of wine and spirits merchant Emmanuel Courvoisier and his associate Louis Gallois in the Paris suburb of Bercy in 1811. So impressed was Napoleon by the quality of the merchandise that he took several barrels of cognac with him to St Helena. This version is somewhat slapdash with the facts. Napoleon may well have taken a few barrels of cognac to ease the pain of exile, but the brand name Courvoisier was not officially established until 1835 by Emmanuel's son, Felix. It was based in Jarnac, not far from the town of Cognac itself. Less debateable is the fact that Napoleon III granted Courvoisier the title 'Official Supplier to the Imperial Court' in 1869 – a certificate to this effect is on display in the brand's museum in Jarnac.

Fragrance house Guerlain is another French company that emphasizes its ancient imperial connections. Pierre-François Pascal Guerlain opened his perfume shop at 42 Rue de Rivoli in 1828. 'Inspired by the beauty and elegance of Empress Eugenie, [he] created Eau de Cologne Imperiale in her honour. Seduced by this refined *eau*, the Empress conferred on Guerlain the title of Her Majesty's Official Perfumer, the very pinnacle of imperial ranking' (www.guerlain.com). Time, it seems, cannot dim a royal connection.

FABERGÉ: JEWELLER TO THE TSARS

Arguably the most fascinating historical relationship between craftsman and court was that of Fabergé with the Russian imperial family. The jeweller's legendary eggs would have been fabulous enough in any circumstances, but their connection with the fallen dynasty of the tsars gives them an additional touch of the Romanesque.

The Fabergé name has a new relevance today because – after more than a century in the doldrums – it is being resurrected as a 21st-century luxury brand. The journey back to its roots has been a labyrinthine one.

Peter Carl Fabergé was born Carl Gustavovich Fabergé in Saint Petersburg on 30 May 1846. As his surname suggests, his family had French origins – they were Huguenots who had fled France after the revocation of the Edict of Nantes, which effectively made their Protestant faith illegal. Carl joined his father's jewellery business in 1864 and took over the management of the firm eight years later.

The Easter of 1885 was a turning point for Fabergé. Easter is the most important celebration in the Russian Orthodox calendar. Families had exchanged colourfully decorated folk art Easter eggs for centuries – but Tsar Alexander III wanted a special gift for his wife, the Tsarina Maria Fedorovna, to mark their 20th wedding anniversary. Knowing that Maria was an admirer of Fabergé's, he commissioned the craftsman to create an exceptional egg. Fabergé delivered it to the palace on Easter morning. At first it appeared to be a simple enamelled egg. Inside, however, there was a golden yoke. In Russian doll style, the yoke yielded a golden hen. And nestling within that was a miniature of the imperial crown, encrusted with diamonds, and an egg-shaped ruby. It's easy to imagine the Tsarina's squeals of delight as she uncovered each layer.

The egg started a tradition. Each year, Fabergé was commissioned to produce another, with the sole criterion that it had to be entirely different from those that had gone before. In recognition of the relationship, Fabergé was named Official Court Supplier. When Nicholas II ascended to the throne after Alexander's death, he continued the tradition, presenting Fabergé eggs to his wife and his mother. The Imperial eggs were exhibited for the first time at the 1900 World Exhibition in Paris. This helped to transform the House of Fabergé into an international brand. The orders poured in for fine jewellery, silverware and tableware.

At its height, Fabergé was the largest company in Russia, with more than 500 artisans and branches in Saint Petersburg, Moscow, Odessa, Kiev and London. It produced some 150,000 objects between 1882 and 1917.

During the chaos of the revolution, Fabergé abandoned his company and fled with his family on the last diplomatic train to Riga – and then to Berlin, Frankfurt, Hamburg and Lausanne. He died in 1920 and was buried in Cannes, France.

The fortunes of the Fabergé brand waned considerably after that. Fabergé's sons Eugene and Alexander set up shop in Paris, where they ran a small workshop called Fabergé & Company, dedicated to restoring original Fabergé objects and making a limited number of new items. Details of what happened next are cloudy, but most accounts suggest that the pair attempted to take legal action against a businessman who had begun marketing cosmetics and perfumes under the Fabergé name.

Samuel Rubin (1901–1978) had been a trader in soap and olive oil from Spain until the Civil War forced him out of business in 1937, when he set up a new concern making cosmetics and toiletries. One of Rubin's acquaintances was the oil tycoon Armand Hammer, a collector of Fabergé eggs. It was Hammer who suggested that Rubin name his fragrance house after the jeweller to the Tsars, perhaps assuming that the brand had died with the Romanovs. Unable to pursue their litigation against the wealthier Rubin, the Fabergé heirs eventually ceded the brand name to him for US $25,000. Rubin himself later sold his business to another company, Rayette, for US $26 million. He used the money to set up The Samuel Rubin Foundation in New York, dedicated to fighting 'the immorality and inequity of the disparity between rich and poor' (Transnational Institute biography of Samuel Rubin, www. tni.org). Now renamed Fabergé Inc, the company sold products like the aftershaves Brut ('Splash it all over') and Denim ('For the man who doesn't have to try too hard') and the perfumes Babe and Cavale. Another company, McGregor, briefly owned the Fabergé brand before Unilever acquired it for US $1.5 billion in 1989.

Having plummeted from the heights of intoxicating luxury to the depths of the mass market, Fabergé was ready to be rescued. The lifeline arrived in 2007, when Pallinghurst Resources, a London-based mining investment group, unexpectedly announced that it had purchased the Fabergé brand name from Unilever. Not only that, but it planned to spend as much as US $450 million developing a gemstone and luxury goods business under the Fabergé name. 'Pallinghurst is all about identifying unrecognized, unloved or overlooked assets and developing them with a strong vision,' said Sean Gilbertson, a partner at Pallinghurst. 'The Fabergé acquisition is a good example of a downtrodden brand whose value was not being realized within the Unilever stable' ('Fabergé to be revived by Pallinghurst-led investment group', Bloomberg.com, 24 October 2007).

The new owners would even seek advice from Tatiana Fabergé, Carl Fabergé's 77-year-old great-granddaughter. 'I've dreamed of this moment for decades,' she said. 'It's been my life's ambition to restore the unsurpassed standards of design and workmanship that characterized my great-grandfather's treasures.'

At the time of writing, Pallinghurst was poised to unveil its new collection of Fabergé jewellery.

But what of the original jewel-encrusted eggs made by the Official Court Supplier to the Tsars? There were 50 of these legendary items in all. Nine were acquired in 2004 by a Russian energy tycoon from the family of the late publisher Malcolm Forbes. Ten are housed in the Kremlin. Five are at the Virginia Museum of Fine Arts. Queen Elizabeth owns three (and perhaps even gazes upon them while eating her toast with Frank Cooper's marmalade). Most of the others are divided among collectors around the world. And eight have vanished entirely.

14

In champagne country

'If the name Champagne means anything today, it's because we have gone to great lengths to ensure that it is respected.'

The train glides through the Marne Valley on a fine autumn morning. Gazing out of the window, I can see a light ground mist drifting over fields of rich, dark, tilled earth. A silhouette of hills languishes below a pale strip of sky. In the distance there is the squat grey tower of a village church. Slowly, the fields fall away and the hills draw nearer. And here at last are the serried ranks of deep green vines, marching up the hillsides like advancing armies. Cheerful red and yellow markers delineate each grower's territory.

It is late September – harvest time – and more than 100,000 temporary workers have descended on the Champagne region to pick grapes. At Epernay station there is an energetic, festive air. Passengers are met with a trestle table of croissants and plastic cups of champagne. I've barely had time to sample this impromptu breakfast when I'm greeted warmly by Daniel Lorson, communications director of the CIVC – the *Comité Interprofessionnel du Vin de Champagne*. Among other things, Daniel is responsible for looking after the image of the champagne brand worldwide. After a short car ride to the CIVC's imposing redbrick headquarters – proudly bearing the legend La Maison de la Champagne above its portico – we settle down to talk about the sparkling wine that has become synonymous with luxury.

The first thing Lorson tells me is that few of the champagne houses own vineyards – they are mostly marketers. He explains: 'As in every other wine-growing region, there are two different groups. The first are the *vignerons*, the growers, of which there are about 15,000. In Champagne they own 90 per cent of the vineyards. The second group, the merchants, are known here as 'houses' and control two-thirds of sales. The houses construct and nourish the image of champagne. Consumers in Asia and the United States will talk to you about Moët, Clicquot and so on, but they may not be aware that behind these great names are the largely anonymous people who cultivate the vines.'

Although sparkling wine is produced in other parts of the world, there's no doubt that the Champagne region is unique. Vines rarely flourish beyond the latitudes of 50° north and 30° south. The dual capitals of the Champagne region lie at the northernmost edge of vine-growing territory, with Reims at 49° north and Epernay at 49.5° north. The average annual temperature is 10°C (50°F). This is said to give the wines of Champagne their fresh crispness. Other advantageous factors are the area's limestone and chalk subsoil – which provides good drainage – and gently rolling hillsides exposed to the sunlight.

The original *vignerons* of Champagne did not make champagne at all. The Romans were probably the first to cultivate vines in the region, but the slow evolution that led to the effervescent money-spinner we know today began in the Middle Ages. At that point the Bishop of Reims and the area's great abbeys owned most of the vineyards. They produced crisp whites and the pale reds later known as *clairets* (a term misappropriated by the British in the form of 'claret'). By the 17th century, the monks had become skilled at blending grape varieties in order to create more balanced flavours – a practice that would one day be adopted by the champagne houses.

Like many great inventions, the discovery that was to make the region's fortune came about by accident. Due to the northerly location of the vineyards, the grapes were harvested late in the season. When the musts (freshly pressed juices) were stored in barrels, they began to ferment. This process was halted by the winter chill and recommenced with gusto in the spring. Originally, most of the resulting gas filtered out of the barrels – but by the 17th century the *Champenois* had seen the potential in this phenomenon and began to harness it in a rather acidic sparkling wine called Tocane. The drawback was that the bottles were not thick enough to resist the internal pressure and often exploded in a shower of foam and glass before they made it out of the cellar.

'It was actually the English who helped us out with that one,' smiles Lorson. 'Your glass company Pilkington was one of the first to produce a bottle solid enough to resist the fermentation process.'

There were other reasons why the 19th century was a crucial era for Champagne. Fermentation was still a tricky, barely understood process – but in around 1820 the *Champenois* began adding a small amount of crystallized sugar to each bottle to boost the second fermentation. Tests showed that four grams of sugar per litre resulted in an almost uniform pressure. Meanwhile, in 1860, Louis Pasteur unmasked the microscopic organisms – yeasts – that caused fermentation. After further experimentation, this allowed champagne producers to influence the course of nature. Today champagne is created using a process known as *méthode champenoise*.

Briefly, this involves fermenting the musts in tanks to remove the sugar. The resulting base liquid is then blended with wines from other grape varieties, vineyards and harvests. Each year, base wines with good ageing potential are set aside as 'reserve wines', which are added to the blend to add balance and maturity. Reserve wines can be stored for up to 10 years. Occasionally, they form up to 40 per cent of the final blend. This mixing and matching of wines to arrive at an intended taste and aroma is the art of the champagne winemaker.

When the blending process is complete, the wine is ready to be bottled. Before doing so, however, the producers add a small quantity of yeast and sugar. This provokes a second fermentation within the bottle itself. The bottles are initially stored horizontally so the yeasts can grow and multiply across a wide area – rather than suffocating at the bottom – while feeding on the sugar-producing alcohol and carbon dioxide. This process takes about six to eight weeks. Once all the sugars have been consumed, the yeasts die, forming sediment that is removed before the final corking. By that time the bottles have been tilted downwards and the sediment has gathered in their necks. Removing it is a neat trick – but we'll get to that later on, after touring a couple of dank cellars.

A NAME TO RECKON WITH

The general consensus when writing about champagne is that the region – Champagne – takes a capital 'C', while the drink does not. In the eyes of most of the world, champagne is a generic product, like whisky or wine. But that is not, in fact, that case. Champagne is a brand name, heavily protected and fought over by its guardians at the CIVC. In 1993, for example, the organization blocked Yves Saint Laurent from selling a fragrance called Champagne. The Paris Court of Appeal ruled that the use of the Champagne appellation was 'exclusively reserved for wines originating and produced in Champagne'. This was by no means the first case of its kind.

The struggle dates back to the late 19th century, when a phylloxera epidemic devastated the vineyards. Phylloxera is a tiny bug – a little like an aphid – that feeds on the roots of grapevines, choking the plant. Originating in North America, the insects were thought to have been brought to Europe on the cuttings of more resilient imported vines. The epidemic left the vineyards of Champagne ravaged. Facing ruin, growers and merchants joined forces to replant the vineyards and re-establish the reputation of their wine. In order to promote and protect the region's heritage, the larger champagne houses began taking legal action against producers who used the word fraudulently.

Daniel Lorson of the CIVC says 'Some growers from the Loire were not only using the word "Champagne" on the label, but also the names of villages in our region. From this concern sprang the idea of creating an official "appellation", stating that only wine made here could be sold under the name Champagne. In fact the appellation system, which other wine regions would later adopt, was born in Champagne.'

Although 'Champagne' was proposed as an appellation in December 1908, it lacked the force of law and there was controversy over the borders of the region. Growers from the neighbouring Aube, for example, initially excluded from the territory, staged a minor revolt in 1911 when a poor harvest and their inability to use the Champagne brand name threatened to undermine their livelihoods.

The situation was resolved in 1927, when government legislation strictly delineated the Champagne region. The law also stated that only pinot noir, pinot meunier and chardonnay grapes could be used to make champagne. The final seal of approval came in 1935 when the government created a committee to oversee and classify appellations.

Champagne became an Appellation d'Origine Contrôlée (AOC) on 29 June 1936. But, as we shall see, its problems did not end there.

The CIVC has three main roles. The first is to represent the interests of both the growers and the champagne houses. For example, the CIVC releases all the figures concerning the financial performance of the champagne sector. It also regulates the harvest dates and monitors quality. In addition, the organization has a technical department (with a staff of 50 researchers) that uses the product of its own 13-hectare vineyard to experiment with innovations in champagne production. Among other things, it has studied the phenomenon of champagne bubbles.

Connoisseurs set great store by the choreography of the bubbles in a glass of champagne. Ideally, these should rise gracefully to the surface in a column known as 'the chimney', growing slightly larger en route as they become engorged with oxygen. The ring of bubbles that clusters around the edge of the glass at the surface is called 'the necklace'. Uniformity of bubble and a certain restraint, as opposed to vulgar popping and fizzing, are the desired effects.

Finally – and most importantly for our purposes – the CIVC is responsible for protecting and nurturing the image of champagne.

'It's a public relations task, certainly – but it's also one of education,' says Lorson. 'We rely a great deal on the press to help us spread the fundamental message that champagne only comes from Champagne.'

To make sure the message is spread globally, the CIVC has 13 bureaux around the world. The first was set up in 1953 in the United States, which is where most of the 'attacks' on the champagne brand occur. In Europe, the champagne appellation is protected under European Commission regulations – but in the wider world it is nakedly vulnerable. Certain California producers still insist on labelling their sparkling wine 'champagne'. The US office of the CIVC has run print advertising acknowledging that this practice 'may be legal – but it's not fair'. In an effort to avoid sounding pompous, the ads humorously turn the tables. 'Alaska salmon from Florida? Monterey Jack from Alaska? Washington apples from Nevada? Florida oranges from Maine? Gulf shrimp from Nebraska? Champagne not from Champagne? No way!'

The most recently opened offices are in Beijing, Moscow and Delhi. The CIVC also has access to a network of 60 legal firms around the world. 'It's a big machine,' says Lorson, 'but it's crucial to the health of this region's economy. If the name Champagne means anything today, it's because we have gone to great lengths to ensure that it is respected.'

GOLD BENEATH THE STREET

After leaving the CIVC building, I follow Lorson's advice and head for a wide, gently ascending street called Avenue de Champagne. Once upon a time it was known as Faubourg de la Folie – the street of extravagance. Its more recent name derives, of course, from the fact that it is lined with prestigious champagne houses: Moët & Chandon, Perrier-Jouët, De Castellane and Mercier, to name but a few. Residents of Epernay will tell you that it is the richest avenue in France – worth far more than the Champs Elysées – due to the thousands of bottles of champagne stored in cellars deep beneath its surface.

As we know, the church produced the bulk of the early champagne wines, which at that stage were not effervescent and were transported in wooden casks. In 1728 a royal decree allowed for the transportation of champagne in bottles in order to preserve its sparkling quality. (Prior to that time it was felt that glass was too fragile to transport.) This seemingly innocuous change uncorked a champagne revolution.

First into the market in 1729 was a young draper called Nicolas Ruinart, who initially sent bottles of champagne to his wealthy clients. Soon he was running a fully-fledged champagne house. He certainly had the right connections – his uncle, Dom Thierry Ruinart, had been close friends with a Benedictine monk and celebrated cultivator of vines named Dom Pérignon.

The house that would later become Moët & Chandon was established shortly afterwards, in 1743. Today, Ruinart, Dom Pérignon and Moët & Chandon are all owned by the luxury conglomerate LVMH – among with Veuve Clicquot, Krug and Mercier.

Because it is the market leader, Moët & Chandon is the first champagne house I visit. Its flagship building certainly suggests great wealth. This is not just a house – it is a manor house: a white-fronted mini-Versailles with formal gardens, ornamental ponds and splashing fountains. The gift shop is a more recent addition. The administrative headquarters of the brand are tucked away in a banal office building around the corner, but the Hôtel Moët is its impressive public face. I hang out in the marble-floored lobby with a clutch of American and Japanese visitors and tag along with them on a cellar tour.

The early champagne houses had an advantage because they found at Epernay a labyrinth of chalk pits that had been excavated by the Romans. These made ideal cellars. Moët & Chandon possesses 28 kilometres (or 18 miles) of cellar space, much of which has been carved out since the 18th century. According to our guide, these dimly lit spaces feature 80 per cent humidity and a temperature of a fairly steady 10° C (50° F).

Although Claude Moët founded the house, his heir Jean-Rémy is said to have established the brand's scintillating reputation. When Cossack and Prussian troops were busy looting the cellars in 1814, Jean-Rémy noted that the drunken soldiers were actually doing him a favour, because they would 'sing the praises' of his product when they returned home. Moët was already on its way to becoming a global brand. Jean-Rémy's grandson Victor Moët and his son-in-law Pierre-Gabriel Chandon took over the business in 1832.

But a more recent – and highly colourful – figure transformed the house into the giant that it is today. He also had a direct impact on the structure of the contemporary luxury industry.

Count Robert-Jean de Vogüé was born in 1896 into a prominent aristocratic family in Ardèche. He volunteered to fight in the First World War at the age of 20, emerging with a Croix de Guerre. He joined Moët & Chandon in 1930 and proved adept at marketing. For instance, although the name Dom Pérignon had long been associated with the production of champagne – the monk was one of the first to successfully blend grape varieties – the brand did not exist in the public domain until 1936, when Vogüé launched it. The idea sprang from a limited edition wine that had until then only been consumed within the family. The *cuvée* (vintage) soon became more venerated than its older brother.

Vogüé's career was interrupted by the Second World War, during which he once again covered himself in glory as a resistance fighter, his exploits earning him the nickname 'The Red Marquis'. He was arrested by the Gestapo in 1943 and sent to a forced labour camp, where he remained until the British freed him just over a year later. He returned to Moët & Chandon and the presidency of the company. In the 1950s, he transformed the champagne house from a family-run concern into a corporation, floating it on the stock market. With the proceeds, he was able to snap up rival houses Ruinart and Mercier.

But Vogüé had more visionary plans for the company. Due to the 1927 legislation that had limited production of champagne to a strictly defined area, he felt that demand would soon outstrip supply, and that Moët should make provision for its future income by expanding into other areas of the luxury industry. In 1970 he bought a stake in Parfums Christian Dior. He also began merger negotiations with the cognac producer Hennessy & Co, leading to the creation of Moët-Hennessy in 1971. Rather than shunning the United States – as a French wine producer might have been expected to do – he launched the California winery Domaine Chandon in 1973. Vogüé died a couple of years later, leaving the company in the hands of his protégé Alain Chevalier. In 1987, the final stage of the transformation was complete: the merger of Moët-Hennessy with luxury luggage maker Louis Vuitton, forming LVMH.

Property developer and financier Bernard Arnault initially arrived on the scene as an investor, but he quickly became embroiled in a three-way battle for control of the company between himself, Chevalier and Henry Racamier, the distinguished chairman of Louis Vuitton ('A luxury fight to the finish', *The New York Times*, 17 December 1989). Arnault emerged the victor. He has since taken the group to lofty heights – but the foundations were put in place by Robert-Jean de Vogüé of Moët & Chandon.

Today, as our little tour winds through the cellars of the venerable champagne house, our guide struggles to maintain an impression of artisanal luxury. She tells us that Moët & Chandon owns 1,000 hectares of vines – making it the biggest landowner in the region – and that it also buys grapes from other growers. She apologizes that the house is 'not allowed to talk about production'. In fact, as it has a 20 per cent share of the market, LVMH is obliged to produce champagne on an almost industrial scale: up to 37 million bottles a year, according to the French newspaper *L'Humanité* (*'Bulles financières'*, 20 February 2009), with annual sales of between 25 million and 30 million bottles. Meanwhile, the official website of the Union des Maisons de Champagne reveals that the house had a turnover of €901 million in 2008 (www.maisons-champagne.com).

Bearing all this in mind, it's hard to hold on to the guide's image of the workers known as *remueurs*, who painstakingly turn each bottle by hand to dislodge the yeast sediment (a process known as 'riddling' in English). I later learn that in most champagne houses this task is performed by a machine called a *gyropalette*, which works 24 hours a day, seven days a week.

Moët & Chandon's response to suggestions that it traffics in mass luxury remains Dom Pérignon. Most champagne is made not only of blends of grapes from different varieties and sites, but of grapes from different years. However, the houses also release collectible 'vintage' champagnes, made from the grapes of a single harvest. All Dom Pérignon champagnes are vintage (the French term is *millésimé*) and each bottle is aged in the cellar for eight years. This quality comes at a price. The French business publication *Challenges* suggested that every bottle of Dom Pérignon represents a profit margin of 50 per cent for its producer. ('*LVMH fait mousser ses champagnes*', 3 March 2009). As one of the magazine's anonymous sources explained, the cost of producing a Dom Pérignon is not much higher than that of producing a Moët. The difference is that one bottle sells for about €150 – and the other for €30.

KINGS, TSARS AND RAP STARS

The second of the Champagne region's twin poles, Reims – pronounced *ruhns* with a slight guttural inflection – lies behind the drink's association with upmarket revelry. The first king of France, Clovis, was baptized here and it became a tradition that French kings were crowned at the city's cathedral. These occasions were inevitably accompanied by joyful carousing, much of which involved swigging the local wine.

Today Reims is a calm, pleasant city of wide, tree-lined boulevards. One of the passengers who alighted from the train with me was a young man with a Louis Vuitton bag and a large shaggy black dog in a matching collar. I put the stately boulevards and the wealthy visitor together and came to the conclusion that Reims was a rich town. I was wrong. Unemployment is high and there is a large divide between the fortunate families who run the champagne houses and just about everybody else.

My next scheduled visit is with Louis Roederer. Compared to Moët & Chandon it is a small house – selling some 3 million bottles of bubbly a year – yet it makes one of the world's most famous champagne brands: Cristal.

The Louis Roederer headquarters is a 19th-century mansion. I perch gingerly on a Louis XVI chair in a lobby decorated with potted ferns and tapestries, before gratefully rising to meet the house's spokeswoman, Martine Lorson. And, yes, that name does sound familiar: Martine is married to Daniel Lorson of the CIVC. Champagne is a sociable business.

It's possible to argue that the champagne houses have been far more successful at marketing than 'conventional' wine producers. This may be because the champagne houses are merchants, while the chateaux of Bordeaux, for example, are located in the midst of their own vineyards. 'Originally this region was noted for its textiles,' Martine explains, as she shows me into a boardroom lined with family portraits. 'But when it became evident that sparkling wines were about to develop into a major business, some of the families who worked in the textile trade transformed themselves into champagne merchants.'

Perhaps that objectivity gave them an edge. Champagne houses are sophisticated, urban creatures, located in town centres above the cellars where their precious product is stored for between 15 months and three years, on average. Louis Roederer wines remain in the cellar for five years. In some ways this is an old-fashioned champagne house – independent and family owned.

Louis Roederer inherited the house from his uncle, one Nicolas Schreider, in 1833. By 1868, Louis was selling 2.5 million bottles a year, mostly to Russians who had – as Jean-Remy Moët had predicted some 50 years earlier – developed an unquenchable thirst for the drink. Of all the family members who followed Louis, the most remarkable was Camille Olry-Roederer, who became director of the house in 1932 after the death of her husband, Léon. This determined and energetic woman ran Louis Roederer for more than 40 years. 'By the time she took over, the house was suffering,' recounts Martine. 'Sales had sharply declined after a succession of disasters: the Russian Revolution, which robbed it of its biggest market, the phylloxera epidemic, the depressed global economy… it's fair to say that, were it not for Camille, the house would have gone under. Her husband had been considerably older than she was, so when she took charge of the house she was still in her early thirties. She was dynamic and persuasive.'

Camille was not afraid to exercise her charismatic charms, throwing extravagant parties to which the fashionable set clamoured to be invited. These boosted the reputation of the house and its champagne. (There is quite a tradition of strong women leaders in Champagne. Madame Clicquot took over her family's business in 1805, when she was only 27. In the mid-19th century, Louise Pommery grew her late husband's relatively small winery into a leading champagne house. Mathilde Emile Laurent-Perrier ran the show for 38 years from 1900. And Lily Bollinger was a contemporary of Camille's, managing the house through the Second World War and receiving the Ordre du Mérite from the French government in 1976.)

Camille's grandson, Jean-Claude Rouzaud, headed Louis Roederer until 2006. A modernizer, he made a foray into enemy territory by opening the Anderson Valley winery in California in 1987. The following year, he oversaw the launch of an American sparkling wine called Roederer Estate (marketed under the name Quartet in Europe). He has since handed over the reins to his son Frédéric.

Frédéric Rouzaud's name is occasionally evoked in marketing circles alongside that of Cristal, the Louis Roederer *cuvée* favoured – until recently – by American rap stars. Cristal was originally created for the Tsars of Russia on the orders of Alexander II in 1876. Sweeter than conventional champagnes, it came in a flat-bottomed, transparent lead-crystal bottle (necessary, legend has it, because Alexander feared that conventional green bottles might disguise the presence of poison or booby traps). While the Russian revolution put an end to Cristal's extremely niche market, Camille Olry-Roederer resurrected the brand in 1945 as a *cuvée prestige* that would play a role similar to that of Dom Pérignon at Moët & Chandon. It later became known for its gold-tinted cellophane sleeve, designed to protect the wine from damage by light.

It's not entirely clear why rappers adopted Cristal as opposed to any other champagne brand. Some have suggested that the evocative name slips easily into a lyric. Others say the gold label and distinctive packaging were the attraction. According to one article, 'Rapper Biggie Smalls (aka the Notorious BIG)… is believed to have been the first performer to mention Cristal. He started off elegizing Moët & Chandon champagne, then switched to 'Cristal forever' on the song 'Brooklyn's Finest' on Jay-Z's album *Reasonable Doubt*. References to Cristal started popping up in the lyrics of Lil' Kim, Snoop Dogg, P Diddy, Jay-

Z and 50 Cent' ('Bring on the bling – rappers give Cristal and Hennessy street cred', *San Francisco Chronicle*, 16 December 2004).

The trend should have been viewed as solid gold at Louis Roederer, exposing Cristal to a young, entirely new audience for zero marketing dollars. But back in Old Europe, not everyone was certain that the brand benefited from being associated with the ostentatious universe of rap. The grapes hit the fan when Frédéric Rouzaud, freshly appointed as Roederer's managing director, responded to a question posed by a journalist from *Intelligent Life*, a lifestyle magazine published by *The Economist*. 'Frédéric Rouzaud… says that Roederer has observed its association with rap with "curiosity and serenity". But he does not seem entirely serene. Asked if an association between Cristal and the bling lifestyle could actually hurt the brand, he replies: "That's a good question, but what can we do? We can't forbid people from buying it. I'm sure Dom Pérignon or Krug would be delighted to have their business"' ('Bubbles and bling', *Intelligent Life*, summer 2006).

The fact that the comment appeared under the sub-headline 'Unwanted attention' compounded the diplomatic error. The news quickly flowed to the rap community, which pledged to boycott Cristal. Today, Martine Lorson admits that the incident was unfortunate. 'In my view it was a misinterpretation: we mustn't forget that Monsieur Rouzaud was not speaking in his native language. But it's true that, while it was by no means our intention to upset anyone, rappers were not our traditional clients. During the short period of controversy that followed, we received many supportive calls and letters. To a certain extent, this slip of the tongue merely returned Cristal to its usual positioning.'

She adds that Roederer did not sell 'a single additional bottle' of Cristal thanks to the rap phenomenon: the wine is produced in such limited quantities that upping production to satisfy increased demand was not an option. When the rappers and their fans abandoned the brand, other buyers quickly filled the vacuum.

Like many luxury brands, Louis Roederer does not consider that it engages in anything as tawdry as 'marketing'. However, it deploys certain communication techniques that seem to fall into that category. They are the responsibility of executive vice-president Michael Janneau.

'It's true that we consider marketing something of a dirty word,' he says, with unexpected good humour. 'No doubt you think there's an element of snobbery in that. But in fact it's a very logical stance for us to take. If you consider that the aim of marketing in the classic sense is to sell more of your product and thus gain a greater market share, then that is not the business we're in. In fact, we do quite the opposite. We produce a limited number of bottles and we decide to whom we will allocate them. We're practising a policy of inaccessibility, which is the essence of luxury. In fact the real challenge for us – and here is where an element of marketing comes in – is to control with the precision of a jeweller exactly where and in what circumstances our brand appears.'

When Janneau arrived at the house in 1998 he found it to be 'almost advertising-phobic'. Nonetheless, it had achieved a couple of publicity coups, notably in 1992 when it sponsored a search for the missing plane of French writer and airman Antoine de Saint Exupéry. Known as 'Saint Ex', the revered author of *Wind, Sand and Stars* and *The Little Prince* disappeared in his P-38 Lightning off the coast of Corsica in 1944. (The search backed by Roederer was unsuccessful, but the plane's wreckage was discovered in waters not far from Nice a few years later.) The champagne house had also sponsored the restoration of a statue of the Empress Sabine – the wife of Hadrian – at the Louvre.

Sponsorship remains key to Roederer's strategy. 'Creating print advertisements and buying space in magazines does not make much sense for a brand like Roederer,' Janneau observes. 'You find yourself drowned out by six or seven pages of advertising for brands owned by LVMH.'

Janneau stumbled across a much better opportunity in 2003. Through mutual friends he was introduced to Thierry Grillet, cultural director of the Bibliothèque Nationale de France (the French national library). This vast archive of almost anything that's ever been published in France – or at least since 1368, when it was established as the royal library of Charles V – is also a museum with two sites in Paris. Grillet told Janneau that the library possessed more than five million photographs, which were at that moment lying dormant in a cellar under the library's building in rue de Richelieu, just up the street from the Louvre. 'And they didn't have a cent to spend on exhibiting them,' Janneau says. 'After that, we very quickly decided to become the sponsor of the Bibliothèque Nationale's photography collection. Our first move was to fund the installation of a gallery in the very heart of the building on rue de Richelieu.'

Thanks to that piece of smart thinking, the Louis Roederer brand has been attached to a series of widely reviewed photography exhibitions and names such as Eugene Atget, Sophie Calle, Robert Capa, Stéphane Couturier, Mario Giacomelli and Sebastião Salgado. 'Personally, I get a great deal of satisfaction from the relationship. I believe it's important for a luxury brand to contribute to society. One can face oneself more easily in the mirror.'

At the same time, Roederer redesigned its website to emphasize its involvement in culture and the arts (www.louis-roederer.com). Each new exhibition is accompanied by an interactive preview online. The brand has not entirely rejected traditional advertising – 'We do a modest amount,' says Janneau – but there is little doubt that it has reaped greater benefit from a far more innovative approach: placing itself at the intersection of art and the web.

Before leaving the brand's headquarters, I am taken on a brief tour of its cellars. They naturally seem smaller and more claustrophobic than those of Moët & Chandon. Here, it's a little easier to believe that the *remueurs* turn each bottle by hand. They also return periodically to set the bottles at a new angle in the racks. As I mentioned earlier, during the fermentation period the necks of the bottles are gradually inclined towards the floor, so that the debris of dead yeast gathers below the cork. In the corking and labelling area above, I learn why.

The question has been bugging me since my first cellar tour: how is the sediment removed from the bottle without losing any of the champagne? Now I get my answer. The neck of the bottle is flash-frozen. The cork is removed and the pressure forces out the neck-sized lump of ice, with the sediment neatly encased inside. This process is known as 'disgorgement'. The small amount of champagne lost in the process is replaced with a dose of the same type of wine, mixed with a dash of cane sugar. Alternatively, some winemakers prefer to add a liqueur made from a personal selection of reserve wines, to give the resulting champagne a more complex aroma.

Once re-corked, a bottle of Louis Roederer is returned to the cellar for a 'rest' period. It will spend six more months in the dark before it finally gets a chance to gleam on the table of a fancy restaurant.

CHAMPAGNE BUBBLES OVER

A great contradiction lies at the heart of Champagne country. Although many of the houses rely on the scarcity of their product for their allure, they are also in business. If demand can't be satisfied, or prices rise from high to astronomical, customers will go elsewhere – to the sparkling wines of the United States, for example. And the simple fact of the matter is that there is not enough champagne to go around. The entire territory of the Champagne AOC region as determined by the 1927 legislation is planted with vines. Production is at a maximum. But new customers from China, Russia and India have developed a taste for champagne.

Faced with this dilemma, the growers and the champagne houses have come to a radical decision – to revise the official borders of the Champagne region. A request from the growers' union (the Syndicat Général des Vignerons) to the INAO (the Institut National de l'Origine et de la Qualité, part of the Ministry of Agriculture) was granted in 2008. The first new plots are likely to be authorized by 2015.

This, as you can imagine, is a delicate process. The existing region covers some 33,000 hectares and 319 villages (or 'communes'). The revision could mean that 40 new villages are added.

For the villages concerned, there is a great deal at stake. Daniel Lorson of the CIVC estimates that one hectare of land planted with vines within the official Champagne region is worth €1 million. A hectare of normal farmland is worth between €5,000 and €7,000. 'Imagine you're a farmer with a plot of land worth €5,000,' he says. 'Then, overnight, you find that your land falls within the Champagne appellation. Jackpot!'

But Lorson emphasizes that 'not just any land' will be chosen: 'The process is of course being conducted scientifically. A committee of independent experts has been drawn from different fields: geography, geology, agricultural engineering and history. There is even a plant sociologist, which was a term I'd never come across before. They study the relationships between different types of plants and how they interact with their environment. This committee is analysing the entire region, almost under a microscope, to determine which land should be selected. At the end of the first phase, they've already determined 40 likely villages.'

The initial report attracted more than 2,000 comments and protests from landowners and communes when it was made public. The second six-year phase, which began in 2009, involves choosing the precise parcels of land that should be planted with vines. 'You can imagine the work that represents, especially when you consider all the subtle factors that go into the making of a great wine: the soil, the subsoil, exposure to the sun, the micro-climate... And finally, there is the historic aspect. We want to choose land that forms part of the heritage of the Champagne region. The committee wants to retain a certain consistency and homogeneity during this process.'

The aim is to boost champagne production just enough to satisfy rising demand, but not so much that the market is destabilized and the golden nectar is transformed into a commodity. And making adjustments to the existing territory, as well as expanding it, should safeguard the quality of champagne. Not that there aren't voices of protest. Some growers aren't keen on seeing their slice of the pie reduced. And certain champagne houses would have been happy to sit back and watch prices rise until their wine became accessible only to the very rich. Finally, though, the region decided that it wanted to hold on to its 12-to-15 per cent share of the global effervescent wine market.

In the meantime, ironically, the depressed economy has meant slowing sales. Lorson is confident, though, that champagne will survive with its mystique intact. 'This region has known hard times before. In any case, what's the best remedy when you're feeling down? The first hint of celebration – a birthday, a wedding, an anniversary – and you'll hear the popping of champagne corks again.'

15

The wines of paradise

'It's like comparing a flint to a pebble.'

For some people, wine is not merely a civilized pleasure – it is a passion, even an obsession. Take the man sitting before me in the bar of the Crillon Hotel. With an open suntanned face and a light sprinkling of silver hair, François Audouze looks like a fairly unassuming person – a successful businessman, perhaps. He is even drinking a glass of mineral water. Nothing about him would lead one to suspect that, in a secret location somewhere near Paris, he has a cellar stocked with thousands of the world's most rare and valuable wines. And his mission in life is to drink some of them, preferably in good company. Several times a year, Audouze invites friends, connoisseurs, fellow collectors and the merely curious to a lavish dinner. For the occasion, he selects 10 or so bottles from his cellar.

'I was in the steel business, which on the face of it has nothing to do with gastronomy,' he says. 'But as a businessman, you are fortunate enough to visit great restaurants and drink very good wines. At a relatively young age, in my early 30s, I developed a taste for old wines. The wine that changed my life was a 1923 Château Climens, a Sauternes. When I sipped it, I lost all my bearings. It was like no other wine I had ever tasted. I knew that the essence of winemaking – its soul, if you like – was here. I was determined to further explore this magical world. And because I had the means, I built up a considerable cellar.'

To be precise, Audouze owns more than 40,000 bottles of wine, of which 10,000 are over 50 years old. I am astonished by this figure. I buy CDs fairly regularly, I tell him, but I still don't have 35,000 of them. 'When you're passionate, when you're driven to explore, you just keep buying,' he says. 'I buy a bottle of wine practically every day. I picked one up just before I came to meet you.'

At a certain point he realized that he had collected far more bottles than he would ever be able to drink in his lifetime. So why not share the pleasure? 'I decided to organize dinners at which I could drink these wines with others. More than that, my aim was to provide the ultimate in gastronomy: the perfect food with the perfect wines. I consider a dinner to be like a symphony, with an overture, a drama and a finale. The wine plays a crucial role.'

Audouze works with leading chefs to ensure that the flavours are perfectly choreographed. Each dinner takes place at a restaurant that has been awarded a minimum of two Michelin stars. Audouze invites nine guests who contribute just under €1,000 each to attend. It's possible to apply for a place at his website: www.wine-dinners.com. At the time of writing he has staged more than 120 dinners, each one different. 'It's important to stress that these dinners are open to anyone, whether you have an enormous experience in wine tasting or not. Obviously, it's a bit like music – the more you listen, the more you become attuned to the subtle role played by each instrument – but during the dinner I explain exactly why each wine has been chosen, so you need not be an expert to understand.'

The bottles opened at the dinner are an average of 50 years old. Some are considerably younger, others are far more ancient: one was an 1828 Muscat des Canaries. ('Just imagine,' he says. 'Truly a wine from another world!')

Audouze does not turn his nose up at younger wines – far from it – but he insists that they can never have the complexity of a wine from a bygone age. 'It's like comparing an 18th-century Aubusson tapestry to a modern hand-woven rug. The modern rug might be pretty, even exceptional, but it can't compare to a tapestry from the 18th century. It does not have that plenitude, that fullness, or the colours that are impossible to recreate today. That's the case with old wines: the palette of aromas and flavours is infinitely more complex. It's like comparing a flint to a pebble.'

He has, he will tell you, supped the wines of paradise: a 1929 Romanée-Conti, a 1945 Mouton Rothschild, a 1947 Cheval Blanc, a 1900 Margaux, even an 1861 Yquem. While rare wines are collected and traded like any other valuable commodity, Audouze buys all his bottles with the aim of one day opening them. 'That does not mean a bottle or a label cannot be beautiful. And, indeed, I keep my empty bottles as souvenirs. But I'm not ashamed to admit that what interests me most is their contents.'

Some of the wines in Audouze's cellar are worth tens of thousands of dollars, which is why he never reveals its location. To give you an idea, a single bottle of great wine like the '45 Romanée-Conti might fetch more than US$30,000 at auction. Moving from the sublime to the ridiculous, a 1787 Château Lafite Bordeaux that had supposedly once been owned by Thomas Jefferson was sold at Christie's for US$156,000 in 1985. It has since become the subject of a book called *The Billionaire's Vinegar* (2008), a title that reveals something of the plot. Audouze was neither the buyer nor the seller of that particular bottle, but it inspires me to ask him how he can be certain that he's getting the genuine article. How prevalent is wine fakery?

'That is a vast subject,' says Audouze. 'Obviously you have to rely on your experience to avoid falling into traps, but it's fair to say that nobody is really safe.'

An article in French newspaper *Le Figaro* at the end of 2008 estimated that the market in counterfeit vintage wines was worth in excess of €200 million a year ('*La traque aux bouteilles falsifiées*', 3 November 2008). Marc-Antoine Jamet, president of the Union des Fabricants (set up in 1872 to protect French businesses from intellectual and industrial copyright infringement) told the paper that fraudsters were often able to obtain empty bottles bearing the original labels and fill them with low-quality wine. If this was not an option, no matter: the label could be counterfeited. The great vintages of Bordeaux, Burgundy and Champagne are the main victims of fakery, while the traffickers have been linked to the Italian Mafia. Inevitably, China has also come under scrutiny – Jamet told *Le Figaro* that wines were being counterfeited there 'on an industrial scale'. A common trick is to steal an empty bottle of vintage wine from the kitchen of a leading hotel or restaurant, then refill it and sell it to a collector.

Perhaps for this reason, wine collectors tend to keep a low profile. Audouze feels that's a shame, given that wine is such a convivial pleasure. One of the highlights of his year is a meeting with a fellow collector from the United States, at which they each uncork a bottle of the most prestigious vintages in their collections. Presumably, I joke, these wines are French rather than American?

'There is a theory that American wines dating back to before 1970 are no longer drinkable, but that's simply not true,' asserts Audouze. 'There are very few, but they exist. There are also some great Italian wines. But France has by far the greatest wine heritage in the world.'

Which brings me on to another question. Many of the wines I've mentioned above are brand names of a sort: Mouton Rothschild, Château Margaux, Château d'Yquem... even if we don't know much about wine, they strike a chord. But surely the dusty chateaux of France deny the very existence of 'marketing' – don't they?

VINTAGE BRANDING

The French wine sector is in trouble. Although the country is practically fused in our imaginations with the art of winemaking – and names like Burgundy and Bordeaux are brands in their own right – it has been losing global market share for years. As early as 2001, a report written for the French Agriculture Ministry by the consultant Jacques Berthomeau warned that 'New World' wines – from the United States, Australia, Chile and Argentina – had seized 20 per cent of the world market virtually from scratch in two decades. They had 'gained ground through clever marketing, large-scale production and competitive pricing' ('France's wine industry losing global market share to New World producers', *Food & Drink Weekly*, 20 August 2001).

France is now the world's third largest exporter of wine in volume, after Italy and Spain, according to April 2009 figures released by the International Organization of Vine and Wine (OIV). And consumption of French wine in France itself is falling as younger consumers turn to soft drinks, mineral water or (*'Quel horreur!'*) wines from the New World. Many factors are blamed, from the variable quality of French wines to the confusion caused by their labels, which communicate the names of chateaux and regions rather than grape varieties, making it difficult for everyday consumers to determine exactly what they are buying. Many British consumers defected long ago to Australian wines, with their clear, modern and occasionally humorous labels, while American drinkers have the splendid wines of the Napa Valley to turn to.

The shaky position of France in the global market has sparked various trends, some of them alarming. There have been reports of French 'wine terrorists' expressing their support for domestic growers by attacking delivery trucks filled with imported wines. Less dramatic but more far-reaching is the suggestion that some French wines are becoming 'Parkerized'. This accusation is based on the power wielded by the American wine critic Robert M Parker and his influential periodical *The Wine Advocate*. In it, Parker rates wines according to a 100-point system. A good Parker rating can have a positive impact on a wine's price and sales. Parker's critics – notably Jonathan Nossiter, maker of the 2005 wine world documentary *Mondovino* – claim that his influence has prompted some winemakers to deliberately adjust their production techniques in order to cater to his taste for powerful, fruity wines. Parker himself dismisses this as nonsense. 'You can't simplify my taste and say "Parker likes big wines" because it's simply not true,' he told *The New York Times*, adding that those who did so had not read his work properly. Later in the article, he said: 'I think the diversity of wines today is greater than it's ever been' ('Decanting Robert Parker', 22 March 2006).

'Parkerized' or not, French wines have been trying to regain their high profile abroad. In 2006, the CIVB (Conseil Interprofessionel de Vin de Bordeaux), which represents growers, producers and merchants, ran a print campaign created by the advertising agency M&C Saatchi. Placed in upmarket newspapers and magazines, it played on the association of Bordeaux with grand chateaux. For instance, an image of a man and a woman looking at one another flirtatiously over glasses of wine was accompanied by the slogan: 'If the lady refuses a glass, treat her to a chateau.'

As ever, then, the French are banking on the prestigious image of their product. Indeed, the International Organization of Vine and Wine confirms that France is still the largest exporter of wine in *value* terms, even as export volumes shrink, suggesting that it is still a successful producer of expensive wine. For a great many connoisseurs, French wines have lost little of their allure. When asked to name the greatest luxury wine brands, Evelyne Resnick, a wine marketing consultant and the author of the (2008) book *Wine Brands*, unhesitatingly names Château Haut-Brion, Romanée-Conti and Château Palmer among her top choices (along, admittedly, with the Napa Valley brands Opus One and Dominus).

Legendary French wine brands tend to have enjoyed what is described in Resnick's book as an 'organic growth', which means that their very age has contributed to their status. Dig a little further, though, and you'll find some canny marketing. Take Château Haut-Brion, for example. The wine owes its notoriety to the English – or rather, to a Frenchman's grasp of the English market in the 17th century.

In 1666 François-Auguste de Pontac opened a tavern in London called 'L'Enseigne de Pontac' exclusively to promote his family's claret. The wine was made in Bordeaux on the ancestral estate, Haut-Brion ('on the hill'). The estate had been in the family since 1525, when Jean de Pontac cleverly married Jeanne de Bellon, daughter of a powerful local landowner.

But the most influential member of the Pontac family was Arnaud de Pontac, owner of Château Haut-Brion from 1649 until his death in 1681. Alongside the power conferred by his wealth, he was president of the first 'Parlement' in Bordeaux. His word, quite literally, was law. More importantly, however, he was a winemaker of genius.

According to a profile of the estate in *Wine News*, 'it wasn't until the property came... into Arnaud's hands that the quality of its wine improved dramatically. He introduced the practice of regular racking from barrel to barrel, separating young wine from its coarse, early lees to avoid spoilage, and was among the first to realize that frequent "topping up", to compensate for evaporation, allowed the wine in cask to improve rather than oxidize. These techniques, innovative for their time, allowed the true greatness of the vineyard to reveal itself in the wine' ('Haut-Brion: the world's first cult wine', April/May 2001).

Pontac was well aware of the market for red wine in London, where it was known simply as 'claret' – and ordered as such, with little regard for its origin. But Pontac's wine was of such obviously superior quality that the patrons of London taverns and coffee houses began asking for it using an approximation of its name: 'Ho Bryen'. The diarist Samuel Pepys noted on 10 April 1663 that he had drunk 'a sort of French wine called Ho Bryen that hath a good and most particular taste I never met with' (*Oxford Companion to Wine*, 3rd Edition, 2006). This incident is said to have taken place at the Royal Oak Tavern, in which the Pontac family had a stake.

Very soon the family had its own London tavern, run by Arnaud's son, François-Auguste. As well as selling the esteemed wine, François-Auguste hired a skilled chef to cook up more elaborate fare than was generally available at such establishments, effectively creating London's first upmarket restaurant. The wine was sold at higher prices than its competitors, but it was the perfect accompaniment to the sophisticated cuisine and the tavern's convivial surroundings. Haut-Brion had established itself as a luxury brand.

The family lost the Haut-Brion estate during the French Revolution, after which it fell briefly into the hands of Talleyrand, the wily diplomat who had served under both Louis XVI and Napoleon. A succession of owners followed down the centuries, one of the most notable being Jean-Eugène Larrieu, who bought the estate at auction and whose family owned it until 1923.

The modern era began on May 13 1935, when an American banker named Clarence Dillon bought the estate. Most accounts maintain that Haut-Brion's continuing success was due not to Dillon, but to his nephew Seymour Weller – who was named president of what had now become a business – and its director Georges Delmas. The company they ran, Domaine Clarence Dillon, still owns the estate today. Its honorary president is Madame la Duchesse de Mouchy (the former Joan Dillon, granddaughter of Clarence), while its president is her son Prince Robert de Luxembourg, and its director is Jean-Philippe Delmas, grandson of Georges.

As well as various technological advancements that are well known within the winemaking community (for instance, the introduction of stainless steel fermentation vats and research into clonal selection, which involves taking cuttings from the 'best-performing' vines), Haut-Brion is notable for its savvy marketing. For a start, it comes in a distinctive bottle, with sloping shoulders and a medallion bearing the wine's name embossed into the glass just below the neck. This design was introduced in 1958. As Evelyne Resnick points out, by rights 'no estate needs an original bottle less than Haut-Brion, classified First Growth [*Premier Cru*] in 1855 and since then served on all royal and presidential tables throughout the world.' Not to mention on the tables of lesser mortals who might wish to appear presidential – and can telegraph their status to an entire restaurant via the bottle.

THE REIGN OF *TERROIR*

Haut-Brion also appears to have grasped the importance of a snappy name for overseas customers. For years its 'second' wine was named Château Bahans Haut-Brion, after the parcel of land on which the vines were planted. 'Difficult to pronounce, even for French people,' observes Evelyne Resnick drily. In 2009, to celebrate the 75th anniversary of Clarence Dillon's first visit to the chateau, the name of the wine was changed to 'Clarence', which would also appear on the embossed medallion. The decision adhered to one of the classic strategies of luxury marketing, which is to repurpose one's heritage in order to tell an attractive story to the potential consumer. Still, one has to admit the name has an attractive ring to it: make mine a bottle of Clarence.

Haut-Brion was by no means the first of the Bordeaux titans to launch a new brand. In 1998 Château Palmer unveiled Alter Ego. The wine can be drunk younger than its big brother and is positioned as 'spontaneous and uninhibited', which seems designed to appeal to younger consumers.

Château Palmer itself attracts an almost slavish following. This is not entirely due to the inarguable quality of its wine. The estate – acquired in 1814 from the Gascq family by Charles Palmer, a major general in the British army – has also used a digital strategy to generate customer loyalty.

Evelyne Resnick notes that Château Palmer 'came rather late to the web: their first site was launched in 2001, when most of the estates in the Bordeaux area were already working on their second or even third versions.' This, however, allowed the château to learn from its neighbours. One of the challenges faced by the estate was the fact that, like many others in Bordeaux, it sold its wine through brokers, which meant that it rarely came into contact with its customers. The website helped it solve that problem. In order to gain access to the full content of the site, visitors had to sign up to become members of a Château Palmer 'club'. In return for leaving valuable data, they received several privileges, the best of which was an invitation to spend a day in the vineyards during the harvest. While picking grapes may not be light work, visitors revelled in the experience and the exclusive access to the estate and its management. Château Palmer's website still lies at the heart of its communications strategy. Highly interactive, it includes a blog with written, audio and video content.

Needless to say, some connoisseurs find it disheartening that commercial realities force even the greatest winemakers to resort to branding and marketing techniques. 'Branding' a wine undermines the cherished ideal of the *terroir* – the land where the wine is grown and which lends it its distinct character. The implication is that customers who rely on a brand name to identify a wine are uneducated dolts who would not know – to use François Audouze's metaphor – a flint from a pebble.

Citing Micheal Havens, founder of Havens Wine Cellars in California, Eveylyn Resnick suggests that there are two different marketing techniques in the wine business: one for entry-level brands and one for luxury brands. Entry-level brands focus on 'synthetic marketing', which emphasizes the brand's concept, label and price, only then followed by the wine itself. 'Organic marketing', on the other hand, focuses on the wine and the region first.

If wine snobs – sorry, 'connoisseurs' – insist that wine should be categorized by place of origin rather than brand name, how did the winemakers of California generate any form of respectability during the 'new wave' of the 1970s? Although wines had existed in California since the 18th century, Prohibition had largely destroyed the industry and by the 1960s the region was associated with underwhelming sweet wines. The renaissance that began at the end of that decade owes a great deal to the knowledge and marketing instincts of one Robert Mondavi.

Mondavi – who died in 2008 aged 94 – was born in 1913 to an Italian immigrant family in Hibbing, Minnesota. A few years after his birth, his father decided to become a winemaker and the family moved to California. When Robert graduated from Stanford in 1943, he persuaded his father to buy the Charles Krug Winery in Napa Valley. Robert worked at the family business with his brother Peter right up until 1966, when a simmering difference of opinion over winemaking techniques led him to quit and start his own winery – at the age of 52. Mondavi had been inspired by several trips to Europe, where he 'began a quest to understand *terroir* – the French notion of how soil and climate affect grapevines and shape the character of a wine' ('Robert Mondavi dies at age of 94', *Wine Spectator*, 16 May 2008).

Mondavi had a gift for inspiring others. He welcomed visitors to his winery for tours, tastings, art exhibitions and concerts. He and his wife Margrit created cooking classes with great chefs – such as Julia Child and Paul Bocuse – who experimented with different matches of food and wine. As *Wine Spectator* comments, 'rather than limit wine to fine dining, Mondavi championed making it a part of everyday life and of a healthy lifestyle.' His friend and public relations advisor Harvey Posert told the magazine: 'The programmes – comparative tastings, harvest seminars, great chefs, summer concerts, the mission programme – all had the sole purpose of explaining wine's positive values to the public and to the industry he served.'

Mondavi also understood and appreciated the importance of Europe's winemaking heritage. In 1979, he joined forces with Baron Philippe de Rothschild, of Château Mouton-Rothschild in Bordeaux, to create Opus One. The resulting wine, which sprung out of a marriage of French and Californian winemaking traditions, 'caught the attention of vintners and businessmen worldwide. Baron Rothschild's desire to partner with Mondavi validated the quality of California wine and ushered in a new era of foreign investment in California. By the 1980s, dozens of international firms had bought land or built or bought wineries in the state.' The mythology around French winemaking helped California wines win the respect they deserved.

A strange footnote to Mondavi's adventures occurred in 1976 at the so-called 'Judgement of Paris', a wine-tasting event organized in Paris by the British wine merchant Paul Spurrier. French judges were challenged to a blind tasting of chardonnay and cabernet sauvignon wines from France and California. In the event, California wines were rated best in each category. The French wines on the table included a 1970 Haut-Brion, a 1970 Mouton Rothschild, and a 1973 Domaine Leflaive Puligny-Montrachet Les Pucelles. But a 1973 Chateau Montelena Chardonnay from Napa Valley was the top-rated white, while a 1973 Stag's Leap Wine Cellars Cabernet Sauvignon, also from Napa, was ranked highest among the reds.

Thus 24 May 1976 was the day when the reputation of French wine began its slow decline. To an extent, at least; on the 30th anniversary of the event, an article in online magazine *Slate* observed that although the French had been 'blindsided by aggressive competition' from other markets, 'the very finest French producers... thanks in part to the Judgement of Paris... recognized early on that the New World was capable of making excellent wine, and they worked hard to improve their own offerings... The good French wines have never been better.' Still, gone are the days when, in the words of one Burgundy winemaker, 'there is a belief that you don't need to market your wine, that France's reputation is enough' ('The judgement of Paris', 24 May 2006).

Today, the borders of the New World are being extended – and French *savoir faire* is once again playing a role in the expansion. In March 2009, Domaines Baron de Rothschild – owner of Château Lafite – announced a plan to make wine in China. In a partnership with state-owned Chinese investment company CITC, the French winemaker had selected a 25-hectare site on the Shangdong peninsula, near the town of Penglai. It added that wine was already produced in the region, which is known as 'China's Bordeaux' as it lies roughly at the same latitude.

In common with many luxury brands, Domaines Baron de Rothschild has a taste for emerging markets.

16

The chef

'In a restaurant, everything counts – nothing is trivial.'

If luxury is about enjoying goods and services that have been elevated to the highest levels of quality and refinement, then eating in a fine restaurant is one of the greatest luxuries of all. There are many reasons for choosing a particular restaurant: the location, the decor, the service, the wine list – I've even heard two French businessmen debating the quality of the bread at their potential lunch destinations – but ultimately our judgement rests on the cooking. We might come the first time for the smart crowd or the quirky design, but the food is why we'll come back. The proof is in the *moelleux au chocolat*.

We may also come for the chef. Most of us can cook, but not all of us can cook well. And very few of us can turn basic ingredients into the kind of culinary magic that makes diners close their eyes and groan with pleasure when they take a bite. Those who combine this ability with an attractive personality, a flair for marketing and an eye for all the elements that make up a great restaurant are rewarded with cult status in our society: they become celebrity chefs.

One thinks of British firebrands like Marco Pierre White and Gordon Ramsey – with their *commis*-searing tempers – or the more cerebral Heston Blumenthal, whose scientific approach at the three-Michelin-starred Fat Duck in Berkshire frequently earns him comparisons to Ferràn Adria of El Bulli. Adria's restaurant on the Costa Brava is said to be the best in the world, although it's so hard to get a table that few people you know will be able to confirm or deny this claim. In America there is Thomas Keller, of Per Se in New York and The French Laundry in California – although the Alsace-born Jean-Georges Vongerichten may have a stronger claim to global brand status. In France the restaurants of Pierre Gagnaire and Joël Robuchon regularly earn rave reviews from the toughest of critics.

When I started researching this chapter, however, the name that sprang to mind was that of Alain Ducasse. And it wasn't just because I'd recently been hanging out on his home patch in Monaco. With his eponymous company, his 25 restaurants worldwide (as either owner or consultant), his nine Michelin stars and his 1,000 or so employees, Ducasse is a global luxury brand. Indeed, in the introduction to the company brochure, CEO and co-founder Laurent Plantier compares Groupe Alain Ducasse to Ferrari and Louis Vuitton. So how does Ducasse feel about this? How did the man become the brand?

A BRAND NAMED ALAIN DUCASSE

'Let's get one thing straight first,' replies Alain Ducasse, 'I have no marketing theories and no lessons to give about how to construct a brand. I can simply look back at my 35-year career and try to understand, retrospectively, how things happened. And even then, one must remain prudent: I did not, at the age of 25, have a clearly established plan that would enable me to progress in a coherent manner. There are lucky breaks, desires and encounters that orientate you little by little in a certain direction.'

Let's establish some background. Alain Ducasse was born on 13 September 1956 on a farm in the Landes region, which is located below Bordeaux in the southwest of France. This is the legendary region of Gascony, also known as Aquitaine. Gascons have a reputation for earthiness and courage: d'Artagnan was from Gascony, as was Cyrano de Bergerac. It is an area of rolling Atlantic breakers and vast pine forests, of Armagnac and *foie gras*. Ducasse fits right in to this bucolic scene: 'His grandfather was a carpenter, his father a farmer,' reads the company brochure. 'His rustic upbringing, surrounded by chickens and ducks, influenced his taste early in his life.'

Apparently Ducasse did not want to rear fowls and grow vegetables – he wanted to cook them. He apprenticed at the age of 16 at a restaurant called the Pavillon Landais in Soustons, not far from home. Then he studied at the Ecole Hôtelière de Bordeaux. His next job was with Michel Guérard, the inventor of *nouvelle cuisine*, who had moved with his wife to Eugénie-les-Bains in Les Landes. Soon, Ducasse found himself on less familiar territory near Cannes, where he worked at Le Moulin de Mougins under Roger Vergé. 'If Guérard's lesson was to remove the shackles of old culinary habits, Vergé initiated the young chef into the tradition of Provençale cuisine and healthy, natural, authentic and joyful cooking.'

But Ducasse considers that his next mentor, Alain Chapel, had the greatest influence on his cooking style. By the time Ducasse arrived at Chapel's La Mère Charles in Mionnay, near Lyon, in 1978, the restaurant had been proudly sporting three Michelin stars for five years. Ducasse says that everything he had learned since childhood was brought into focus by Chapel's cooking. He learned that cooking was not about mixing flavours and aromas, but dextrously highlighting each one to create a sensorial landscape.

By the time he left, a couple of years later, Ducasse was ready to take the helm of a restaurant. At the age of just 25, he took over La Terrasse, the restaurant at the Hotel Juana in Juan-Les-Pins. And in 1982 he received his first two Michelin stars. This promising career was almost cut short in 1984 when Ducasse and four friends boarded a Learjet from Courchevel to Saint Tropez. The jet crashed – and Ducasse was the sole survivor. After numerous operations, Ducasse emerged a subtly different character: stronger and more rigorous. And during all those bedridden months, unable to cook, he had learned to conceptualize dishes in his head, designing and refining them long before he instructed others in how to make them. His teaching, management and delegation skills are among his greatest strengths today.

In 1987, fully recovered, Ducasse accepted the position of head chef at Le Louis XV, the restaurant at the Hotel de Paris in Monaco. He bet Prince Ranier III that he would gain three Michelin stars for the restaurant within four years. He did it with a year to spare in 1990 – incidentally, at the age of 33, becoming the youngest French chef ever to achieve three-star status. Many more restaurant ventures were to follow, including the Bastide des Moustiers in Provence, the Plaza Athenée in Paris and Beige in Tokyo. And in 1998 – also in Paris – Ducasse opened the first branch of Spoon Food & Wine. This pioneering concept enabled diners to assemble their own meals from lists of elements. It also included an extensive list of wines from overseas.

In France – where the traditional image of the chef in the tall white hat remains practically set in stone – Ducasse established a reputation as a modernizer. He certainly wasn't above turning his name into a brand. In fact, after a chance meeting in a bar, he teamed up with MIT graduate and finance wizard Laurent Plantier to do just that. Groupe Alain Ducasse was formed to expand into overseas markets and diversify into sectors beyond haute cuisine. Apart from its many restaurants, it now owns a hotel chain – Chateaux & Hôtels de France – a culinary publishing arm, a training department and a consulting service. The chef's range of interests is so wide that he has even designed meals for manned space flights; some of them were consumed on the International Space Station in 2006.

Although he is clearly a skilled businessman, Ducasse does not consider himself a marketing expert. 'If one looks upon branding as a marketing strategy, with cynicism, it's the beginning of the end. Turning one's own name into a brand signifies a genuine personal engagement.'

Marketing may add a garnish of glamour, he suggests, but chefs generally rise to prominence because they are extraordinarily good at their jobs. 'There is a fundamental truth in cooking as in any other artisanal métier: you cannot cheat. At a given moment, you serve the meal and it is tasted. The magic works or not – that's to say, you grant the client a moment of happiness or not. Whatever else happens, you should never lose sight of that essential truth.'

Honesty is a strong theme in Ducasse's discourse, along with the importance of being true to one's vision – while remaining clear-sighted and flexible. 'When I arrived at the Louis XV in Monaco in 1987, I was an advocate of Mediterranean cuisine. It was the style of cooking that inspired me and therefore it was the one that I developed. There were quite a few negative comments, because my approach did not remotely correspond to the accepted canons of gastronomy at that time. Nevertheless, I stuck to my guns and now I can say that I was right.'

Almost 10 years later, when he arrived in Paris, the critics assumed that he would bring his Mediterranean-themed cooking with him. 'But of course not! I'm not blind: Paris is not Monaco, the culinary cultures are not the same and the customers have different expectations. So I invented something else. And I take that same "adaptive" approach to every restaurant I open.'

In fact, says Ducasse, if he has a style at all, it is *'la différence'*: 'When I create a new restaurant, everything starts with the place. You know, when I was young I thought for a while that I might become an architect. I'm very sensitive to locations, to buildings, to their environmental context and the comportment they suggest. I spend a lot of time soaking up the spirit of the place, trying to understand its story. Whether you're in Paris, London, Tokyo, Osaka or New York, each city has a distinct personality. I opened Adour in New York for New Yorkers and, when I took the idea to Washington, I adapted to the particular atmosphere of that city. So – I start with the place and then I create the cuisine that goes with it.'

I wonder if he chooses the place – or whether the place chooses him?, he replies: 'More than the place, it's the entire cultural context. Take for example Le Comptoir de Benoit, in Osaka. That city has a particular atmosphere, very different from that of other Japanese cities. In Osaka, eating is a leisure activity that takes a wide variety of different forms, from the simplicity of *udon* to the delicacy of *takoyaki*. Osaki also has an infinite palette of different establishments, from the earthy *kappo* to the refined *ryotei*. The quality of the products, the long culinary tradition and the passion for eating well make it a place apart. In that context, there was no question of simply copying Benoit in Paris, which is a classic French bistro. So we put a lot of work into harmonizing the two cultures. Le Comptoir de Benoit is the result of that work: it offers the diners of Osaka the exotic elements of a French bistro while paying homage to local ingredients and culture. Even the interior designer was Japanese.'

This desire to adapt, observes Ducasse, prevents him from being boxed into a certain style. Having said that, he admits that there are recurring themes. 'Rather than a style, I have certain convictions, certain principles to which I adhere. The first is the most essential: the quality of the ingredients. Nature provides us with products that are already excellent. The skill of a cook is to remain modest and not try to detract from nature. I don't like clever techniques that put virtuosity before taste. The flavours should remain perfectly discernable – not too many ingredients, not too much seasoning.'

Ducasse's sardonic comment on self-consciously fancy cooking appears at the beginning of his group's brochure: 'A turbot without genius is better than a genius without a turbot.' Additionally, each chef is a product of his predecessors. 'Cooking is a story of encounters – with the great chefs of the past, with one's mentors. One can't cook today as if nothing has happened for the last two centuries. Yet, at the same time, it's a story that's written in the present and in the first person. Everyone has followed their own path, experienced their own encounters. It's a combination of creativity and shared knowledge.'

Sharing is one of the delights of the job. 'To eat is a marvellous moment: all the senses are involved. Above all, it's a shared moment. Beyond that, there are a million and one ways of creating pleasure because everyone is different. Tastes are not exactly the same: here one steams a fish, there one grills it; elsewhere it is eaten raw or marinated. The nuances of taste are infinite – they reflect the world's diversity and they fascinate me.'

I wonder if his customers have become more sophisticated and demanding since the beginning of his career. Is he under more pressure to perform, to innovate? 'Indisputably, eating well has become a more democratic pleasure. [Former Cartier president] Alain-Dominique Perrin has an interesting phrase: "luxury was once the ordinary in the lives of the extraordinary; now it is the extraordinary in the lives of the ordinary." There is an increasing interest in cooking classes, which is paradoxical because we know that people cook less on a daily basis. But the phenomenon demonstrates that interest in cuisine has grown and changed in its nature. It has become a leisure activity for more people. Flourishing restaurant guides and the multiplication of articles and broadcasts about cooking reflect the same trend.'

And, like every other luxury sector, the phenomenon has globalized. 'Two generations ago, haute cuisine was very European, if not to say rather French. Today, enthusiasts can be found all around the world. At the same time, talents are emerging worldwide and, above all, local culinary traditions are evolving and melding. Consequently, cuisine is becoming multicultural. We're dealing with clients who have widely varying approaches and reference points.'

While restaurants like El Bulli and The Fat Duck have grabbed headlines and plaudits with their scientific approach to cooking, Ducasse comes from a more classical tradition. On the other hand, his website is sleek, accessible and bang up to date. Does he appreciate technology? He says, 'I like it so much that I try and make it invisible. The best car is the one that never forces you to open the bonnet. In my job, technology has two very different facets. The first concerns service, and the second the way we do our jobs. Naturally, we've developed extremely sophisticated tools for management, reservations, human resources and so on. But we also appreciate technology that helps us in the kitchen. Such tools permit us to be more accurate, to obtain exactly the right cooking temperatures by controlling humidity levels, for example. They also enable us to innovate in terms of flavours: I'm thinking of slow cooking, at extremely low temperatures, which enables us to concentrate flavours in a remarkable way.'

Inevitably, I'm keen to hear a chef's definition of luxury. What separates an extraordinary restaurant from an ordinary one? And how has Ducasse been able to replicate the formula with such apparent ease? 'It's the obsession with detail. In a restaurant, one must master a multiplicity of details. That's the challenge: absolutely everything counts. In the kitchen, of course, the timing and the seasoning are fundamental. In the dining area, the placement of the tables and the decor are key. Nothing is trivial or unimportant: if the vegetables are not perfectly peeled and the tableware is not impeccable, a chef can have all the talent in the world, but the meal will not be of quality.'

Service, then, is crucial: 'During the meal the most difficult elements to control are the intangible ones. The detail, in this case, is in the natural smiles of the staff, the way they move, the well-judged word, the right advice on the choice of wine. These are the concerns of men and women who are committed to their work and have a feeling for perfect service. It's the most fragile aspect of what we do and the hardest to get right. It's essentially a live performance: you don't get another chance to shoot a badly judged scene. You must perform perfectly, every day, for every client.'

Not surprisingly, Ducasse is rarely convinced that the performance merits a standing ovation. 'In the end, luxury is a perfection that one strives for every day, without ever being entirely satisfied.'

17

Well-being

'Sanctuaries for the senses.'

In the 1966 film *Alfie*, the titular working class philanderer played by Michael Caine worries about two things: his health and his peace of mind. 'If you ain't got that – you ain't got nothing,' he observes, sounding surprised by his own insight. Somewhere along the line, health and peace of mind hitched up to give rise to the concept of 'well-being'. Happily, there are many spots around the world where one can seek this elusive physical and mental condition. If Alfie wanted to pick up wealthy women today, he'd undoubtedly cruise a spa.

Spas have been around forever – certainly since long before François Blanc had ever heard of Homburg or Monaco. When I was growing up in the West Country of England, one of the places my family regularly visited on weekend motor trips was the city of Bath, in Somerset. Of course, it was named after its natural hot springs – the only such springs in Britain, we were always informed – although the Romans had called it *Aquae Sulis*. The city they built around the source was essentially a giant spa complex. I would stand on uneven flagstones amid the noble ruins of the Great Bath, staring through wraiths of steam into the murky green water and wondering how anybody could have considered even dipping a toe into the stuff.

Not far away, the hot water that fed the baths gushed constantly from a dark, mossy aperture in the wall. At that point it still looked sparkling and pure. But a strong whiff of sulphur provided evidence of its long subterranean journey. We were told that this very water had originally fallen on the Mendip Hills as long as 80,000 years ago, seeping towards the hot core of the earth and rising again through a crack in the carboniferous limestone to emerge at a constant temperature of 46.5°C – more than a million litres of the stuff blasting from the depths every day. Not surprisingly, the Celts and the Romans felt that the spring waters had healing powers. They were said to cure rheumatic and muscular disorders, skin ailments and respiratory problems, as well as promoting ease and – naturally – well-being.

The Romans were by no means the last civilization to exploit the power of the hot springs. In the 18th century, Bath Spa became a fashionable destination – an English Monte Carlo. *The Strangers' Assistant and Guide to Bath*, published in 1773, speaks of 'the Hot Springs, their several Qualities and Impregnations, the Disorders to which they are adapted and some Cautions respecting their Use... Also, an account of the Public Amusements there'. The latter included a full programme of balls and dances as well as several cafés serving spring water. The grandest – The Pump Rooms, adjacent to the Great Bath – can still be visited. The guide mentions that the waters offered relief from gout, bowel disorders, bilious colic, jaundice and the horrifying-sounding 'wasting of the flesh... generally called a *nervous atrophy*'. It does not take a physician to summarize these disorders as afflictions of the rich, idle and overfed, which explains the appeal of Bath to Georgian luxury nomads.

The city continued to vaunt the waters' health-giving qualities well into the 20th century – until, suddenly, it could no longer do so. In 1979, a girl contracted amoebic meningitis after swallowing some of the source water while swimming in the baths. She died five days later. Tests confirmed that the water contained a bug called *Naegleria fowlerii* and the baths were closed.

Inevitably, the demands of heritage marketing and the sense that the city was sitting on an untapped goldmine meant that attention eventually turned back to the hot springs. As the infectious organism had been discovered in only one of the water sources, it was felt that with careful design and frequent testing this neglected tourist attraction could be reactivated. In the 1990s, plans were drawn up for a modernized and safe bathing complex. The city authorities applied for a grant from the Millennium Commission, which was funded by the National Lottery and designed to support heritage projects. Originally scheduled to open in 2002, the project hit a number of obstacles, ranging from technical and construction problems to political wrangling and even vandalism. Thermae Bath Spa finally opened in August 2006, having cost £45 million – more than £32 million over-budget.

The centrepiece of the complex is the New Royal Bath, a contemporary glass and stone cube designed by the architect Sir Nicholas Grimshaw. By far its most attractive feature is the naturally heated rooftop pool, in which one can relax while admiring the city's honey-coloured Georgian buildings and the distant Cotswold Hills. The building is linked to the restored Cross Bath, a round structure that would have been familiar to 18th-century bathers. Prices range from the £70 'Entrée' two-hour spa package to the £250 'Ultimate Thermae' full-day session, which includes a pedicure and a 'Luxury Caviar Facial'. This is accessible luxury, then, whose marketing plays less on exclusivity and more on the benefits of taking time out from the rigours of daily life. 'Bathe in the warm, natural, mineral-rich waters and choose from a range of spa treatments designed to ease the body and soothe the mind,' coos its website (www.themaebathspa.com).

The potential health benefits of visiting a spa are merely flimsy justifications. The 21st century encourages us to think that successful living is borne of striving and long hours. Padding around a spa in the cocoon of a towelling robe is the opposite of that existence. Like all of the most appealing luxuries, it feels faintly illicit. As the marketers of spas have intuited, we need to be reassured that it is doing us good, too.

SPAS: THE FINAL FRONTIER

Naturally, there are spas that push the luxurious elements of the experience to their outer limits. One of these is the Banyan Tree Al Areen Spa and Resort in Bahrain. It is part of a Singapore-based group and its positioning combines Arabian exoticism with 'the ancient wellness philosophies of the Far East'. It is also the Middle East's largest spa, at 10,000 square metres, and includes secluded villas with individual pools, an extensive hydrotherapy garden, spacious treatment pavilions, saunas and even an igloo – which in the middle of the desert is quite something. Alongside international expatriates, it attracts a large number of Saudi Arabian guests who zip across the causeway.

The Independent newspaper described it as 'the most luxurious and expensive hideaway in the Middle East' ('Top 10 pamper palaces', 11 February 2007). A three-night stay in a Royal Deluxe Villa, with a 120-minute hydrotherapy treatment, could cost around US$1,500 depending on the season. Add treatments and watch the price rack up.

The spa's director, Hylton Lipkin, is a great advocate of the Asian approach to spa treatments. 'It's very different from the European interpretation, which tends to have a slightly clinical side to it: lots of people in white coats. The Asian experience is far more sensual, with aromatherapy candles burning and a strong sense that you have left the real world behind.'

Banyan Tree opened its first establishment in Phuket, Thailand, in 1994, describing it as 'the first luxury oriental spa in Asia'. Reintroducing 'ancient health and beauty practices which have been passed down from generation to generation', the chain focuses on 'spiritual, mental and physical harmony' (www.banyantreespa.com). For many spas, this emphasis on spiritual renewal is a further method of convincing guests that they are indulging in something more profound than pure physical pleasure. They are making progress, improving themselves in some undefined way.

Behind the Banyan Tree Group is an entrepreneur named Ho Kwon Ping – affectionately called KP Ho by the Asian press – and his wife Claire Chiang. KP initially worked as a financial journalist, including a stint as the economics editor of the *Far Eastern Economic Review*, before joining his family's modest conglomerate, the Wah Chang Group, in 1981. He entered the resort business almost by accident, when he and his wife came across an abandoned strip of land by Bang Tao Bay in Thailand in the 1980s. It was a disused tin mine and on the face of it highly unattractive. 'Struck by the tranquillity of the area, the young couple decided to tackle the challenge of healing the scarred, post-apocalyptic landscape and replacing it with a lush resort paradise' ('What makes Banyan Tree grow', *Hotels Magazine*, 1 September 2007).

Now Banyan Tree has 25 resorts and hotels, 68 spas, 65 retail galleries selling local crafts and two golf courses. It has successfully expanded into China, taking advantage of the growing interest in spa culture there. KP is frequently quoted as saying that he does not want the group to resemble a spider's web of resorts and hotels, but rather a 'necklace' of luxurious properties strung around the globe.

'It's definitely a premium experience,' confirms Lipkin, referring to the Bahrain property. 'You only have to take a look at the design of our treatment pavilions to see that. There are 12 of them, and when you're inside one you feel as though you're in an oriental palace.'

Not in a conventional sense, though: when KP Ho launched the Phuket resort, he imagined something more along the lines of a boutique hotel than The Ritz. According to an article on the website Hospitality Net (www.hospitalitynet.org), he saw it as 'a sanctuary for the senses' aimed at city dwellers. 'I have heard there are resorts that furnish their suites with luxury brands, like Christofle crystal glasses... You will not find that kind of luxury in Banyan Tree Phuket, or any of our other resorts. What we do is try to create a magical, intimate setting for guests to play out their romances. We aim for an emotional response. That's how we build brand loyalty. One couple has been coming here every year since it opened' ('Paradise regained', 25 April 2005).

Along with rejuvenating 'rain showers', various massage therapies are on offer, with treatments originating from Sweden, Hawaii, Bali and elsewhere. Lipkin says that therapists at Banyan Tree spas must undergo at least 300 hours of training at a central Banyan Tree Spa Academy, which is accredited by Thailand's education and public health ministries. 'The therapists are trained not to give one-size-fits-all massages, but to follow their instincts and adapt to the body of the person lying before them, ironing out specific tensions and problems,' he says. As usual in the luxury world, it all comes down to personal service.

And to being totally over-the-top: the hydrothermal garden mentioned above is a series of therapy stations far too vast to be visited in a single session. It includes various shower experiences – such as the 'warm rain mist corridor' and the 'monsoon shower' – a salt scrub, a detoxifying steam room and the igloo. Rubbing ice on the body is said to combat cellulite. Even more amusing is the 'bucket drench shower' – 'an age-old unique hydrotherapy as one is drenched from head to toe with a massive amount of water falling from a bucket'. Primitive tech meets Hollywood jungle fantasy: you too can be Ava Gardner in *Mogambo*. Moving on, the 'brine cavern', a combination of steam and salt, is recommended for 'respiratory disorders'. This suggests that the health concerns of the wealthy have changed little since Roman times.

As I've illustrated with that last sentence, it is tempting to make fun of the rich. This relatively harmless exercise can turn toxic in a luxury resort situation, where there is often a large disparity in income between the workers and the consumers. The result is that the employees can end up resenting the guests. KP Ho is aware of this danger and tries to ensure an emotional connection between the staff and consumers, reminding employees that the situation is mutually beneficial. Staffers are also given a chance to experience some of the resort's facilities, putting them in the place of the customer.

Hylton Lipkin certainly has no concerns about the attitude of his staff. 'They are people who have a flair for hospitality. They see this as more than a job – they actually want to provide the customer with an experience to remember. And at a resort like this, it's important that the guests feel spoiled.'

REHAB

One of the many odd facets of celebrity is the need on the part of the famous to atone for their excesses from time to time by getting themselves to the contemporary equivalent of a nunnery. Reading the newspapers, it can sometimes seem as if fame, a sense of entitlement and access to unlimited funds lead to addiction as inevitably as night follows day. In order to regain their equilibrium and show a measure of humility, the men and women concerned occasionally pull out of the fast lane to check themselves into an establishment that will help them 'recover' from their 'exhaustion'. This pattern has created a mythology around expensive rehabilitation clinics.

Perhaps the most famous of all such clinics is the Betty Ford Center, founded in 1982 by the former First Lady when she had recovered from addictions to alcohol and painkillers. Ford underwent her own treatment for chemical dependency at the US Naval Hospital in Long Beach, but emerged determined to set up a treatment centre for others. A friend, Ambassador Leonard Firestone, supported the project and together they founded the non-profit Betty Ford Center in Rancho Mirage, California. Its treatment is based on the 12-step programme devised by Alcoholics Anonymous. Although it is a perfectly serious and worthy establishment – and one of the cheaper of its type – the centre owes its prominent image to celebrity guests. Liza Minnelli, Elizabeth Taylor and Kelsey Grammer are among those who've talked openly about their stays.

As early as 1987, *The New York Times* ran a report attempting to demystify the centre. 'This sheltered desert oasis in Rancho Mirage, set on 14 manicured acres and framed by purple mountains, has a year-round occupancy rate of 100 per cent. But for its 80 carefully screened guests, there is no entertainment to speak of and the daily routine can be long and gruelling.' Pointing out that celebrities made up 'less than 1 per cent' of the centre's guests, the article painted a picture of bland single-storey beige buildings, Spartan shared rooms, a tough regimen of chores and strict rules. These days it is considered somewhat old-fashioned and far from glossy ('A day in the life of The Betty Ford Center', 27 February 1987).

The British equivalent of The Betty Ford Center in terms of notoriety is The Priory, which features almost as often as Yves Saint Laurent handbags in the lives of certain supermodels. In fact the Priory Group operates more than 50 hospitals, schools and care homes throughout the United Kingdom, but it is best known for The Priory Hospital in Roehampton, London's oldest independent psychiatric hospital, which was established in 1872. It treats a variety of conditions including addictions and eating disorders. Its facilities include a fully equipped gym with trained fitness instructor, tai-chi, yoga, aerobic classes, swimming, aromatherapy and shiatsu massage. Patients stay in their own en-suite rooms with television and are encouraged to have their meals in the main dining room. Fees are assessed individually, but are said to be in excess of £2,500 per week.

With all the free publicity it receives, one would not have thought that The Priory needed to advertise. And yet that is precisely what it did in 2003, when it offered free assessments for people with alcohol and drug problems. The Priory said the goal of the campaign was not to turn callers into clients, but to 'raise awareness of the huge problem of alcohol and drug addiction in society'. One of the print ads featured a picture of a glass of whisky next to another of a telephone, and the line 'It's a tough call'. Another showed a blurred list of drunken comments. The copy read: 'If this is all you can remember about last night, call The Priory' ('Ad drive launched by celeb clinic', BBC News website, 2 October 2003).

The public learned a little more about The Priory Group when it was acquired by Dutch bank ABN AMRO in 2005 for £300 million. Reports at the time stated that the company earned £120 million a year from its various mental health, rehabilitation and special education services.

Like the Betty Ford Center, The Priory lacks glamour once you've peeked behind the headlines, and does not feel like a luxury brand. Where, then, are the truly upmarket rehab clinics? How about Promises Treatment Center in Malibu, California? Variously described as 'the king of celebrity rehab' and 'the first place on the speed dial' of actors who want to dry out, it features gourmet meals, masseuses, private rooms with fireplaces and sweeping beach views, according to an Associated Press feature ('Britney's rehab is the choice of many stars', MSNBC.com, 6 March 2007). 'It sounds like a high-end resort and it is – for the rich and famous looking to kick an addiction,' the article continues.

A 30-day stay is said to cost more than US $40,000. Founder and director Richard Rogg, who launched the facility in 1989, deliberately designed it to appeal to guests who usually enjoyed a five-star lifestyle. 'Flying in on your jet plane, or somebody coming from a 20,000-square-foot house into our programme, you know this is a step of humility for them... It gives them the treatment and it gives them the environment where they feel safe and comfortable' ('Promises: the Ritz of rehab', ABCNews.com, 25 February 2007). Although based on the 12-step programme, it created a gentler approach known as 'Malibu-style' treatment and spawned a string of lookalike centres down the coast. Some of these facilities are even more relaxed, allowing celebrities to leave the grounds in order to work, shop or socialize while supposedly undergoing treatment.

Levels of scepticism about such rehab programmes are high. An investigation by *The New York Times* uncovered very little evidence that they work:

> The quiet truth in the upper-crust rehabilitation industry is that $49,000 a month may buy lots of things – including views of the Pacific, massage therapy and blue-ribbon chefs. But whether it buys sobriety is very uncertain. Reliable statistics about drug rehabilitation as a whole are hard to come by, and are near impossible to isolate for the luxury-level rehab programmes that attract so much attention in the news media...
> And experts in the field seem to agree that the success rate for rehab programmes, most of which are based on the 12-step therapy created by Alcoholics Anonymous, hovers somewhere between 30 per cent at best, and below 10 per cent at worst.

Even Rogg admitted that it was difficult to measure success rates, other than keeping in touch with alumni ('Stars check in, stars check out', 17 June 2007).

A rival Malibu operation, Passages – which costs more than US $67,000 a month, according to *The New York Times* – rejects the 12-step procedure in favour of an intensive one-on-one treatment. Guests 'do not generally leave the property' says founder Chris Prentiss – a former real estate developer – who claims an 84.4 per cent success rate based on interviews with more than 1,000 alumni. *The Independent* called the property 'a beachside resort whose faux-classical Doric columns positively drip with bougainvillea'. It added: 'Facilities include a library... a media room with flat-screen TVs, a meditative koi pond, massage room, hypnotherapy, acupuncture, "metaphysical classes"... and a restaurant catering to each individual's dietary whim' ('The celebrity guide to detox: pass out, check in, and dry out', 6 January 2007).

Living in a luxury world means that even the nastier things in life – addiction, stress and trauma – take place against a paradisiacal backdrop.

18

The knowledge economy

'They wanted the Louvre, the Guggenheim and the Sorbonne like ladies want handbags from Christian Dior.'

When it comes to the Tate Modern art museum in London, I am an iron filing. Every time I get within walking distance of the building, I am helplessly drawn towards it. Even if I only have time to pop in to the former power station's vast Turbine Hall, I know that something amazing awaits me there: over the years I've been captivated by Louise Bourgeois' giant metallic spider, Olafur Eliasson's blazing sun (part of 'The Weather Project'), a giant crack in the floor made by the Brazilian sculptor Doris Salcedo (called 'Shibboleth', it symbolized racial division) and a post-apocalyptic hospital – complete with metal-framed military bunks and the sound of monotonously drumming rain – installed by Dominique Gonzalez-Foerster. I could go on – and I will continue going, again and again.

Although these artworks are serious in their intent, the Tate knows that they are also publicity-grabbing blockbusters. Nobody makes any secret any more of the fact that museums are brands with marketing strategies. Indeed, there are many books about the subject. Here's an extract from *Museum Marketing: Competing in the global marketplace* (2007): 'It would be nice if museums did not have to worry about marketing. It would be nice if the money just rolled in by itself. Sadly, new economic realities mean cash-strapped museums cannot afford to be complacent about attracting visitors through the doors to exhibitions. To stay afloat, they need to attract new audiences as well as keep established ones. Marketing is no longer an option: it's a survival tool rather than a dirty word.'

Museums were 'outed' as brands in 1988, when Saatchi & Saatchi caused raised eyebrows with its campaign for London's Victoria and Albert Museum. The copy read: 'An ace caff with a rather nice museum attached'. More than 15 years later, nobody was shocked when the Museum of Modern Art in New York emphasized its upmarket dining facilities as part of its reopening campaign.

You may be protesting at this point that museums are not luxury brands. But they are competing for a luxury in the lives of many people: leisure time. More specifically, they are competing for the tiny window of time that many adults set aside for self-improvement – for the acquisition of knowledge. One of the reasons that I compulsively visit the Tate Modern whenever I am in London is that I want to take away something more valuable than a high-end fashion item or the memory of an expensive meal.

The book mentioned earlier refers to 'constructive chilling', an activity that 'allows visitors to do something worthwhile and relax at the same time'. Surveys of visitors to museums have shown that looking at permanent collections or the latest exhibitions forms only part of a wide range of activities that they expect to enjoy – also high on their lists are 'meeting friends', 'visiting the cafe/restaurant' and 'browsing or making a purchase in the museum shop'.

The Tate has proved particularly adept at branding. Building on the values of accessibility and education established by the original Tate Gallery on London's Millbank – founded by the sugar magnate Sir Henry Tate in 1897 – it has expanded into a 'family' of four galleries: Tate Britain (the renamed original gallery), Tate Modern, Tate Liverpool and Tate St Ives (in Cornwall).

Tate Modern is by far the most spectacular. It was largely made possible by Sir Nicholas Serota, director of the Tate Gallery, who put forward a two-pronged argument for the establishment of the new site: the original gallery was too small to display the museum's permanent collection, and London lacked a significant modern art gallery to compete with New York's MoMA and the Centre Georges Pompidou in Paris. The latter criticism highlights another important fact about museums: not only are they brands in their own right, but they also contribute to the brand reputations of cities. The arrival of the Guggenheim Museum in Bilbao, for instance, has transformed the identity of that formerly rather rusty port in northern Spain.

The Guggenheim is another outrageously successful museum brand. Rather like Tate Modern, the original Frank Lloyd Wright building in Manhattan (1939) and the Bilbao site designed by Frank Gehry (1997) confirm the theory that people visit museums not only for the artworks within them, but also for their architectural grandeur and their prominence as monuments. They are on the list of 'sights'. Other museums associated with the Guggenheim brand are the Peggy Guggenheim Collection in Venice, the Deutsche Guggenheim Museum in Berlin and the Guggenheim Las Vegas (designed by Rem Koolhaas).

Thomas Krens, director of the Solomon R Guggenheim Foundation, has occasionally been criticized for his global branding initiatives. But he argues that museums have a right – even a mission – to engage with a globalized society. 'It's a discourse on an international scale. In a contemporary society, for contemporary art, with everything becoming ever more interconnected, I think it's an essential aspect of how museums have to confront the world.'

The foundation's latest project is the Guggenheim Abu Dhabi, on the Saadiyat Island complex. Further study of this extremely interesting island leads us right to the heart of the knowledge economy. The Guggenheim is only one of several cultural brands that have been lured to the ambitious development project. Led by its crown prince, Sheik Mohammed bin Zayad al-Nahyan, Abu Dhabi wants to position itself as the cultural capital of the Middle East. The US $27 billion Saayadit Island will include 29 luxury hotels, space for a biennial arts festival and a clutch of illustrious museums and educational institutions, designed by architects like Frank Gehry, Zaha Hadid, Tadao Ando and Jean Nouvel. 'We're bringing together the top architects of the past 100 years,' Mubarak al-Mahairi, director of the Abu Dhabi Tourism Authority, told *Newsweek.com* ('Buying Culture', August 2007).

One of the cornerstones of the project is an outpost of a revered museum brand: the Louvre. There was an outcry in France when the news emerged in 2007 that the Louvre had leased its name to Abu Dhabi for 30 years in return for €400 million, along with further payments for loans of art and consultancy. 'This, according to critics, amounts to using France's artistic heritage for basely commercial ends. "Our museums are not for sale", proclaims an online petition signed by 4,700 people – including many curators, art historians, and archaeologists' ('Gulf Louvre deal riles French art world', news.bbc.co.uk, 6 March 2007).

Nevertheless, work went ahead on the dome-shaped building, designed by French architect Jean Nouvel and scheduled to open in 2012. But the Louvre is not the only slice of French patrimony that will be available on the island – there will be a branch of the Sorbonne, too. According to the *Newsweek* piece cited earlier, the university's president Jean-Robert Pitte initially had misgivings about the arrangement. He suspected that 'they wanted the Louvre, the Guggenheim and the Sorbonne like their ladies want handbags from Christian Dior.' Finally, however, he became convinced of the cultural significance of the project. At the inauguration in 2006, he told students that they were writing 'an historic page' in the relationship between occident and orient. The new university would become a beacon of 'liberty of thought' (*'Les cheikhs du Golfe s'offre la Sorbonne'*, Lefigaro.fr, October 2006).

It can't hurt that students at the Abu Dhabi faculty pay over €6,000 per term to attend, many times more than their French equivalents.

EDUCATION BRANDS

Other universities have opened branches in the Middle East, too. New York University is set to join the Sorbonne on Saadiyat Island. In Qatar's Education City complex there are outposts of Cornell's medical school, the Virginia Commonwealth University's art and design programme, Georgetown's foreign service school and Northwestern University's journalism programme ('In oil-rich Middle East, shades of the Ivy League', *The New York Times*, 11 February 2008). Elsewhere, Harvard offers a summer programme in Beijing, also known as the Harvard-Beijing Academy.

Although they are somewhat less vocal about it than museums, universities and other educational establishments accept that they, too, are brands. And some of them are premium brands. Names like Harrow, Eton, Oxford, Cambridge, Yale and of course Harvard spring to mind.

'Harvard', began an article in *USA Today* in 2005. 'Just the name exudes superiority, if not smugness. From its "Veritas" coat of arms to the Georgian-era brick edifices that dot its campus, everything about this storied institution, founded in 1686, smacks of that most un-American trait, elitism.' The piece goes on to quote Stanley Katz, director of the rival Princeton University's Center for Arts and Cultural Policy studies. 'There isn't any doubt that brand matters and Harvard is the prestige brand,' he says. 'It's the Gucci of higher education, the most selective place' ('Does Harvard "brand" matter any more?' 6 June 2005).

Harvard's history, its alarming fees – more than US $48,000 a year for tuition, room and board – and its influential 'old boy network' make it the school of choice for America's elite. In addition, its notoriously exclusive admissions policy, which includes a strong focus on the 'personality and character' of each candidate, ensures that its lofty image is maintained. The writer Malcolm Gladwell takes a wry look at the Ivy League admissions system in his classic *New Yorker* article 'Getting in' (10 October 2005). He suggests that these universities, with their insistence on admitting potential 'winners' and 'leaders', rather than the merely academically gifted, are behaving like modelling agencies. 'You don't become beautiful by signing up with an agency. You get signed up by an agency because you're beautiful.' He concludes that the schools' admissions directors are in 'the luxury brand management business'. Certainly, Harvard is acutely aware of its brand identity. In an article for brandchannel.com, Barry Silverstein describes the university as 'a branding empire'. He explains: 'The school's name appears on such separate entities as *Harvard Business Review*, an internationally known magazine, *Harvard Health Letter*, one of six eponymous health newsletters, Harvard Business School Press, a major publisher of business books, Harvard Planners, Harvard Business Organizers, and Harvard University Global System and Software. And then there is the Harvard-emblazoned merchandise that is licensed for sale in every corner of the globe.' He adds that the Harvard Trademark Program is 'a model of sophistication', with six staff members managing licensing agreements and monitoring the use of the Harvard name ('Brands in a league of their own', 27 October 2008).

The Ivy League itself is an evocative umbrella brand embodying the values of tradition and excellence. The members of the league are Brown, Columbia, Cornell, Dartford, Penn, Princeton and Yale. Although there is some debate about the origin of the name, most accounts suggest that a sports writer coined the term in the 1930s, when the schools competed against one another during the football season. The league later became an official athletic conference, but the phrase took on a broader meaning. The members accept that the collective title gives them even greater clout and they often refer to it in their marketing initiatives.

Silverstein writes: '[T]he term connotes an exceptional education, prestige, and business connections that virtually guarantee career success. While other colleges and universities may be of equal or even better quality, they can never achieve the perceived status of the Ivy League. To demonstrate the point, Stanford University and Massachusetts Institute of Technology (MIT), two outstanding universities in their own right, are sometimes referred to as the "Ivy Plus" schools.'

Oxford and Cambridge are the clear equivalents of the Ivy League schools in the United Kingdom. The University of Oxford even has a widely recognized 'brand colour' – Oxford Blue (Pantone® 282). On a section of its website aimed at staff, the university offers an extensive 'branding toolkit' (www.ox.ac.uk). An introduction reads: 'There is nothing new about the cultural potency of visual images, but their public significance in communicating something of the purpose and meaning of institutions and of organizations has probably never been greater... The University of Oxford has long been responsive to these realities and has devoted time and attention... to trying to ensure that its own visual branding reflects the institution appropriately and has resonance in the increasingly sophisticated and competitive global arena in which it is viewed.'

This preamble goes on to suggest that the university's brand identity – which is legally protected – 'should seek to combine a powerful sense of both past and future: we are a forward-looking university of world repute with a rich history.' Advice follows on how the university's identity should be reflected in the use of the brand colour and official typeface (Foundry Sterling) on brochures and other printed items, as well as on wallets, folders and business cards and even PowerPoint presentations.

Oxford and Cambridge have a sticky branding problem in that they are agglomerations of independently run colleges: 38 at Oxford and 31 at Cambridge. This is an accident of the history, as the venerable universities slowly swallowed up independent academic institutions within their respective cities. The result is that students are more likely to identify with their college (be it Exeter, Jesus, Magdalene or Trinity) than with the university as a whole. This situation makes it even more understandable that Oxford and Cambridge should want to devote time and energy to promoting the 'parent' brand on a global scale.

Another contributor to brandchannel.com, Patricia Tan, highlighted the above situation a few years ago. She also drew a useful parallel between educational and more conventional brands:

> As in most industries, universities offer very similar 'products' at first glance. But the best universities define a world of difference behind the BA, MBA, MEng, or PhD… The students from the top universities will tell you that the degree is merely an excuse for the overall experience, in the same way 'I need new shoes' really means 'I want those Nikes.' No one remembers the mathematics class, or even that groundbreaking seminar on the Middle East. They will remember the annual football game, the 'Full Moon on the Quad' tradition, the fountain-hopping, and the breakfasts with the President' ('Branding lessons at the world's top universities', 3 September 2001).

In other words, as with other luxury brands, the 'brand experience' is often the real attraction. On a smaller scale, I've personally witnessed the impact of prestige and brand experience on an educational establishment. For the last couple of years I've taught an advertising history class at Parsons Paris School of Art and Design, which is an offshoot of the far larger Parsons The New School for Design in New York. While the Paris school is located in a rambling building in the placid 15th arrondissement, it attracts bright students from all around the world. When I quiz them on their (or their parents') motives for choosing the school, two factors come to the fore: the power of the Parsons brand (the school in New York, after all, counts Donna Karan, Marc Jacobs, Tom Ford and Steven Meisel among its alumni) and the appeal of Paris.

These elements combine to attract a very particular type of student. When one of my friends – a strategic planner at an advertising agency – accepted an invitation to give a guest lecture, her first comment after the class had emptied out was: 'Did you see those heels and handbags? You have the most glamorous bunch of students I've ever seen.'

19

The gift of time

'Successful people have somebody to organize their lives.'

'Service is the future of luxury,' says Emmanuel Isaia, personal shopper and author of the blog Luxemode. When your luggage is stranded back at JFK and you need an ensemble for tonight's cocktail party in Paris, Emmanuel will fix you up. But there's a lot more to him that that. He can also tell you about the hottest new restaurants, the trendiest art galleries and the singer you should be talking knowledgeably about. A blend of concierge and style counsellor, Emmanuel says that his real selling point – the thing that clinches the deal – is that he helps his devoted clients save one of the most precious commodities of all: time.

The length of days is shrinking, don't you think? There are theories about this: one of them suggests that, as we grow older, a year represents a much smaller fraction of our overall lifespan. And so it appears to pass more quickly. Thus, when we were kids, a day seemed long and full of possibilities. As an adult, it passes in the blink of an eye. If we want to get anything done, the only option seems to be to load up on caffeine and postpone sleep for as long as possible.

Stressful urban lifestyles have led to sleep disorders. And not just for the overworked: financial worries, unemployment – or fear of it – and vague 21st-century anxieties about terrorist attacks, pandemic viruses and extreme climate change are turning us into sleep-deprived zombies. The National Institute of Health in the United States recommends seven to eight hours of sleep a night for adults, but the average achieved by most of us is a measly 6.1.

A couple of years ago, an entrepreneur named Arshad Chowdhury realized that there might be a business opportunity in this phenomenon. He created MetroNaps, a company that makes 'snooze pods'. These white, ovoid, futuristic-looking capsules were installed in the Empire State building and at a number of airports, where passers-by paid around US$14 to score 20 minutes of refreshing sleep. The 'energy napping' concept took off and the business rapidly expanded to the United Kingdom and Australia. As well as leasing the pods to businesses, MetroNaps provides 'fatigue management' advice.

It has been suggested that there is a 'sleep economy': 'a burgeoning US$20 billion business of aromatherapy pillows, high-tech beds, face masks, biorhythmic alarm clocks, and, yes, naps' ('US$20 billion for a good night's rest', *Business 2.0*, 15 March 2007). The same article goes on to inform us that the MetroNaps service is an affordable luxury. 'Toward the high end, there's the Gravity Zero, a five-figure bed made by Israeli firm Hollandia International. The company hired Philadelphia consultant Kanter International this year to market the Honda Civic-priced beds in the United States. With fully adjustable positioning, a microprocessor, aloe vera fibre, body massage, and even stereo speakers, the beds retail for US $10,000 to US $20,000.'

All very nice if you can afford to take time out and lie down. But aren't there ways of ensuring that we squeeze more out of our day, so we can get some shuteye at the end of it?

YOUR WISH IS THEIR COMMAND

A butler must be the ultimate luxury: somebody to lay out your clothes, fetch your newspaper, comment wryly on current matters and generally organize your life while you revel in Woosterish incompetence. On the other hand, the concept of butlers has stood the test of time rather less well than the novels of PG Wodehouse, in which Bertie Wooster and his unflappable manservant Jeeves appear. Far more modish are personal concierge services. These ensure that polite, efficient, well-informed men and women are at your beck and call at the end of a telephone line, 24/7.

The trend began in the 1990s, around the same time that the internet, e-mail and mobile phones started eating large chunks of our personal time. But the technology that caused the problem also helped to enable the solution. Credit cards began providing concierge services for time-poor customers with large credit limits. American Express is closely associated with the phenomenon, having launched a concierge service for its Centurion and Platinum cardholders. The idea has since been adopted by other, more accessible credit cards like Visa's Signature and Mastercard's World Elite. These have far lower annual fees than the Amex products.

Soon, personal concierge services began cropping up in more unusual contexts. We've already discussed the emergence of concierges in department stores as an extension of personal shopping services. Vertu, the Nokia-owned maker of jewel-like, outrageously expensive mobile phones, also provides a concierge service to its customers. This is accessible via a dedicated button on the side of the phone – a perfect example of marketing by design.

And of course there are stand-alone concierge services launched by entrepreneurs. US-based VIPdesk started out as Capitol Concierge in 1987, when founder and CEO Mary Naylor began installing corporate concierge services in offices in Washington, DC to organize the lives of harassed workers. Building on the success of the concept, Naylor created VIPdesk in 1997 as a virtual concierge service using a network of 'home office'-based assistants. This trend, known as 'home-shoring', is an alternative to overseas call centres. Among its first clients were MasterCard and Citibank.

Another US success story is Circles, started in 1987 by Janet Kraus and Kathy Sherbrooke. Today it bills itself as 'a concierge, events and experiences company'. 'Besides garden-variety perks like Super Bowl or World Series tickets, Circles can arrange for celebrities to show up at your cocktail party, get you a flight in a jet fighter or even land you a bit part on a TV show' ('My concierge will call your concierge', *The New York Times*, 21 February 2006). It also provides concierge services to companies that want to make their employees' lives easier – or at least enable them to work more efficiently. But it means that instead of marketing its services to individuals, Circles now has a network of client companies that are paying its fees and promoting its services to customers and employees.

In order to retain a sense of exclusivity and avoid being swamped by callers, concierge services tend to rely on word of mouth and press coverage rather than advertising. Indeed, some are accessible by invitation only. One of the most famous is Quintessentially, the UK-based 'private members' club and 24-hour concierge service'. One of its founders was 'movie-star handsome Ben Elliot, whose aunt just happens to be Camilla Parker-Bowles' ('Beyond the black card', *Forbes*, 26 February 2003). Elliot told *Forbes*: 'Yes, we can charter yachts and jets, but we can also find you the best tea in town for 10 bucks. We do not try to offer the most expensive, but the very best.'

Although it's not very time-consuming to reserve a place for dinner, good concierge services have the connections and clout that encourages 'fully booked' restaurants to conjure tables out of the ether. In order to find out how some of the world's most demanding customers use concierge services, I spoke with Anna Isaeva, director of travel services at Primeconcept in Russia. This invitation-only lifestyle club charges an annual membership fee of US $5,000, which includes a credit card and a special mobile phone tariff. Members receive a magazine called *Prime Traveller*, which is packed with ads for Bentley, Aston Martin, Cartier and dozens of other luxury brands.

Primeconcept describes its 500 or so clients as 'the Russian business, political and cultural elite'. Getting them a table for dinner is the least of its problems. 'One guy wanted a pink elephant for his birthday,' Isaeva recalls, with a chuckle. 'We had to borrow one from the zoo and paint it.' Another client was organizing a party in Dubai when he discovered that the singer had left a vital playback CD in Moscow, so Primeconcept arranged to courier it to him within 10 hours. And when yet another client wanted to send flowers to his girlfriend – a model who happened to live in Irkutsk in Siberia – he also required a photograph of her expression when she received them.

But Isaeva points out that it's just as tricky to find a last-minute hotel room in Courchevel at peak season or one in Paris during fashion week. The travel department has a full-time staff of 12 people who handle everything from tickets to visas and accommodation. 'One of the reasons for using a service like ours is that we know all the best rooms in all the best hotels.' The favoured travel destinations remain timeless: Dubai for the shopping, Courchevel or St Mortiz for the skiing and the Côte d'Azur for the good life.

Hasn't the financial crisis left Russia's rich a little chastened? 'They continue to spend, but there's a trend towards a more "modest" Russian lifestyle,' says Isaeva. 'The image of the Russian with loud, flashy and obviously expensive items is becoming a cliché.'

One of the benefits being touted by lifestyle clubs is that, although they charge a fee at the outset, they might actually end up saving you money: the assistants can often negotiate upgrades and preferential rates. And the general trend of the concierge market is downwards, as a wider range of brands experiment with add-ons to please their customers. Hence the theory that – like many luxuries – concierge services are for those who aspire to status rather than those who've made it. One marketing consultant told *The Times*: 'Most successful business people already have people to organize their social lives... They don't need help getting tickets for this and that or getting a table at a restaurant' ('Dinner for six at Claridge's tonight? Certainly', 14 February 2006).

For the truly elite, then, it's back to the butler.

20

Sustainable luxury

'It's about taking the time to do something well, using excellent ingredients – and then savouring the results.'

Given the increasing keenness of brands to convince us that they are helping to save the planet rather than contributing to its ruin, it was inevitable that a certain segment of the luxury industry would get in on the act. As mass luxury brands are also fashion brands – with an obligation to constantly update their offering – they are doomed to scurry after trends. I couldn't help smiling when Louis Vuitton announced that it was backing a foundation dedicated to the preservation of Easter Island. Louis Vuitton had read the writing on the wall, as well as on the glyphic stone tablets. Consumer attitudes had changed, and corporate ones with them. In the summer of 2008 I was surprised to see an article headlined 'Farewell to consumerism' in *Campaign* magazine: the advertising industry heralding the end of the consumer society. The article centred on a quote from Sir Martin Sorrell, CEO of the giant marketing communications group WPP, which owns advertising agencies JWT and Ogilvy & Mather.

'All of our instincts as clients, agencies and media owners are to encourage people to consume more – super-consumption,' he said. This had given rise to consumer demand for bigger cars, more jet travel and bigger or multiple houses. 'Our view, counter to what you expect our industry to argue, is that conspicuous consumption is not productive, and should be discouraged.' Sorrell cast doubt on the flimsy efforts made by companies to slow global warming. 'It is increasingly common for companies to have targets to reduce their carbon footprint – but look closely, almost all of these are ex-growth... In other words, they will reduce the impact per unit of sales, or on the basis of like-for-like operations. Businesses that feel they know how to de-couple growth from increased climate impact are few indeed' (11 July 2008).

The equation is starkly simple: in order to make more money, companies must produce more. But are people still buying? The article spoke of a 'profound change' in consumer habits provoked by the 'perfect storm' of climate change, a resurgent sense of social responsibility and the democratizing force of the internet.

Paradoxically, luxury brands may have an advantage in this new consumer landscape. Beyond opportunistic one-off marketing ploys, they could – and do – argue that they offer an alternative to mass consumption. As we've established, in the 1990s many luxury companies transformed themselves into fashion brands in order to create more product lines and fuel demand for their goods. Now they must decouple from the fashion industry and insist that they offer products of rare and lasting quality.

This discourse was heavily apparent at a Sustainable Luxury conference organized by the *International Herald Tribune* in New Delhi in March 2009. François-Henri Pinault, chairman and chief executive of the luxury group PPR, said: 'Today, more than ever, people want a return to genuine values, such as timelessness, sincerity and exemplary standards... And these are all qualities which – as we have seen – are inherent in sustainable luxury.'

At the same conference, Jem Bendell, an environmentalist who has advised luxury brands on corporate responsibility, warned that 'luxury brands are promoting consumerism in countries at a time when we need to reduce consumption in order to avert a climate catastrophe.' But he offered them a potential get-out clause. 'The shirts on our backs each took a few thousand litres of water to create. If we cherished them more, we would use less water... The great thing about luxury brands is that the way consumers relate to them actually prefigures the way we need consumers to relate to all their products. To look after them, to repair them, to see them as becoming vintage not garbage.' In other words, he concluded: 'Luxury brands have the margin and the mandate to create the most environmentally responsible products.'

The brands got the message and changed their tunes accordingly. Expensive items were no longer delicious treats, but 'investments'. When luxury bag maker Smythson of Bond Street advertised its £775 Enid handbag, it described it as 'this season's investment accessory of choice'. Pam Danziger of Unity Marketing was quick to scoff at this new positioning. 'The idea that any of these consumer goods are going to grow in value is just ridiculous. They're like cars: the minute you take them out of the store, they lose half their value' ('Luxury as an investment?', Reuters, 6 May 2009).

Although there's clearly no such thing as a 'seasonal investment', there is something to be said for saving up your cash until you can afford the good stuff. I'm thinking of my great uncle, who had a small collection of highly polished and seemingly indestructible bespoke shoes. The secret is being able to spot when the quality claim is real, and when it's just advertising mystique.

The return to a more profound, thoughtful version of luxury has given rise to the phrase 'slow fashion'. Just as Italy's 'slow food' movement promotes honest cuisine over burgers, slow fashion requires products that are handcrafted to last – preferably by artisanal, family-run concerns. I came across one of them in Paris. Appropriately enough, it's called Slowear.

SLOW FASHION

Slowear is an unusual concept in lots of ways. For a start, it is an umbrella label embracing four different Italian brands: Incotex, which makes only trousers, Zanone, which specializes in knitwear, Montedoro, which makes rainwear and jackets, and Glanshirt, which as its name suggests makes only shirts. The brand has done very little marketing, but it attracted the attention of Tyler Brûlé, the founder of *Monocle* magazine, which has run articles about it. This has given Slowear something of a cult following. When the brand opened a new store – its second permanent location in the world after Milan – in rue Royale, Paris, I found myself at the launch party chatting to Massimo Gambaro, its marketing and communications director.

'The first thing you must understand is that Slowear is not really a brand in the conventional sense,' he told me. 'It's more like a curator, a selector of high-quality products. Slowear is a portfolio of brands that meet, debate and complement one another, so that when we put all the collections under one roof there is a coherence.'

He stresses that each brand is a specialist. 'They're the exact opposite of brands that over-extend. These companies do one thing and they do it extremely well. We were looking for a kind of perfection in each domain.'

The first brand in the portfolio was Incotex, which has its roots in a 1951 company founded by Carlo Campagno. Initially it made trousers and uniforms, but later it concentrated on trousers under the brand name Industrie Confezioni Tessili. In 1981, Carlo's sons Roberto and Marzio inherited Incotex. At the end of the 1990s, they decided to expand the business not by moving into other areas of fashion, but by acquiring brands that placed a similar emphasis on quality and performance. Montedoro joined the group in 2001, followed by Zanone in 2003 and Glanshirt the following year. They are considered Italian 'heritage' brands: Marcello Mastroianni and Federico Fellini are both said to have favoured Glanshirt's products. The Slowear umbrella brand was created in 2007, but the brands continue to operate as separate units.

Slowear is not really a fashion company. In fact it provides classic apparel. The look is timeless and unfussy: pristine button-down shirts in cotton or Oxford weave, V-neck pullovers, slim-cut trousers in cotton or wool, discreet windcheaters and raincoats that might have been made any time over the last 40 years. Gambaro calls it 'basic chic'. He adds: 'Quality is not necessarily something that makes you go "wow". It's all about the detail and the finishing. Sometimes you have to look closer in order to recognize it. Our target customer has a certain amount of knowledge and they can see what sets our clothes apart.'

I asked Gambaro if the company felt a kinship with the promoters of 'slow food', a concept that also derived from Italy. 'We don't have direct links, but there's definitely a common thread,' he said. 'It's about taking the time to do something well, using excellent ingredients – and then savouring the results.'

Slowear is a lifestyle, too. Its stores stock books, objects and furniture. Like the store fittings, the furniture leans towards 1950s Scandinavian: streamlined yet warm. And the brand's website incorporates a *Slowear Journal*, a magazine covering 'art, design and wellness'. 'It captures the tone of the brand by discussing the things we like,' says Gambaro. Visitors are invited to contribute articles, adding to the impression that Slowear consumers are part of a small yet savvy club. As the site itself explains, the journal 'is a way of forging connections and affinities, available to anyone who identifies with the values of excellence' (www. slowear.com).

Slowear's products are not cheap, Gambaro admits, but they do offer value for money. The smartest thing about the brand is that, by subtly implying that it is preserving a small part of Italy's textile heritage, it bucks the anti-consumerism trend by making you feel good about 'investing' in luxury.

SLOW LIVING

When you arrive at a Six Senses resort, the first thing they do is take away your shoes. These are placed in a bag and labelled with your name. The message is clear: you can relax now. The concept is sometimes referred to as 'barefoot luxury'. But Sonu Shivdasani – who founded Six Senses Resorts & Spas with his wife Eva – describes it another way. 'We call it Slow Life,' he says. As far as Shivdasani is concerned, the idea comprises a whole range of elements that go far beyond well-being. He has even devised an acronym to explain the proposition. Slow Life stands for Sustainable, Local, Organic, Wholesome, Learning, Inspiring, Fun Experiences. To stay at a Six Senses resort, he says, is to experience a different way of living.

Sonu and Eva opened their first resort in the Maldives in 1995. They had always loved travelling to the islands, but found the standard of accommodation to be generally low. 'It was three-star stuff – plastic chairs and white tiled floors,' says Shivdasani. Resort operators would lease land from the locals, give them a cut of the takings, and then abandon the properties when the profits failed to meet targets. That's how Sonu and Eva came across the site that would become their first venture. 'It had been closed for two years. Part of the problem was that it was only accessible by boat from Mali. We organized an air service, which immediately made it more accessible. Today's travellers want destinations that are at the same time remote and easy to reach.'

Combining their names, the pair named the resort Soneva Fushi. Beyond the Maldives, Six Senses now has resorts in Thailand, Vietnam, Oman, Fiji, Jordan and Spain. The slow living concept is the connecting theme. 'You have to bear in mind that the traditional norms of luxury were defined in the 19th and early 20th centuries. Time was less of an issue then. People travelled less often. Homes were larger. Now you have executives who are travelling 300 or 400 hours a year in stuffy aircraft. Time is important to them, as is space. So in our resorts we give you big spaces and plenty of fresh air. The bathrooms are bigger than some of their apartments. And you can shower under the stars.'

There's nothing primitive about the surroundings, however. The villas are kitted out with Bose sound systems and the resorts come equipped with skilled chefs and sommeliers, who can recommend European and local wines. 'Most of our guests enjoy a more local experience. They quickly discover that one of the many great aspects of this new form of luxury is the ability to eat a fresh salad that has been plucked that very morning from an organic garden.'

Foodstuffs are sourced locally and imported bottled water is banned: most of the resorts have their own desalination and bottling plants. (In an aside that is definitely not for the sceptical, Shivdasani describes how the water is bottled while classical music plays softly in the background. Before the bottling, minerals are added and the water is poured over crystals with healing properties.) Local materials are also used to construct the villas. And local craftsmanship often comes in handy. In Hua Hin, Thailand, local builders constructed the resort walls and a spa using traditional materials, including earth. The spa did not require air conditioning because the design creates a naturally cooling environment.

Green concerns are central to the Six Senses positioning. For example, it builds a carbon-offsetting scheme into the price of its vacations. The sun, the wind and the sea provide power. At Soneva Fushi, even the air conditioning comes courtesy of naturally cold seawater piped in from the ocean. 'Soneva Fushi is one of the most luxurious resorts in the world and it's zero carbon,' says Shivdasani proudly. His next goal is to 'decarbonize' all his resorts through 'oversupply of clean, renewable energy and carbon offsets of unavoidable emissions'. 'This means that rather than leaving a small footprint on the land that we develop, we will in fact be erasing the footprints and the damage caused by others.'

At the Soneva Kiri resort on the Thai island of Koh Kood, Six Senses commissioned the construction an 'eco-villa' as a showcase for its philosophy and a template for the future. Thai craftsmen built the entire structure. As the manufacture of concrete contributes to carbon emissions, none was used in the project. Instead, the foundations were made from sandstone boulders excavated at the site. A local boat builder handmade the dowels that secured the villa's post and beams, some of which were made from driftwood. Others were sourced from local plantations. The interior walls were made from adobe mud bricks. The 'green roof' is a garden, as if the little round building has sprouted hair. Recycled egg crates were used in the drainage layer of the roof, while soda water bottles were used as glass bricks for the shower. 'Non-toxic' adhesive and wood treatments were used throughout. Wireless technology has been banished. The building is 'therefore entirely suited to guests suffering from allergies or sensitive to electro-magnetic fields'.

It's interesting to note that developments regarded as luxuries not so long ago – mobile communications and the ability to keep in touch wirelessly – are now portrayed as intrusive and undesirable. Shivdasani would say that this is one of the differences between conventional luxury and the new 'intelligent luxury' of which Six Senses is a purveyor.

Shivdasani admits that he is partially motivated by business, as it seems certain that more travellers will demand 'eco-friendly' vacations. But he adds that he is genuinely concerned about the future of the planet. After all, he lives in the Maldives. 'Climate change becomes personal when your home may be underwater in a few years' time.'

Conclusion: The rehabilitation of luxury

'Cultivated people appreciate luxury.'

Inevitably, the sports car caught my eye. Flame orange, built of carbon fibre, the Tesla Roadster costs €84,000 and can accelerate from 0–100 km/h in 3.9 seconds. It is powered entirely by electricity. As I've already mentioned, I don't own a car right now. But the Tesla had such boyish charm that it made my palms itch.

It was only one of the items on show at the 1.618 Sustainable Luxury Fair, held at the Palais de Tokyo contemporary art space in Paris. The event was backed by the WFF (the World Wide Fund for Nature) and the French Ministry of Culture. The figures in the name are the so-called Golden Number, representing perfect balance in nature. The three-day fair showcased high-end yet eco-friendly products from the worlds of hospitality, design, furniture, automotive, jewellery, technology and cosmetics. When you walked in, the air was filled with busy rainforest sounds, an ambient sigh of music and a distant pattering of water; projections of jungle foliage and waterfalls chased across the walls. Strolling around, I lingered by the sleek Alter catamaran in polished mahogany – 'a material with an unlimited lifespan' – and a line of jewellery called JEL (Jewellery Ethical Luxury), made from gold that is either recycled or mined using traditional techniques. There was even a travel organization called Ecoluxury.

The word 'luxury' has so many potential meanings – and can be adapted to such a wide variety of circumstances – that it flexes easily with the times. Right now, conspicuous consumption is out of fashion. The logo-driven excess of the past decade is being looked upon – at least in the Western world – with distaste. And so luxury is showing us a gentler, more discreet face. Quality has become a watchword again. Authenticity is all the rage. A rehabilitation process has begun.

How will this affect the evolution of luxury? By combining some of the strands running through this book with advice from various experts, I've detected five trends that may have a bearing on the luxury sector over the next few years.

TREASURING

'Emilie is more interested in embroidery than marketing,' wrote a friend of mine on her Facebook status update recently. When I remarked on this a few days later, she told me that she was not entirely joking. Emilie is a nightmare to go shopping with: she scrutinizes every item of clothing like a forensic scientist, tugging at it to see what gives. Now she refuses to buy expensive pieces unless they show some form of creativity beyond the advertising campaigns that have made them 'desirable' – hence her enthusiasm for embroidery. 'I want to buy things that I will treasure.'

'Treasuring' is in vogue. There is a renewed appreciation of the hand-made. Craft is respected. At the Milan Design Fair in 2009, Italian brand Fendi teamed up with the organizers of the Design Miami exhibitions and invited designers to create what they called 'Craft Punk'. Participants were invited to work 'low-tech design magic' on discarded materials from Fendi's production process: leather, fabrics, plastic decorative elements and metal. Visitors could watch the live creation of sculptures and installations – such as animal figures made from scrap leather and wire. Embroidery, collage and old-fashioned printing techniques were also on show. As the design blog Unbeige commented, that's what you get when 'you mix design, innovation [and] a shaky global economy' ('Design Miami teams with Fendi for Craft Punk in Milan', 14 April 2009).

Only in that climate, too, would we have seen the creation of the Authentic Luxury Association, set up by individuals from the worlds of environmental concern, luxury branding and design. 'Luxury must be something meaningful and lasting. It is our conviction that superior social and environmental performance is becoming a defining aspect of elite design, quality and consumer experience. It is our conviction that luxury can lead, not lag, in the transition to a fair and sustainable world' (www.authenticluxuryfoundation.org).

While the ALA feels quite new, the trend is a throwback to our grandparents' version of luxury. I keep thinking about the watch brand whose advertisements read: 'You never actually own a Patek Philippe – you merely look after it for the next generation.' On a darker note, I was haunted by the image of the Jewish refugees boarding the Red Star Line steamers at Antwerp, bound for New York with diamonds sewn into the lining of their clothes. Some items are worth treasuring, even in the most extreme circumstances.

SOCIAL LUXURY

At quite an early point in your life – around about school age – you realize that society is riddled with cliques. If you're not in the right one, you're simply not in. The English, with their class obsession, know this very well. But class snobbery exists in France, too, despite its claim to equality and fraternity.

The moment you arrive at a restaurant in Paris, a snap judgement is made. It could be based on your clothing, your posture or on the way you talk – often it's made before you've even shown up, based on your accent on the phone. In any case, the pigeonhole your greeter mentally puts you in has an immediate impact on the position of your table. If you're unlucky, you may find yourself beside the toilets, or the swinging kitchen door, or in some annexe away from the buzzing salon. And this being Paris, the restaurant is a metaphor for the whole of French society.

The secret, I've discovered, is to visit the same restaurant regularly. After a while, the waiters recognize you. With every visit, you move up a rank. Everything is based on personal contact. The same is true of receiving invitations to gallery openings or getting on the guest lists of nightclubs. All cities work this way. Without the right connections, you can feel like Woody Allen in the film *Stardust Memories*: Woody is sitting on a gloomy train, the carriage filled with grotesque and miserable passengers. Outside, another train passes. In the brightly lit carriage opposite, beautiful people are drinking champagne and laughing. Woody stares bitterly as the glamorous train speeds on, leaving him sitting in the murk.

But there is a remedy to this situation. When I spoke to concierge services, they set great store by the fact that they had excellent contacts. *You* may not be able to snag a table at that hot restaurant, or get invited to an exclusive party at the Cannes Film Festival – but they can get you in because *they know the right people.*

I believe this kind of service will become increasingly desirable. Wealthy aspirants are aware that 'status' is about more than just logos. After all, anybody can buy an expensive handbag – but what use is it when you're freezing in line outside a club instead of sipping cocktails in the VIP area? Not only that, but the circles of power have become less visible. The elite are not who they used to be. They are not politicians or bankers – they are stylists and gallery owners, restaurateurs and DJs. The rules of entry are vague and breaking in is much harder.

Some luxury automobile brands – Lexus, for one – already sell concierge services with their cars. Other luxury brands will soon offer access to elite social networking assistance when customers spend a certain amount. The status object as a ticket to social status: it's not just what you buy, it's who you buy.

ANALOGUE SNOBBERY

The world is becoming digital. Pretty soon, like the fabricated universe depicted in *The Matrix*, it will be composed entirely of zeros and ones. That's a pretty alarming thought – but it only partly explains analogue snobbery. The other explanation is that technology is becoming common, and thus inexpensive. Objects from the analogue era are growing rare – treasured, even.

Evidence of this trend is all around us. You go over to your hip friend's apartment and he puts a crackly vinyl disc on his record player. Nearby, a collection of albums lovingly hunted down on eBay – of course, he tells you that he never stopped buying vinyl – sits proudly on display. Similarly, when I was at a party the other day, a self-consciously 'cool' girl took my picture on a battered analogue camera. 'It's getting harder and harder to find the film,' she sighed. Dali was right when he said that what is unfashionable today becomes fashionable tomorrow.

Newspapers will become the next icons of analogue snobbery. Everyone accepts that news has migrated online and that printed newspapers are facing extinction. Those that survive will become more expensive, and they will adopt some of the attitudes of luxury brands. They will distance themselves from the web by saying that their cultivated readers appreciate the time it takes to peruse a well-written article. They will portray their journalists as wordsmiths – craftsmen. They will tell you that they use traditional printing techniques and paper from sustainable forests. And so on. Many magazines have already taken this route, positioning themselves as glossy coffee table publications.

With the arrival of electronic reading devices like the Kindle, books are next on the list. The other day, when a friend arrived late at a cafe where we had arranged to meet, he picked up the hardback book I was reading. He ran a palm appreciatively over its cover and peeked inside to look at the endpapers and the binding. 'It's rather beautiful,' he said. It was a gift. A hardback book is a luxury item.

DISRUPTION FROM ASIA

An acquaintance of mine works for an event organizer. Not so long ago, her company organized a seminar for the employees of a large French luxury brand. My friend sat in on the event. At a certain moment, the marketing director showed PowerPoint images of all the advertising campaigns being run by the brand's rivals. My friend thought the marketing director would then unveil an innovative new marketing strategy that would blow his competitors out of the water. Instead, to her dismay, he said: 'This is the direction the luxury industry is moving in at the moment. And we should be going the same way.'

Most big luxury brands are risk-averse. Their slowness to embrace the internet is another example of their disinclination to explore new terrain. But risk taking is necessary if innovation is to occur. You may be familiar with the theory of disruption, devised by Jean-Marie Dru of the advertising agency TBWA. Disruption is a three-stage process that enables brands to innovate. First, you examine the conventions that bind your sector. Then, you challenge yourself to overturn those conventions. The result is an original vision – one that allows your brand to stand out.

Arguably, the last disruption of the luxury sector took place in the 1990s, when venerable companies like Louis Vuitton began transforming themselves into instant-gratification fashion brands. Now they are busy trying to dissociate themselves from that image, but it feels more like communications gloss than genuine creativity. The trend forecaster Genevieve Flaven speaks of a 'creative crunch', suggesting that the new generation of designers are not attracted to the luxury titans. 'In the past, talented designers were happy to find themselves designing the latest "it" bag. But now they've grown disenchanted with that world.'

If the luxury giants have become sluggish and predictable, there are opportunities for others. Nokia cleverly filled a niche with Vertu, its luxury mobile phone. There is a similar Chinese brand called Veva, launched in May 2008 by Qiao Xing Mobile. The slender Veva phones come in gold-plated and crystal-studded versions.

A Chinese luxury brand – that's a pretty disruptive concept. The convention is that Asian markets are consumers rather than producers of luxury goods. But what if a new wave of luxury brands were about to emerge from Asia?

In fact, Asia has a history of bringing disruptive ideas to the luxury market. The group of avant-garde Japanese fashion designers that rose to prominence in the 1980s included Yohji Yamamoto, Issey Miyake and Comme des Garçons, launched by Rei Kawakubo in 1973. Not only is Kawakubo one of the world's most visionary designers, she has also mentored younger names like Junya Watanabe and Tao Kurihara. Kawakubo's Dover Street Market concept store in London (in which other designers are invited to set up 'creative spaces'), her temporary 'guerrilla' stores around the world and her unashamedly synthetic fragrances make her brand a model of alternative luxury.

Meanwhile, Wang Xiao Lan, owner of Taiwan's largest publishing company, has owned prestigious French fashion house Lanvin since 2001. This brings us neatly on to Shanghai Tang, the upmarket fashion brand started in 1994 by David Tang. Based in Hong Kong and partly owned by Cartier parent group Richemont, it now has branches all over the world. It originally made tourist-friendly takes on Mao jackets and cheongsam skirts, but lately it has been channelling a more contemporary version of Chinese culture. Its chief designer, Joseph

Li, has a Masters from Central Saint Martins in London – and he apprenticed under Alber Elbaz at Lanvin. He told the *New Straits Times* newspaper that a recent collection was inspired by 'the current new wave of contemporary artists from China like the politically quizzical Zhu Wei and the avant-garde Cai Guo-Qiang' ('East and West turned inside out', 12 April 2009).

Another interesting Chinese brand is Qeelin, which positions itself as 'China's first luxury jewellery brand' (www.queelin.com). It's jewel-encrusted pandas may not be to everyone's taste, but the brand has apparently been given the seal of approval by fashionistas like Marc Jacobs and Mischa Barton – and the fact that it has been stocked by trendsetting Paris concept store Colette is also a positive sign. Its designer, Dennis Chan, was educated in Hong Kong and started his career in London before returning to his home town. He describes his designs as 'a startling fusion of distinctive Chinese design with influences of Western contemporary concepts'. The brand's co-founder is Guillaume Brochand, a French marketing specialist who has held posts in Asia for Tag Heuer and Ebel. He writes on the website: 'With its 5,000 years of heritage in arts and craftsmanship together with the rising interest of its people for luxury brands, Dennis Chan and I believe that China is bound to become a major world player in the luxury goods industry, as a market itself as well as a source of creativity.'

Chinese students are currently studying fashion and luxury brand management. French business school HEC runs an 'Advanced Management Programme in Fashion and Luxury' in association with Tsinghua University in Beijing. There are certainly many others. When it comes to innovation in the luxury market, China is the next Japan.

GUILT-FREE LUXURY

It's fair to say that the word 'luxury' can have negative connotations. It may imply elitism or status seeking, not to mention greed. In other contexts, it might suggest idleness or dissipation. In *War and Peace*, Tolstoy describes how Napoleon's entire invading army vanished into Moscow as if absorbed by the streets. They were ruined by a familiar temptation. 'The men who had recently made up an army drained away all over this wealthy, deserted city, so richly supplied with goods and luxuries.'

Luxury, in this interpretation, should be resisted by the pure of spirit. But the notion of 'authentic' luxury offers an alternative approach. It encourages a sense of moderation and taste, of saving up for the best instead of squandering on the disposable. Perhaps the dream of luxury – as Alain Ducasse suggested – speaks of a yearning for perfection, the pursuit of an ideal.

I was particularly struck by the viewpoint of Patrizia Pressimone, director of architecture at the Paris department store Printemps. She told me: 'Luxury is an aesthetic pleasure. It is a form of evolution, a sign that we have learned how to enjoy life beyond the basics. It is no coincidence that cultivated people appreciate luxury. If we did not crave beautiful surroundings, there would be no Venice, no Paris. But it is a mistake to assume that luxury is about possessing a gold bath with jewelled taps. Luxury is not measured in dollars – it is measured in details.'

The next time we covet a luxury of some kind, or admonish somebody else for doing so, it may be helpful to remember Patrizia's theory that the pursuit of luxury has contributed to art and culture – and perhaps to civilization as a whole.

In any case, even if we finally decide to turn our back on it, luxury is impervious to our scorn. Consumers come and go, economies boom and bust – but luxury endures.

References

BOOKS

Benaïm, Laurence (2002) *Yves Saint Laurent*, Bernard Grasset, Paris

Berry, Christopher J (1994) *The Idea of Luxury*, Cambridge University Press, Cambridge

Blume, Mary and Lartigue, Jacques-Henri (2001) *Lartigue's Riviera*, Flammarion, Paris and New York

Castarède, Jean (2007) *Histoire du Luxe en France*, Groupe Eyrolles, Paris

Chadha, Radha and Husband, Paul (2006) *The Cult of the Luxury Brand*, Nicholas Brealey International, London and Boston

Chevalier, Michel and Mazzalovo, Gérald (2008) *Luxury Brand Management: A world of privilege*, John Wiley & Sons (Asia), Singapore

Cologni, Franco (2001) *Hallmarks of History: Piaget*, Assouline, Paris

Grumbach, Didier (2008) *Histoires de Mode*, 2nd edn, Editions du Regard, Paris

Fraser, Antonia (2001) *Marie Antoinette: The journey*, Weidenfeld & Nicholson, London

Philips, Tim (2005) *Knock-Off: The true story of the world's fastest growing crime wave*, Kogan Page, London

Rentschler, Ruth and Hede, Anne-Marie (2007) *Museum Marketing: Competing in the global marketplace*, Butterworth-Heineman, Oxford

Resnick, Evelyne (2008) *Wine Brands*, Palgrave Macmillan, London

Ring, Jim (2004) *Riviera: The rise and rise of the Côte d'Azur*, John Murray, London

Robinson, Jancis (2006) *Oxford Companion to Wine*, 3rd edn, Oxford University Press, Oxford

Thomas, Dana (2007) *Deluxe: How luxury lost its lustre*, Penguin Press, New York

Thompson, Don, (2008) *The $12 Million Stuffed Shark*, Aurum Press, London

Thornton, Sarah (2008) *Seven Days in the Art World*, Granta Publications, London

White, Edmund (2001) *Le Flâneur*, Bloomsbury Publishing, London

ONLINE RESOURCES

Academie des Vins Anciens (www.academiedesvinsanciens.org)

Admap (www.admap.com)

Asahi Shimbun (www.asahi.com)

Bloomberg (www.bloomberg.com)

Brandchannel (www.brandchannel.com)

Brand Republic (www.brandrepublic.com)

Business 2.0 (http://money.cnn.com)

Federation of the Swiss Watch Industry (www.fhc.ch)

Fractional Life (www.fractionallife.com)

Haute Horlogerie (www.journal.hautehorlogerie.org)

Hospitality Net (www.hospitalitynet.org)

Luxury Culture (www.luxuryculture.com)

Slate magazine (www.slate.com)

Transnational Institute (www.tni.com)

Unity Marketing (www.unitymarketingonline.com)

Union des Maisons de Champagne (www.maisons-champagne.com)

World Advertising Research Center (www.warc.com)

Index

ALSO AVAILABLE FROM KOGAN PAGE

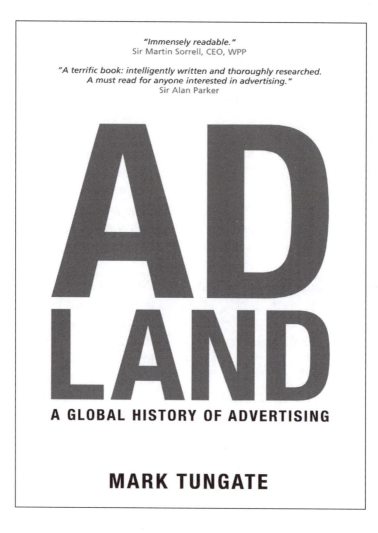

"*Immensely readable.*"
Sir Martin Sorrell, CEO, WPP

"*A terrific book: intelligently written and thoroughly researched.
A must read for anyone interested in advertising.*"
Sir Alan Parker

AD LAND

A GLOBAL HISTORY OF ADVERTISING

MARK TUNGATE

ISBN: 978 0 7494 4837 0   Hardback 2007

ALSO AVAILABLE FROM KOGAN PAGE

Mark Tungate

FASHION BRANDS

Branding Style from Armani to Zara

2nd edition

"An essential primer for anyone wanting to make it big in the fashion biz."
Nicholas Coleridge, Managing Director, Condé Nast

ISBN: 978 0 7494 5305 3   Hardback 2008

ALSO AVAILABLE FROM KOGAN PAGE

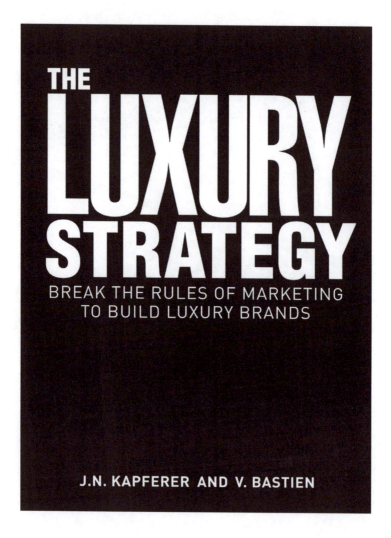

ISBN: 978 0 7494 5477 7 Hardback 2008